ESPECIALLY FOR

....

FROM

....

DATE

....

DAILY WISDOM
FOR MEN

2021
Devotional Collection

BARBOUR BOOKS
An Imprint of Barbour Publishing, Inc.

© 2020 by Barbour Publishing, Inc.

Print ISBN 978-1-64352-518-1, 978-1-64352-831-1

eBook Editions:
Adobe Digital Edition (.epub) 978-1-64352-816-8
Kindle and MobiPocket Edition (.prc) 978-1-64352-817-5

Scripture quotations marked KJV are taken from the King James Version of the Bible.

Scripture quotations marked NKJV are taken from the New King James Version®. Copyright © 1982 by Thomas Nelson, Inc. Used by permission. All rights reserved.

Scripture quotations marked NIV are taken from the HOLY BIBLE, NEW INTERNATIONAL VERSION®. NIV®. Copyright © 1973, 1978, 1984, 2011 by Biblica, Inc.™ Used by permission. All rights reserved worldwide.

Scripture quotations marked MSG are from *THE MESSAGE*. Copyright © by Eugene H. Peterson 1993, 1994, 1995, 1996, 2000, 2001, 2002. Used by permission of NavPress Publishing Group.

Scripture quotations marked ESV are from The Holy Bible, English Standard Version®, copyright © 2001 by Crossway Bibles, a publishing ministry of Good News Publishers. Used by permission. All rights reserved.

Scripture quotations marked NLT are taken from the *Holy Bible*. New Living Translation copyright© 1996, 2004, 2015 by Tyndale House Foundation. Used by permission of Tyndale House Publishers, Inc. Carol Stream, Illinois 60188. All rights reserved.

Scripture quotations marked AMPC are taken from the Amplified® Bible, Classic Edition © 1954, 1958, 1962, 1964, 1965, 1987 by The Lockman Foundation. Used by permission.

Scripture quotations marked NASB are taken from the New American Standard Bible, © 1960, 1962, 1963, 1968, 1971, 1972, 1973, 1975, 1977, 1995 by The Lockman Foundation. Used by permission.

Scripture quotations marked NLV are taken from the New Life Version copyright © 1969 and 2003 by Barbour Publishing, Inc. All rights reserved.

Published by Barbour Books, an imprint of Barbour Publishing, Inc., 1810 Barbour Drive, Uhrichsville, Ohio 44683, www.barbourbooks.com

Our mission is to inspire the world with the life-changing message of the Bible.

Member of the
Evangelical Christian
Publishers Association

Printed in China.

INTRODUCTION

Welcome to 2021—and to this year's edition of *Daily Wisdom for Men*!

The key word for this year's *Daily Wisdom for Men* is *endurance*. As you make your way through the Bible—and through this book's daily readings—you'll see that God has a lot to say to us men about endurance. Along with important subjects such as love, holiness, peace with God—and many, many others—you'll see that endurance is an overarching theme in God's written Word.

The inspiration for this year's daily devotionals is taken from each day's scripture readings in our popular "Read Thru the Bible in a Year Plan," which means you can read the daily Bible passages and then spend a few minutes reading that day's writing in this book. You will find this year's "Read Thru the Bible in a Year Plan" at the end of this book.

God wants to grow you into a man of endurance—a man who can face up to this world's trials and temptations and come out a winner every time. It is the hope of the seven men who wrote this year's *Daily Wisdom for Men* devotionals, as well as the people at Barbour Publishing, that God will use your daily Bible reading, as well as the writings in this book, to help make you a true man of endurance, a man whose faith in Christ will continue growing and thriving each day of this year and beyond.

The Editors

HOW IT ALL STARTED

This is the story of how it all started,
of Heaven and Earth when they were created.
GENESIS 2:4 MSG*

God drew from His imagination and created a world illuminated by light He created, populated by animals He imagined, and filled with lakes and oceans teeming with life. It was mankind's first chance to prove faithful. They failed.

The story of mankind started with a God who went above and beyond to offer the first second chance. He set the example of endurance and asks you to follow His lead. His second chance is for the *nearly faithful*, the *sometimes faithful*, and the *hardly ever faithful*.

God made the earth and everything in it. He sustains what He made. He sets the pace in the rhythms of grace. He has endured mankind's failure from the very first act of disobedience. That's important because the book of Genesis recalls the, "Story of how it all started."

God is the enduring One who invites you to show His character to others by withstanding trials and bearing up under temptation so you can follow Him. This is your journey. Endure to the end and find encouragement to make each step a choice of endurance. It's a new year. It's a new day.

God, I want this year to be the one when my spiritual
muscles get in shape and my will bends to Your direction.
Let today begin the story of how it all started in me.

*A 365-Day Genesis to Revelation Bible Reading Plan that follows
each devotion can be found at the back of this book.

THE MOCKED BOAT BUILDER

*[God told Noah], "Build a large boat from cypress wood
and waterproof it with tar, inside and out. Then construct
decks and stalls throughout its interior. Make the boat
450 feet long, 75 feet wide, and 45 feet high."*
GENESIS 6:14–15 NLT

I magine living in a time, place, and culture where the only people who believed in God were your immediate family. When you mentioned God to neighbors, friends, and even extended family members, they thought you were delusional. After all, no one could recall ever seeing or hearing God, and the only one talking about Him was building a huge boat on dry land.

It took Noah several decades to build the boat described in Genesis 6. He likely suffered through just as many years of ridicule by building a boat that only made perfect sense to God. Noah bore the weight of negative public opinion. If there were polls, Noah paid no attention. If neighbors wanted to argue, Noah just put his back into his work.

If you find yourself being mocked because you follow God, remember Noah. God never asks you to do something that doesn't serve a purpose. Follow His Word. Follow His steps. Follow His plan. He's leading you somewhere you could never find on your own. It's a protection. It's a *blessing*.

*Father, when people argue with me, it's easy to argue
with You. When I believe I've misunderstood Your plan,
help me endure the hard-to-believe steps.*

AN ETERNAL SAFE SPACE

Only Noah and those who were with him in the ark remained alive.
And the waters prevailed on the earth one hundred and fifty days.
GENESIS 7:23–24 NKJV

F lood waters filled every valley in the world. Water climbed mountains until it covered every peak. The human life saved from the devastation had to withstand a year in an enclosed zoo. The people spent nearly half of that year floating in a world silent except for life in the ark.

The purpose of the ark was to protect a remnant of the living from death. The ark represented promise and perspective. Those who faced less-than-ideal living conditions would have a future to share with family and with the God who rescues.

Jesus is your ark of protection. Come to Him for rescue. Don't be surprised when hardships come. The trials you face can never be compared with the future He's prepared for you and the past He's rescued you from.

If life that's really life is found in Jesus, then those who follow Him will be the ones who discover it. Just like Noah, you're faced with a choice. You could cave to the pressure of people who don't understand, or you can trust the Rescuer who invites you to an eternal safe space.

Lord, I'm aware that You save and rescue. I'm grateful that
You love me. I'm willing to live for You even when trouble comes
because You have promised to go through it with me.

PROMISE KEPT

Abram went, as the LORD had told him. . . .
Abram was seventy-five years old when he set out.
GENESIS 12:4 NIV

A bram spent his life living with and for his family. They meant something to him. If he had a bucket list, it was probably filled with cherished memories. But Abram had no son.

God would eventually tell Abram to leave family behind and follow Him on a great adventure. God said, "Go from your country, your people and your father's household to the land I will show you. I will make you into a great nation, and I will bless you" (Genesis 12:1–2 NIV).

How long have you waited for an answer to a prayer? Is it easy to give up when it seems God is silent? Abram would leave his childhood home, his family, and the security he felt in order to experience God's answer to prayer, but he waited twenty-five years for His answer.

Giving up would have been easy, and no human would have blamed Abram. While this aging adventurer tried to find the answer in all the wrong places, God made a promise He would keep.

Trusting God isn't about making you wait but about proving beyond a doubt that when God promises, *He delivers*.

God, help me to be patient when I have to wait on You.
When You have given a promise, help me to remember that I just
haven't seen it fulfilled—yet. Help me trust You while I wait.

NEVER TOO LATE

Is anything too hard or too wonderful for the Lord?
Genesis 18:14 ampc

———◆———

Abram and his wife, Sarai, recalled God's promise that a nation would start with their offspring. He was ninety-nine. She was ten years younger. Hadn't they done what God asked? Hadn't they followed where God led? Where was the promised child? Wasn't it too late?

It must have *felt* that way. But when three divine strangers dropped by, things changed. The promise became more specific. A boy named Isaac would arrive in a year. Abram's name was changed to Abraham and Sarai's name was changed to Sarah. And when Sarah laughed in what must have been disbelief, one of the heaven-sent guests said, "Is anything too hard or wonderful for the Lord?"

The toughest life assignments come with the answer. *Nothing* is too hard for God. *Nothing* is too wonderful for Him. *Nothing* is beyond His ability.

Endurance led this couple to new names, new outlooks, and new futures. Several months later, the laughter of a child erased all doubt.

In those moments when you've grown tired of the wait, you will need reminders of God's faithfulness. You will need to recall prayers already answered. You will need to remember that nothing is too hard for the Promise Keeper.

———————————————

Father, when things are too hard for me, remind me that there has never been anything too hard for You. As I remember, calm my anxious heart.

JUSTICE WILL WAIT

*"For we are about to destroy this place, because the outcry
against its people has become great before the LORD,
and the LORD has sent us to destroy it."*

GENESIS 19:13 ESV

God told Abraham about His plan to destroy two cities. God could no longer endure the law-breaking sin committed in Sodom and Gomorrah. God is the greatest example of endurance, but He cannot endure sin forever.

Abraham's nephew Lot lived in Sodom with his family. They were told to leave before the city was destroyed.

Does this sound cruel? You should know that Abraham pleaded with God to save the twin cities if ten righteous people lived there. God agreed, but they didn't exist.

You might witness injustice and wonder when God will step in and set things right. God prefers mercy when most think justice should blaze. Jesus paid the price for sin. When mankind accepts the opportunity to become right with God, then justice waits a little longer. God wants everyone to accept His rescue. He's been willing to endure the slander, disbelief, and ridicule—though He's never deserved it.

Choose to walk away from a lifestyle defined by disobedience. God wants to adopt you into His family rather than see sin destroy you. He longs for sinners to discover a Savior.

*Lord, thank You for mercy. I'm grateful for Your patience.
Help me show my appreciation by showing mercy to those
I think deserve justice. It's what You've done for me.*

A PROMISED SON

"Don't lay a hand on that boy! Don't touch him! Now I know
how fearlessly you fear God; you didn't hesitate to place
your son, your dear son, on the altar for me."
GENESIS 22:12 MSG

God put Abraham's faith to a test most couldn't imagine facing. God asked Abraham to offer his young son as a sacrifice.

Could Abraham face such a loss? Would he object? Would anyone blame him if he said no? Abraham had learned that God could be trusted even when he didn't understand. So this aging father walked with Isaac to Mount Moriah. He built an altar and prepared for the unthinkable. Abraham proved himself willing to do what God asked.

Enduring faith made Abraham courageous. God wanted to see if Abraham was willing to trust. Just before Abraham reached the point of no return, he heard the welcome words, "Don't lay a hand on that boy!"

This story serves another purpose. Jesus was God's promised Son. He would become the rescuer of mankind, but that meant *sacrifice*. And in His death a heavenly nation opened to mankind.

Christians have citizenship in a forever home because when Jesus bore the brunt of mankind's worst affliction, He was able to rise once more to put out the welcome mat to new family on their journey home.

God, no matter how hard things may be for me,
I have never had to face the choices You made because
You love me. Let this good news change me.

ENOUGH SPACE

Isaac moved on and dug another well.
This time there was no dispute over it.
GENESIS 26:22 NLT

Famine caused a grown-up Isaac to leave the land of his birth and find a place to raise his own family. When he became wealthy in one place, he was asked to leave: "Go somewhere else. . .for you have become too powerful for us" (Genesis 26:16 NLT).

Isaac moved on. The men who worked for him dug several wells, and each time someone else claimed ownership of a well they hadn't dug. Isaac was on the move once more. Isaac didn't give up. He kept digging wells until one day no one came to take the new well away. His family, workers, and livestock had fresh water. Isaac said, "At last the LORD has created enough space for us to prosper in this land" (v. 22).

It may not be a dispute over a well, but there may have been times in your life when something made it impossible for you to live life without interference from others. Every human being will have hardships to endure, and if you are in tune with the God who rescues, then He can carve out a place filled with promise. He will give you a purpose. He will develop His plan in your displaced heart.

Father, give me patience. I want what I don't have now. Help me want what You want so that I have enough space to grow into new life living.

ROOM TO WAIT

So Jacob served seven years for Rachel, and they seemed only a few days to him because of the love he had for her.
GENESIS 29:20 NKJV

I saac had twin sons—and they didn't get along. Jacob was the more mild-mannered son. Esau made brash decisions that got him in trouble. Esau married quickly and everyone regretted it. Jacob was sent back to his mother's family to find a bride. When Jacob met Rachel, he was certain she was the one. Jacob agreed to work for her dad, Laban, for seven years. If Jacob had that kind of tenacity, then he could marry Rachel. But seven years turned into fourteen.

Waiting is one of the hardest things you will face. You might find yourself waiting on a spouse, on children, on a promotion, on a home, or on a car—and you wonder if there is *purpose* in the delay. When you have to wait for something you really want, it develops perseverance (a willingness to do something in spite of the hardships faced).

Instant gratification does nothing to develop endurance. It almost always creates disappointment, a lack of contentment, and decreased life satisfaction (Esau). Trouble might actually be a gift that finds you asking for God's help, waiting for His answer, and following His better set of directions (Jacob).

Lord, I hate waiting. I want what I want, and now would be a good time to get it. But You say I should wait on You, for You, and with You. Teach me to wait well.

A TIME TO PREPARE

*Jacob said to Laban, "Send me on my way
so I can go back to my own homeland."*
GENESIS 30:25 NIV

———————

M any years had passed since Jacob began working for Laban so he could marry Rachel. He was more than a little eager to leave. He now had eleven sons and had worked hard to make a living that would allow him to free himself from Laban. His father-in-law made leaving hard.

God was blessing Jacob, and his time in the *divine waiting room* was almost over. Laban changed Jacob's wages repeatedly, but God blessed Jacob repeatedly. No matter how unfair the labor talks became, God found a way to bless Jacob. Laban didn't like it.

When it comes to waiting, you need to know that it will eventually come to an end. There will be relief—you'll discover an open door, and God will lead you through. Waiting is not stopping. It's not giving up. It's not even a crushed dream. Waiting is a time of preparation for God's next step for you. You're going to need to be ready when God's "No waiting on aisle five" sign lights up.

What are you waiting for? Is it something God can bless? Will it be worth the wait? Endurance is certainty that difficulties will seem small when the answer arrives.

*God, I've been in Your waiting room and I have wondered why.
Help me remember the wait prepares me for Your answer.*

THE NEVER-EXPECTED REUNION

But Esau ran to meet him, and embraced him
and fell on his neck and kissed him, and they wept.
GENESIS 33:4 AMPC

Twin brothers separated by time and choice—neither certain a family reunion would be possible. Esau gave Jacob his birthright for a pot of stew. Jacob took the blessing of his father when he knew it was meant for Esau. It's likely they hadn't seen each other in more than twenty years. Time had changed both men.

When Jacob heard Esau was on his way to meet him, he assumed the worst and created a contingency plan to help save his family. The plan wasn't needed. Jacob was Esau's only brother. It had been a long time since he'd seen family.

You're probably different today from how you were twenty years ago. It's equally likely that the people you grew up with—the family you grew up with—have also changed. The paths some people choose leave them unrecognizable and you uncomfortable. Some people take a path you never expected, and a deeper friendship becomes possible.

Take a personal assessment. Is your today better than yesteryear? Is your heart bent in a God-shaped direction or elsewhere? God transformed Jacob and Esau. He can change you. It's called *new life living*.

Father, let me never think it impossible that You could
change anyone's life. You're the God of lost causes, and You
can change what seemed unchangeable in me—and in others.

SEEKING GOD

And God said to him, "Your name is Jacob; no longer shall
your name be called Jacob, but Israel shall be your name."
GENESIS 35:10 ESV

Jacob could have stayed and continued working for his father-in-law, Laban, but he would have missed God's plan. He could have been satisfied with where he was, but he would have missed where he needed to be. He could have hidden from his brother Esau and missed a memorable and welcome reunion. It seems choices have consequences—and not all of them are bad.

Jacob was seeking God, raising boys, and tending livestock. It was the *seeking God* part that resulted in a meeting with the Almighty One. God promised Jacob the land of his father, Isaac, and grandfather, Abraham. He was given a new name—he was no longer Jacob, but Israel. This name was God's blessing for the man who had endured so much setback.

Perseverance can lead a man to an outcome he didn't see coming. God is aware that you will break His law—that you will sin. He is aware that you will be impulsive. He knows you will need forgiveness. But each time you turn away, endurance returns your focus to seeking God. Keep doing that every time you become aware that you've turned away.

Lord, I never want to turn away from You, but I have. I never
want to let You down, but I will. I never want to stay in that
place, so get my attention so that I turn back to You.

SIBLING RIVALRY

His brothers pulled Joseph out of the cistern and sold
him for twenty pieces of silver to the Ishmaelites
who took Joseph with them down to Egypt.
GENESIS 37:28 MSG

Joseph was Jacob's favorite son. He received special treatment—and a special coat. He was the second youngest son and was familiar with sibling rivalry.

When Jacob needed some intel on his sons, he sent Joseph. They didn't just pick on Joseph, call him a dreamer, or destroy his coat. The brothers threw him in a hole, hatched a plan to convince Jacob that a wild animal had killed Joseph, and eventually sold him into slavery at a bargain price.

How would it feel to have your freedom taken away by jealous siblings who preferred you dead? Joseph endured this pain, but God was with him.

The way people treat you has nothing to do with the way God sees you. His plans for you are not limited by the opinions of critics. His love for you is not based on your perfection, but on His.

A lack of acceptance may be common among acquaintances and less common among family members, but it does happen. You'll need to persevere in the midst of that kind of unfairness. So get to know the God who is never petty, short-fused, or abusive. He cares about you.

God, when I feel abused, help me to remember that Your Son was
also mistreated. When I feel alone, remind me that I'm not the
only one. When life seems unfair, remind me of Your compassion.

FORGOTTEN, BUT NOT FORGOTTEN

The chief butler did not remember Joseph, but forgot him.
GENESIS 40:23 NKJV

———————

Joseph came to Egypt as a slave. Falsely accused of misconduct, he was placed in prison. This wasn't where Joseph wanted to be, but it wasn't long before this prisoner ran the prison: "The keeper of the prison did not look into anything that was under Joseph's authority, because the LORD was with him" (Genesis 39:23 NKJV).

Two confused inmates came to Joseph. They each had dreams but no idea what they meant. Joseph said one dream meant bad news for the dreamer. The other meant the dreamer would get out of jail. Joseph asked the good news guest to tell the king about Joseph's situation, but this dreamer forgot.

You've had bad days. You can relate to the struggle Joseph endured. None of this was fair. Yet God was with Joseph.

God never promised you a life free of trouble, but He promised to be with you. He never said today would be perfect, but He said you can live in joy daily because He never leaves or forsakes you. He never said everything would go according to your plans, but He did say that when you love Him, He can transform bad things into something good.

———————

Father, when I feel left behind, help me remember that Joseph felt the same way, but You were with him. You are with me too. You have never forgotten me, even when others have.

THE FAMINE YEARS

[Joseph's brothers] bowed down,
prostrating themselves before him.
GENESIS 43:28 NIV

Egypt's king had a dream and was baffled. When the previously jailed butler heard about it, he remembered Joseph. Joseph met with the king, and God helped him understand the dream. The king took Joseph from prison and made him second only to him in power and responsibility.

The king had dreamed of a coming famine. There was time to prepare. People came from other countries to buy the grain Joseph stored for the famine years. Among the buyers were Joseph's brothers—the same ones who had sold him into slavery. They didn't recognize Joseph. Instead of remembering brothers who wanted to see him dead, Joseph saw men who needed help staying alive.

Maybe you've lived with the memory of someone who's hurt you and made your life miserable. That person's actions may have been unintentional or more malicious, like those of Joseph's brothers. Don't think of their downfall as justice but as an opportunity for restoration and healing. God offers mercy and asks you to forgive. It's part of bearing with others.

Pray for your enemies. Bless those who offer a curse. Love those you find hard to love. Joseph did that for his brothers. Jesus did that for you. Now you have the opportunity to do that for others.

Lord, when I would rather see someone get what's
coming to him, remind me that if I get what's
coming to me, I would have to live without You.

MERCY FOR BAD PLAN MAKERS

[Joseph] sent his brothers away, and they departed,
and he said to them, See that you do not disagree
(get excited, quarrel) along the road.
GENESIS 45:24 AMPC

You can imagine the emotions Joseph's brothers may have felt when he told them who he was—sorrow, shame, defensiveness, and fear. They never expected to see him again. They never expected him to be a ruler. They didn't expect him to be kind.

Joseph said, "Do not be distressed and disheartened or vexed and angry with yourselves because you sold me here, for God sent me ahead of you to preserve life" (Genesis 45:5 AMPC).

Joseph didn't sidestep what happened. He spoke boldly of how God could take their bad plans and offer mercy to the bad plan makers. When Joseph told his brothers not to quarrel when they returned home, he probably knew that someone would be tempted to play the blame game. But there was better news to share.

Joseph was put in the right place at the right time to offer the right outcome to a very bad situation—a *God-directed* outcome.

The struggle you work through today could impact the life of someone else tomorrow. Your struggle may help someone else. Your life experience might be just what someone needs to work through his own issues.

God, I don't want to ignore injustice, but I want to embrace mercy
and forgiveness. Yes, for me, but also for those I've considered enemies.

THE REUNION

[Joseph] presented himself to [his father] and fell on his neck and
wept on his neck a good while. Israel said to Joseph, "Now let me die,
since I have seen your face and know that you are still alive."
GENESIS 46:29–30 ESV

The sin of ten brothers affected many. Each had to live with the memory of selling his brother Joseph into slavery. Joseph had to live with the unwanted circumstances he faced in Egypt. Their father endured many years of lies, believing Joseph was dead.

Many books portray skeletons in the closet. The stories unfold to reveal something about a character you'd never expect. Maybe people can relate to this dynamic because it's real life. It happened in Joseph's family. You may recognize it in yours.

God has always asked His family to confess sin. This means agreeing that God's laws are better than your own judgments, admitting that you didn't make the right choice, and accepting His forgiveness.

He also wants you to make things right with anyone you've wronged as a lawbreaker. You may endure the consequences of sin, but God never wants you to act as if sin is no big deal.

For Joseph's family, it was complete honesty that led to an epic reunion.

Father, why is it so easy for me to hold on to sin
and refuse to admit You are right to call it wrong?
Help me confess to You and to others when I fail.

LIFE LANGUAGE

I wait in hope for your salvation, GOD.
GENESIS 49:18 MSG

Joseph invited his family to live in Egypt, where they were provided good land and plenty of food. Time passed and Jacob (a.k.a. Israel) came to the end of his life. His sons gathered and he shared what he knew about each son and offered hope for the years ahead.

At an odd time, Jacob pauses his recital of future hope and says a prayer: "I wait in hope for your salvation, God." He had lived through the salvation of an exit from his father-in-law's control, from his brother's wrath, and from famine, and now he recognizes that salvation from Egypt is needed for his family.

Today is Martin Luther King Jr. Day. Dr. King could relate to this verse. Oppression had been endured, but salvation was needed. Dr. King would even say, "Someday we will get to the Promised Land." He too was looking at a different, better future when he spoke those words in Washington, DC.

If you are a parent, you have the ability to speak life into your children. That's rarely done by being critical but is accelerated when you envision a good future for them to grow into.

Lord, help me to speak life-giving words to my family. May they be encouraged as I tell them how they can successfully face the future and that their lives are altered when they take hold of Your purpose.

TRUSTED WITH THE OUTCOME

Pharaoh gave this order to all his people:
"Throw every newborn Hebrew boy into the
Nile River. But you may let the girls live."
EXODUS 1:22 NLT

Jacob was right to be concerned about whether his family would think of Egypt as their permanent home. One king of Egypt invited them in as guests, but when a new king took the throne, there was a different view of Egypt's long-term guests.

Jacob's family had grown large and powerful. They were no longer considered guests but slaves—no longer celebrated but controlled.

This new king did something unthinkable. To control the population of Hebrews, he made it legal for the people of Egypt to kill Israelite boys.

It's hard to endure injustice. God asks you to do the right thing, which makes it hard to see other people refusing to do the same. These people seem to celebrate lawlessness and champion what's acceptable over what's right.

Endurance sometimes means believing God can be trusted with the outcome of your worst circumstances. What happens to you may not be God's plan, but the bad choices of others can strengthen your willingness to trust a good God to help you with the choices you need to make.

God, Your standard is best, but not everyone follows it. I can
make popular decisions or I can choose Your plan. Let me
make the right choice and trust You with everything else.

EXCUSES, EXCUSES

Moses said to the LORD, "Pardon your servant, Lord.
I have never been eloquent, neither in the past nor since you
have spoken to your servant. I am slow of speech and tongue."
EXODUS 4:10 NIV

Moses was an Israelite saved from death as an infant. His parents hid him, but when that was no longer possible, they placed him where the king's daughter would find him. She adopted Moses and he was raised in the Egyptian palace.

Forty years later, Moses ran away from Egypt. Forty more years passed and God told him to return to Egypt. It was time for his family to leave oppression behind and journey to the land God had promised. It was a great assignment, but Moses had a list of reasons why he wasn't the right man for the job. God saw through the excuses.

God made sure Moses was qualified. Moses went back to Egypt.

God might call you to step away from your comfort zone and do what He wants you to do. It will be frightening. You will have plenty of excuses. But God will give you the qualifications you need to do something important—*for Him*.

Live through the awkwardness, let God help you through problem areas, and watch as the impossible becomes possible.

Father, it's easy to believe Your plans are for other people,
but You've got an assignment just for me. Help me not
overlook, neglect, or refuse Your next assignment.

OUTLAST

*Then Pharaoh called for Moses and Aaron, and said, "Entreat the
Lord that He may take away the frogs from me and from my people;
and I will let the people go, that they may sacrifice to the Lord."*
EXODUS 8:8 NKJV

When Moses arrived in Egypt, God sent ten plagues with him. The king thought he could outlast each divine blow. Hail, flies, locusts, and seven more plagues rolled into Egypt and left a massive path of destruction. God hadn't rescued His family from famine just to leave them slaves. God intended to deliver His family, and no one could long endure the consequences of telling Him no.

God can endure more than you can. He witnesses disobedience every minute of every day. He's patient and kind, and His mercy leads to changed minds, hearts, and decisions. He can outlast your stubbornness, win against your selfishness, and teach beyond your resistance.

God is making you a new creature. When He starts something, He is faithful to finish it. Resist your own stubbornness and spend more time with the Instructor. Follow willingly and discover friendship with the Father.

You may have endured what it took to get an education, succeeded in learning your job, and learned to drive. What God can teach you has a much greater importance for every *today* you will ever live.

*Lord, I want to learn from You. I want to be a willing student.
I want You to outlast my stubborn tendencies and change me.*

GOD SHOWED UP

And this day shall be to you for a memorial.
You shall keep it as a feast to the Lord throughout
your generations, keep it as an ordinance forever.
EXODUS 12:14 AMPC

It wasn't just the first of what would be an annual celebration. What happened on the last day of the Israelites' slavery in Egypt was the beginning of a memory of God's faithfulness. Just one more night and the king of Egypt would let the people go.

This wasn't a memorial to Moses—he was simply following God's orders. This feast was a celebration of something more. It was remembering the time of endurance and oppression. It was also a time of release and rejoicing. The One who made it happen was God. The king knew it—the people knew it. There was no doubt this was God's doing.

You may not celebrate a specific date, but you probably remember a time when God showed up and did something that could not be explained any other way.

God encourages you to remember His faithfulness—not once, but daily. This is a foundation stone in any act of worship. God is great and deserves honor. This Passover celebration can remind you that God can do what you can't, and when He shortens the time you endure trouble—*praise Him.*

God, I can get into trouble without Your help.
When I need rescue, I will need You. When Your
plan rescues me, help me remember gratitude.

THE TEST

*There the LORD made for them a statute
and a rule, and there he tested them.*
EXODUS 15:25 ESV

When there's trouble to endure, why is complaining the go-to response? The Israelites were rescued from slavery. They saw the Red Sea divide as they walked on a dry seabed to escape Egyptian soldiers. They had heard about the Promised Land. Yet it was the quality of available drinking water that reduced their gratitude to grumbling.

If this was a test, then the people failed miserably. But God had an actual test, and the people continued to fail. Exodus 15:26 says, "If you will diligently listen to the voice of the LORD your God, and do that which is right in his eyes, and give ear to his commandments and keep all his statutes, I will put none of the diseases on you that I put on the Egyptians, for I am the LORD, your healer."

If this was a class, it was a nearly forty-year failure. The Israelites didn't listen to God, do the right thing, or keep His statutes.

There's no use being judgmental. We all face the same struggle. God gives us the keys to a godly life, and we receive them as mere suggestions in the event our way fails. The people of Israel couldn't follow God, and neither can any of us today—*without His help*.

*Father, I can always get through the worst experiences
in the best possible way when You join me in the journey.
When I fail Your tests, keep teaching me.*

THE STEW-AND-BREAD DISTRACTION

*The Israelites said, "Why didn't GOD let us die in comfort in
Egypt where we had lamb stew and all the bread we could eat?
You've brought us out into this wilderness to starve us to death."*

EXODUS 16:3 MSG

When the going gets tough, some resort to complaining. The free become victims. The rescued want an invitation to return to bondage. It's hard to blame the Israelites for doing what every human does. Maybe you've been there.

God rescued more than a million people from Egypt, where conditions were harsh and the people were oppressed. They wanted to be rescued. But when help came, the people seemed to prefer bondage. Why?

Maybe they thought freedom would look different. Maybe they didn't think they would miss their stew and bread. As odd as it sounds, they may have become used to abuse.

When you choose to follow Christ, you experience rescue and freedom. But it's possible to rejoice one minute and then want to return to the bondage of your old life the next.

In a statement of delusion, the Israelites described their slavery in Egypt as "comfortable." It's possible to wrongly identify *your* old life as comfortable too. This thinking always takes a short view and refuses to consider contentment in new life living.

*Lord, when I entertain foolish thinking and want to return to a painful
past, help me remember that You rescued me from something so
I would have access to something so much better.*

REVOLUTIONARY RULES AND RELATIONSHIPS

"Don't be afraid," Moses answered them, "for God has come in this way to test you, and so that your fear of him will keep you from sinning!"

EXODUS 20:20 NLT

It was just a few weeks since the people of Israel had left Egypt. They enjoyed a quail buffet and manna for breakfast, and God even supplied the water they needed. Yet they still grumbled.

The top of Mount Sinai was roiling with thunder and lightning. Smoke covered the peaks. The people were afraid of God. So Moses met with God and then delivered His *revolutionary rules* (Ten Commandments). Each rule enhanced relationships. God came to the mountain in glorious splendor so the people would experience awe and wonder. He wanted the people to obey Him, but His glorious display didn't seem to penetrate their hearts.

Don't make the mistake of seeing God at work and then shrugging it off as if something normal has just taken place. Work through your resistance, and because glory is due, give it to Him. Don't view God's work as commonplace. He steps in because He loves you. He gives you rules because following them brings you closer to Him. He rescues to shorten the time you must endure trouble.

God, I don't want to be ho hum about You. I don't want to shrug off and dismiss Your gifts. I don't want to invite apathy to my journey with You. Help me get rid of these things I don't want.

A TIME TO DISCARD

"You shall not bow down to their gods, nor serve them, nor do according to their works; but you shall utterly overthrow them and completely break down their sacred pillars."
Exodus 23:24 NKJV

God wants His family to endure the things that change lives and enhance futures. He wants you to realize that you will face trouble but that He'll be with you. He wants to be clear that you won't endure alone.

There are things God doesn't want you to endure. The verse above is an example of one of those things. This wasn't the first time God made a command like this. Exodus 20:3 says, "You shall have no other gods before Me" (NKJV).

God doesn't want you to serve anything in place of Him. He doesn't want you to follow other teachings. He wants you to put aside everything that could distract you from Him.

What does that look like? Teachings that contradict His, objects that become more important than Him, and thoughts that cause you to doubt His truth.

Everyone has something that could become more important than God. . .at least some of the time. You are unique and only you can name what that is for you. Enjoy what God has given you, but never let *stuff* become more important than Him.

Father, You are a one-and-only God. No one matches You in power, wisdom, and love. May I never replace Your meaningful with society's meaningless.

FOR EVERY REBELLIOUS HEART

*When Moses went and told the people all the LORD's
words and laws, they responded with one voice,
"Everything the LORD has said we will do."*

EXODUS 24:3 NIV

I t was a case of good intentions. The people of Israel had been temporarily impressed with God on the mountain. They heard the law, and then a million voices raised in unison to say that they would do everything God had said. There was no mention of exclusions, loopholes, or excuses.

That day, one million people lied. By doing so, they broke one of God's revolutionary rules. It would be the first of many ongoing violations of God's commands.

Humans often forget the important things and remember what should be forgiven. For instance, you should always remember the goodness of God and forgive the offenses others commit against you.

God never offers false promises, and He's patient with those who routinely make them. His Son, Jesus, paid the price needed for God to offer forgiveness for breaking His revolutionary rules.

The people of Israel needed God's patience. So do you. It's possible to become discouraged when you can't live up to your own expectations, let alone God's. But God had a plan to make things right for every rebellious heart.

*Lord, thanks for being patient with me. I will make promises
that will be broken. I will look for an out when there isn't one.
I will need Your forgiveness. I will need to be transformed.*

FROM PERSONAL EXPERIENCE

And they shall know [from personal experience] that I am the
Lord their God, Who brought them forth out of the land of Egypt
that I might dwell among them; I am the Lord their God.
EXODUS 29:46 AMPC

You'd think it would be enough to see the evidence of God's handiwork—that awe would be the natural result of seeing how God freed an entire nation from slavery. The imprint of God's goodness had to be on the minds of those who walked through the Red Sea, ate God's special food, and witnessed His presence on the mountain. But memories fade.

The people knew from personal experience that God rescues. But the people were looking for a return policy.

Jesus was reluctant to perform *some* miracles because people had a short memory. They wanted a show to amuse and astound, but they couldn't endure long enough to recall God's previous faithfulness.

Remember (from personal experience) how God took the impossible and made it an answered prayer—the times when you accepted His forgiveness and love. He's the God who rescued you from slavery to sin.

Faith is your endurance test. It asks that you trust without seeing, believe without knowing everything, and remember without returning to what you once were.

God, my personal experience insists that You are God,
but my daily choices don't always show that I remember
what I know is true. Jog my memory, move my heart,
and let me remember that You're faithful.

WELL RESTED

*"Six days shall work be done, but the seventh day
is a Sabbath of solemn rest, holy to the LORD."*
EXODUS 31:15 ESV

D o you work and play hard but find it hard to rest? Do you feel like you'll miss something if you take time to rest? Maybe the Israelites were made to work every day while they were in Egypt, so it seemed unnatural to rest one day a week.

You can always find something to fill time. There's a lawn to mow, a garage to clean, or a car to maintain. But God said to take one day a week—*and rest.*

Rest invites you to be still and discover the God you've avoided while working. It sets aside bustle in favor of blessing. Rest isn't punishment. It's not designed to make you feel guilty. It's not even to make you work harder the other six days.

Enduring a time of rest insists that time with God is more important than the things you want to do. God set the example and rested on the seventh day of creation.

From a practical standpoint, people who don't take the day of rest are often forced to take *days* of rest due to illnesses that result from refusing to slow down.

God asks you to rest because it's good for you, and because it pleases Him.

*Father, a day of rest is a gift from You. I can't restore, replenish,
or revive if I don't have downtime. Help me accept Your gift.*

SOUNDS OF A PARTY

But Moses said, Those aren't songs of victory, and those
aren't songs of defeat, I hear songs of people throwing a party.
EXODUS 32:18 MSG

G od chose Moses to take the Israelites from slavery to freedom, but the people complained and longed to return to Egypt. When Moses climbed Mount Sinai to meet with God, the people waited. But they didn't wait long.

The people could see the clouds, hear the thunder, and witness the lightning. But the people didn't see Moses. With no one to lead, the people went their own way. They commissioned a new god to lead them. Moses' brother Aaron made a gold statue of a calf. The people thought it looked good enough to worship.

This *nongod* was getting in the way of Moses' time with *the God who delivers*. From the mountaintop, Moses heard the sounds of a party—but God wasn't the honored guest.

Is it hard to wait on God? He has answers, but do you look elsewhere when you think He's not paying attention? Can you remember a time when you wondered if following God made practical sense?

If you're going to follow someone, don't follow the Israelites. Don't witness God's rescue and think this same God would ever abandon you.

Lord, I want to worship You and make You the honored
guest in my life. I want to follow and not be distracted.
I want to remember that You never leave me.

THE CONTRACT

The LORD replied, "Listen, I am making a covenant with you in the presence of all your people. I will perform miracles that have never been performed anywhere in all the earth or in any nation."
EXODUS 34:10 NLT

God gave the people of Israel a contract. The contract (covenant) described what He expected from the people and what they could expect from Him. It explained conditions and offered guidance on improving relationships with the God who created the contract.

If there was ever a breach of contract, it could be found among the people who were given the contract—*not with the God who gave it.* This contract wasn't a backroom deal with loopholes and provisions favorable to few. This was a life contract for all—*guaranteed by God.*

Jesus offered a new contract when He paid the penalty for your sin. Actually, it was more like an amendment to the original contract. It offered greater protections for you and incredible restoration of relationship with God when you fail to live up to the letter of the original contract.

The Bible is the source of God's covenant with you. It makes sense to read what it says and do what it commands. When you find yourself in breach of contract with God, remember that it's Jesus who defends and restores you.

God, it's good to know what You expect from me. It's good to know what I can expect from You. And when I don't live up to Your standards, You have provisions for that too.

FULLY COMMITTED

*They still kept bringing him freewill offerings every morning,
so that all the craftsmen who were doing every sort of task
on the sanctuary came, each from the task that he was doing,
and said to Moses, "The people bring much more than enough
for doing the work that the LORD has commanded us to do."*
EXODUS 36:3–5 ESV

I f your church has ever held a capital campaign for a new building, then you know the endeavor can seem nearly overwhelming, especially when you first hear the projected costs. Once you get over the initial shock, it's amazing to watch God work through the extended efforts of His people as they sacrifice for His kingdom.

As Israel built the tabernacle, the place where God would meet with His people in the desert, He asked them to contribute gold, silver, bronze, yarn, linen, animal skins, wood, oil, spices for anointing oil, onyx stones, and more (Exodus 35:5–9). Their hearts were so engaged that the craftsmen had to ask Moses to tell them to stop bringing offerings.

When leaders at your church ask you to go the extra mile for a ministry project, are you as willing as the Israelites were? It requires a long-term commitment and a stick-to-it mentality, but how can you do anything less than go all in?

*Lord, give me the heart of the Israelites to invest my time,
energy, money, and talent into Your kingdom for the long haul.*

A PERPETUAL PRIESTHOOD

"Anoint them just as you anointed their father, so they may
serve me as priests. Their anointing will be to a priesthood
that will continue throughout their generations."

EXODUS 40:15 NIV

God instructed Israel to anoint everything in the newly constructed tabernacle, including the oil, the furnishings, the basin and its stand, and even Aaron and his sons, who would serve as priests. Everything had to be set apart before it could be used in worship.

Aaron's sons were anointed to a priesthood that would continue for generations. In the new covenant, all Christians are considered priests. It too is a perpetual calling. First Peter 2:9 (NIV) says, "You are a chosen people, a royal priesthood, a holy nation, God's special possession, that you may declare the praises of him who called you out of darkness into his wonderful light."

Christ has made you clean, so you don't need to submit to ritual cleansings like Aaron and his sons did, but the spirit remains the same. How serious are you about your calling as the priest of your family? Are you meeting with God regularly? Are you open to correction from Him and other believers? Are you leading and guiding your family spiritually throughout the week?

Father, I need to take my calling as the priest
of my home seriously. Enable me, guide me,
humble me so I may lead my family for Your glory.

GOD'S PERFECT STANDARD

*"You must never eat any fat or blood. This is a permanent
law for you, and it must be observed from generation
to generation, wherever you live."*
LEVITICUS 3:17 NLT

As you make your way through the Levitical laws, it can be difficult to keep them all straight. God had exact procedures that priests, and ultimately His people, were to follow for burnt offerings, grain offerings, peace offerings, and sin offerings—all of which you'll read about today.

As you do, it should remind you that God's standard for holiness is perfection. And as much as He expected priests and His people to be holy, He knew they would fail. Hence, the temporary provisions for atonement here in Leviticus and the permanent provision in the form of the Messiah. As you run the Christian race of endurance, cling to Christ, who has satisfied all of God's requirements for your holiness.

You still have the responsibility of shunning sin while keeping short accounts with God though repentance followed by faith. This is not a one-time occurrence. It's a daily process of self-examination in which you stay sensitive to the Holy Spirit's promptings to repent and believe anew. This is one of your primary roles as a New Testament priest.

*Lord, Your standard is perfection, and I fall woefully
short every day. Draw me close, and create in me a
clean heart, O God. Renew my loyalty day by day.*

CHRIST, YOUR PEACE OFFERING

"Speak to the children of Israel, saying: 'He who offers the sacrifice of his peace offering to the LORD shall bring his offering to the LORD from the sacrifice of his peace offering.' "
LEVITICUS 7:29 NKJV

In an *I Love Lucy* episode titled "The Matchmaker," Lucy and her husband, Ricky, have a fight after Ricky spoils her dinner party. When he comes home the next evening, he wants to apologize so he brings Lucy flowers and a box of chocolates.

Yes, it's a comedy, and yes, hilarity ensues during Ricky's apology, but don't miss the importance of his peace offering. It was his way of saying he knew he had messed up and wanted to make things right.

Christ is your peace offering. You cannot earn His favor or work your way back into good favor with Him. That's not to say you shouldn't perform good works in His name, but you do those out of the gratitude of your heart.

Psalm 51:16–17 (ESV) says, "For you will not delight in sacrifice, or I would give it; you will not be pleased with a burnt offering. The sacrifices of God are a broken spirit; a broken and contrite heart, O God, you will not despise."

Your work, then, is the lifelong task of staying broken, and therefore usable, before God.

O God, I'm willing to have my spirit and heart broken so I may be pliable in Your hands.

KEEP A CLEAR MIND

*"You are to distinguish between the holy and the common,
and between the unclean and the clean, and you are to teach the people
of Israel all the statutes that the LORD has spoken to them by Moses."*
LEVITICUS 10:10–11 ESV

In today's verse, the Lord called Aaron to a lifetime of faithfulness. Consuming alcohol in the tent of meeting (tabernacle) was forbidden (Leviticus 10:9). Their role as priests was just too important to have their thoughts and judgment clouded. They were to help God's people distinguish between the holy and the common.

What clouds your mind? Alcohol? Pornography? Lust? Gossip? Status? Something else? Your job of washing your wife in the Word (Ephesians 5:25–26) and raising godly children (Proverbs 22:6) is far too important to allow such thinking. You are called to distinguish between the holy and the common. That will require long-term persistence to keep you as free of sin as possible. The more you allow sin to take root in your heart, the less effective you'll be in leading your family.

If you are enslaved to a sin, seek help from a Christian brother. Wrestle, fight, and pray. You and your family have too much at stake to not take action.

*Lord, give me the strength I need to confront my
sin so that I can lead my family with a clean
conscience for many years to come.*

BE HOLY

"Make yourselves holy for I am holy. Don't make yourselves ritually unclean by any creature that crawls on the ground. I am GOD who brought you up out of the land of Egypt. Be holy because I am holy."
LEVITICUS 11:44–45 MSG

The people of Israel had an obligation to know which mammals, sea creatures, birds, insects, and creatures that crawl on the ground would make them ceremonially unclean if they ate them, and which ones did not. Working your way through such a list in today's culture may seem like a foreign concept, but this was the call for the believer to maintain holiness.

Jesus changed this. In Matthew 15:10–11 (NIV), He said, "Listen and understand. What goes into someone's mouth does not defile them, but what comes out of their mouth, that is what defiles them." So, if what a person eats or doesn't eat has no bearing on his holiness, then what does?

"What springs from a corrupt unregenerate heart—a perverse will and impure passions—these defile, i.e. make him a sinner," wrote Bible commentator Adam Clarke.

You will be engaged in the process of minding your heart for the rest of your life as you are careful about what you watch and think. Jesus makes you holy, but even so, you are responsible for your thoughts and actions.

Lord, my earnest desire is to be holy as You are holy.
Empower me to mind my heart today and every day.

UNCLEAN! UNCLEAN!

*"So the priest shall make atonement for
him who is to be cleansed before the Lord."*
Leviticus 14:31 nkjv

Three times in today's reading, the Lord uses the phrase "So the priest shall make atonement for him" in reference to the person who needed to be cleansed. He had to present himself to a priest for examination every time he contracted leprosy, boils, sores, or burns from a fire. And if he was found to be a leper, he had to shout, "Unclean! Unclean!" before being put out of the camp to dwell alone.

What if you had to present yourself to a minister every time you appeared to be unclean, spiritually speaking? And after being examined and found guilty, you had to shout, "Unclean! Unclean!" before being put out of the church? It seems harsh, but in reality, God is holy and He required justice for sin.

Praise God, Jesus stepped into the gap and made you clean. Even so, every time you sin, you can turn to Him and declare yourself guilty and then have full confidence that He'll be faithful and just to forgive you. Jesus is your Priest. Make it a habit of conversing with Him daily, asking Him to wipe your slate clean.

*Lord, thank You for sending Your Son to make
me clean in Your sight. May I never desire to
shy away from Him when I have sinned.*

ON BEING "PRAYED UP"

*"Whenever a man has an emission of semen,
he must bathe his entire body in water, and he will
remain ceremonially unclean until the next evening."*
LEVITICUS 15:16 NLT

Your stomach might be a little queasy after today's reading. You won't often hear discussions of bodily discharges from the pulpit or in Sunday school. You might even be a bit confused at why such talk is in the Bible. And given that it is, why would a man be considered unclean after an emission of semen, even in the context of the marriage bed?

Maybe Bible commentator John Gill's explanation will help: "For though marriage is honourable and holy, and carnal copulation in itself lawful, yet such is the sinfulness of nature, that as no act is performed without pollution, so neither that of generation, and by which the corruption of nature is propagated, and therefore required a ceremonial cleansing."

In other words, even (and especially) man's seed was corrupted by the Fall, and any emission of semen (before the Messiah arrived) made a man unclean. This speaks to the totality of sin in your body and should convince you of your diligent need for continual repentance. Christians of old used to call this being "prayed up," meaning, they believed in confessing sin immediately. It's still a great practice today.

*Lord, I acknowledge the seriousness of sin and want
to live in the light by confessing to You often.*

HE IS FAITHFUL

And Aaron shall lay both his hands upon the head of the live
goat and confess over him all the iniquities of the Israelites
and all their transgressions, all their sins; and he shall put them
upon the head of the goat [the sin-bearer], and send him away
into the wilderness by the hand of a man who is timely (ready, fit).
LEVITICUS 16:21 AMPC

Once a year, Aaron was to enter the Holy Place with a young bull for a sin offering and a ram for a burnt offering. He had to bathe, put on the holy linen undergarment, then sacrifice two male goats and one ram before taking a censer full of burning coals of fire, along with two hands full of incense into the Holy of Holies.

He had other rituals to obey, as well, including the one you read about in today's verse about sending the sin-bearing goat away, which is an obvious reference to Jesus, who would one day take on the sin of the world as the ultimate scapegoat.

What ran through your mind as you read about everything Aaron had to do once a year to eradicate sin? As you reflect on what Aaron had to do, rejoice that Jesus paid the full price for sin, once and for all. He was faithful, even when you weren't.

Father, thank You for being faithful to make a way
for us to go to heaven when there was no way.

IDOL FACTORIES

"Do not turn to idols or make for yourselves any
gods of cast metal: I am the LORD your God."
LEVITICUS 19:4 ESV

John Calvin once wrote, "Man's nature, so to speak, is a perpetual factory of idols."

Let that sink in. If what he's saying is true, then your heart manufactures idols continually. Modern-day idols include materialism, approval, money, independence, status, work, success, sex, and even ministries. John Piper put it this way: "Idolatry starts in the heart: craving, wanting, enjoying, being satisfied by anything that you treasure more than God."

This begs the question, as you search your heart today, is there anything you find more satisfaction in and desire more than God? If so, it's an idol and that's serious business. In Colossians 3:5–6 (ESV), Paul said, "Put to death therefore what is earthly in you: sexual immorality, impurity, passion, evil desire, and covetousness, which is idolatry. On account of these the wrath of God is coming."

You'll spend the rest of your life putting your idols to death. Don't lose heart though. Just continue the fight, knowing that a day is coming when sin will no longer be an issue for you. In heaven, you'll be given a glorified body that no longer produces idols.

Lord, I confess to bowing down to idols.
Empower me to put them out on a daily basis.

NO DEFECTS ALLOWED

"In all future generations, none of your descendants who has any defect will qualify to offer food to his God. No one who has a defect qualifies, whether he is blind, lame, disfigured, deformed, or has a broken foot or arm, or is hunchbacked or dwarfed, or has a defective eye, or skin sores or scabs, or damaged testicles."
LEVITICUS 21:17–20 NLT

Why would God have such stringent requirements for priests, especially since a person who has a defect might have been born with it or might have been in an accident in which he wasn't at fault?

It's not that people with defects are of less value to God. But the priest was a mediator between man and God, and, as such, he needed to be without blemish. But what value does any of this have for the church today?

Since Jesus is the perfect High Priest, Christians don't need to worry about personal defects keeping them from God's presence. But such a high standard is a good reminder about the importance of working out your own salvation, as Paul instructs in Philippians 2:12. You do so by staying steadfast in the tending of your heart—making sure to pursue purity and holiness.

Lord, I'm thankful for Jesus' perfect sacrifice. May I never take it for granted by staying mired in sin. Instead, may I remain vigilant in pursuit of holiness.

TEND YOUR LAMP

*"Outside the curtain that shields the ark of the covenant law
in the tent of meeting, Aaron is to tend the lamps before
the LORD from evening till morning, continually. This is
to be a lasting ordinance for the generations to come."*
LEVITICUS 24:3 NIV

In the early 500s, Benedict of Nursia went to Rome for educational purposes. After encountering a dark culture there, he fled to the forest. He ended up becoming a monk and an advocate for monastic life, believing that a peaceful, consistent, structured life helped to maintain the faith during the beginning of what is now known as the Dark Ages.

Benedict believed in monks taking a vow of stability, meaning they would stay in one monastery until their death. In a very real way, monks tended to the flame of the Christian faith during a dark period in human history.

Aaron was charged with tending the lamps in the tent of meeting from evening until morning. Revelation 1:12–20 refers to seven lampstands that represent the seven churches that were to be lights in a dark world. The symbolism in both passages is hard to miss, isn't it? Your church, your family, is called to be the light of the world, just as Jesus said in Matthew 5:14. Shine for Jesus.

*Lord, I live in a culture that is growing darker
and darker. May I be as vigilant at tending
my lamp as You called Aaron to be.*

THOROUGH REPENTANCE

"If they confess their iniquity and the iniquity of their forefathers, in their unfaithfulness which they committed against Me, and also in their acting with hostility against Me. . .then I will remember My covenant with Jacob, and I will remember also My covenant with Isaac, and My covenant with Abraham as well, and I will remember the land."
LEVITICUS 26:40, 42 NASB

I srael was guilty of all sorts of depravity, including idolatry in various forms and hostility toward God (Leviticus 26:27–33). Not that any sin was good, but idolatry was an especially abhorrent scent in God's nostrils. Yet, today's verses say He was willing to remember His covenants with Abraham, Isaac, and Jacob and relent, if only the people would confess their iniquity and the iniquity of their forefathers.

All of this speaks to God's covenantal nature. Matthew Henry says as much in his concise commentary: "Among the Israelites, persons were not always prosperous or afflicted according to their obedience or disobedience. But national prosperity was the effect of national obedience, and national judgments were brought on by national wickedness."

When you think about the sins of your grandparents and parents, and your own sin, have you been thorough in confessing it? Create a list right now of the generational sins in your family, then confess them to God.

Lord, as I pray through the list I just created, hear my prayer and remember Your promise to forgive my family.

LOVE EQUALS OBEDIENCE

The People of Israel did everything the way GOD
commanded Moses: They camped under their respective
flags; they marched by tribe with their ancestral families.
NUMBERS 2:34 MSG

I n the first two chapters of Numbers, God instructs Moses to have each numbered tribe pitch its encampment around the tabernacle (far off, says some translations, out of reverence) in a specific order. Then they were to fly their own respective tribal flags. Israel didn't have a great track record when it came to obedience, but this time, more than six hundred thousand people did everything the way God had commanded Moses.

Today, on Valentine's Day, the people around you at work or school will be caught up in the notion of romantic love, but many will fail to make the connection between love and obedience—especially as it relates to their relationship with God. First John 5:3 (MSG) says, "The proof that we love God comes when we keep his commandments and they are not at all troublesome."

Take some time today to reflect on this. Is there enough proof in your life, through your obedience to God's commandments, to show that you love Him? Would your family and friends agree with your assessment?

Lord, help me to love and honor my wife or girlfriend
well today. But more importantly, empower me to obey Your
commandments, which will show You how much I love You.

TRUE LEADERS ARE SERVANTS

*All those who were listed of the Levites, whom Moses and Aaron
and the chiefs of Israel listed, by their clans and their fathers'
houses, from thirty years old up to fifty years old, everyone who
could come to do the service of ministry and the service of bearing
burdens in the tent of meeting, those listed were 8,580.*

NUMBERS 4:46–48 ESV

D ave Ramsey shares a story about President George Washington you may not have heard. During the Revolutionary War, Washington rode up and saw a group of soldiers trying desperately to put a log on top of a wall. Their corporal was barking orders to finish the project, prompting Washington to ask the corporal why he didn't help.

"Don't you see, I'm a corporal?" he said.

Washington dismounted and assisted the men himself then told them he was available if they needed any other help. The commander in chief was willing to serve when a corporal was not. Is it any wonder that Washington's birthday has been celebrated nationally, going back to 1885? He lived out the "service of ministry" advocated in today's verses. Later, President Abraham Lincoln's birthday was added to the holiday that we now call Presidents' Day. And now we celebrate all past presidents on this day.

When you lead, are you more like Washington. . .or the corporal?

*Lord, give me a spirit of servant leadership.
May I never be like the corporal.*

A LIVING SACRIFICE

"They [the Nazirites] must never cut their hair throughout the time of their vow, for they are holy and set apart to the LORD. Until the time of their vow has been fulfilled, they must let their hair grow long."
NUMBERS 6:5 NLT

The Nazirite vow, which was generally considered to be voluntary, could be taken by men or women who wanted to be set apart for God. It included several key requirements that would be kept until the vow was fulfilled. The Nazirite was to abstain from fermented drinks, avoid dead bodies, and men were not to cut their hair.

This practice has some similarities, at least in spirit, to the New Testament principle the apostle Paul advocated in Romans 12:1–2 (NLT): "I plead with you to give your bodies to God because of all he has done for you. Let them be a living and holy sacrifice—the kind he will find acceptable. This is truly the way to worship him. Don't copy the behavior and customs of this world, but let God transform you into a new person by changing the way you think."

Rather than copying the behavior and customs of this world, how specifically do you set yourself apart for God?

Father, I confess to copying the behavior and customs of this world all too often. Starting today, I want to be a living sacrifice, set apart for You.

WALK IN THE LIGHT

When Moses finished setting up The Dwelling, he anointed it and consecrated it along with all that went with it. At the same time he anointed and consecrated the Altar and its accessories.

NUMBERS 7:1 MSG

Ash Wednesday, which falls forty days (not including Sundays) before Easter, is a practice some Christian denominations use to help congregations reflect on self-denial while forsaking sin and embracing the cross. While believers should always desire to turn from their sin, this holiday is a reminder to do so.

In today's passage, Moses meticulously consecrated everything in the tabernacle. Are you as meticulous about doing so in your own life? Ephesians 5:8–9 (MSG) says, "You groped your way through that murk once, but no longer. You're out in the open now. The bright light of Christ makes your way plain. So no more stumbling around. Get on with it!"

The way you live will look peculiar to unbelievers. They won't understand your earnest desire to deny yourself as you forsake your sin. Do it anyway. As you do, you'll be modeling the transformed life in front of them, and God can, and often does, use that to draw others to Himself.

Lord, on this day, I'm setting aside time to reflect on my sinful nature so I can forsake it. As a new creation in Christ, may I always represent You well.

BLOW YOUR TRUMPETS

"The sons of Aaron, the priests, are to blow the trumpets.
This is to be a lasting ordinance for you and the generations to come."
NUMBERS 10:8 NIV

God instructed Moses to have the sons of Aaron blow two silver trumpets whenever they went into battle in their own land and also at times of rejoicing during the appointed festivals and feasts. The trumpet blasts served to summon God to rescue them from their enemies and as a memorial of God's goodness. This practice was to be a lasting ordinance for generations to come.

What do you do to summon God to rescue your family or to remember His goodness for something He's done in the past? Maybe the way you blow the trumpet in your family is to place your Bible on the breakfast or dinner table to let your family know that they are about to meet with God. Or maybe you blow the trumpet by asking your family to turn off the television and their gadgets to gather around for family devotions. However you do it, make it a lasting ordinance in your family that can continue for generations to come.

Lord, we need trumpet blasts in our family because we
are a people who often need You to rescue us. And we
want to remember Your constant goodness.

NO MORE PASTOR PIE

While they were at Hazeroth, Miriam and Aaron criticized
Moses because he had married a Cushite woman. They said,
"Has the Lord spoken only through Moses? Hasn't he spoken
through us, too?" But the Lord heard them.
Numbers 12:1–2 nlt

In today's passage, Moses' two siblings appear to have been bitten by the jealousy bug. They were both prophets, and Aaron was a priest. Yet they had a brother who didn't speak well and who had married a Cushite woman, and God was using him mightily. What gives?

Most pastors are familiar with what happened to Moses. It's called Pastor Pie, and it's served on Sundays around the dinner table as adults criticize the pastor's sermon or his delivery or an application point he had made. Pastors are fallible. They will tell you that. But God has appointed them to shepherd flocks. And if you are unjustifiably critical, God hears. You also set a negative example for your children that will stick with them.

Resolve to not criticize your pastor or other leaders, especially in front of your children. Instead, recognize disagreements with God-appointed authorities as an opportunity to grow your humility. Submission to authority is easy when you agree. It's much more difficult when you disagree. But this is your calling.

Lord, I repent for criticizing church leaders in the past.
Forgive me! Help me to see future disagreements as
opportunities for my own long-term sanctification.

GRUMBLE NO MORE

" 'The LORD is slow to anger, abounding in love and
forgiving sin and rebellion. Yet he does not leave the
guilty unpunished; he punishes the children for the sin
of the parents to the third and fourth generation.'
In accordance with your great love, forgive the sin
of these people, just as you have pardoned them
from the time they left Egypt until now."
NUMBERS 14:18–19 NIV

In Numbers 14, Israel is grumbling against Moses and Aaron, fearing they would die in Canaan if they took the land as God had instructed. Moses prays and asks for their forgiveness and God grants it, just as He has since they left Egypt.

Grumbling is the one constant throughout humanity. Israel grumbled often—about manna, danger, and its leadership. First Peter 4:9 cautions Christians against grumbling, which means it was a problem in Peter's time too. And today, Christians grumble about a myriad of things, such as worship music style, the length of the worship service, pastors who preach about tithing—on and on the list goes.

Yet, God is faithful to forgive His church, even when His church doesn't trust Him. What do you grumble about regarding your faith? Your church? God? It's time to stop grumbling, ask God for forgiveness, and trust that He is watching out for you.

Father, forgive me, just as You forgave Israel in today's passage.
I grumble when I should trust You. Change my heart, O God.

STOPPING A PLAGUE

*And Moses said to Aaron, "Take your censer, and put fire
on it from off the altar and lay incense on it and carry it
quickly to the congregation and make atonement for them,
for wrath has gone out from the LORD; the plague has begun."*

NUMBERS 16:46 ESV

After the Lord had consumed 250 well-known people in the congregation who assembled against Moses and Aaron, the rest of the congregation grumbled against them too. The Lord planned to consume them also, but Moses acted quickly. You can read what he told Aaron in today's verse. The Lord relented after 14,700 people were put to death.

Consider Moses' heart. He didn't hold a grudge against Israel. Well, if he did, he didn't let it stop him from taking action to help save them. The same could be said for Aaron. Both men acted on Israel's behalf as a mediator between Israel and God, even though Israel didn't deserve it.

Your family will not always agree with your leadership. They may grumble and challenge you. It's not your job to try to convince them of your authority. Continue to be a steadfast advocate for them in prayer. It's the best way you can love them.

*Lord, may my heart never grow bitter toward my family,
even when they oppose my spiritual leadership. Instead,
may I remain a steadfast advocate for them in prayer.*

APPROACH BOLDLY

"From now on, no Israelites except priests or Levites may approach the Tabernacle. If they come too near, they will be judged guilty and will die. Only the Levites may serve at the Tabernacle, and they will be held responsible for any offenses against it. This is a permanent law for you, to be observed from generation to generation."
NUMBERS 18:22–23 NLT

I magine being told that you could not enter a sanctuary for worship ever again—that only pastors and ministers could do so, and that this was a binding law for the rest of your life. After getting over the shock, it might give you a sense of God's holiness. Before Jesus took on flesh and dwelt among humanity, God could only be approached by the priests.

Praise God, Jesus made approaching the Father not only possible, but, as the writer of Hebrews says, He made it possible for us to "come boldly to the throne of our gracious God. There we will receive his mercy, and we will find grace to help us when we need it most" (Hebrews 4:16 NLT).

After you've sinned, do you shy away from God, embracing an old covenant mind-set? Or do you make it a practice to boldly approach the throne to receive mercy and help when you need it most?

Lord, thank You for Jesus, who made it possible to approach You boldly. And thank You for Your mercy and grace!

PASSING THE BATON

"Take Aaron and Eleazar his son and bring them up to Mount Hor.
And strip Aaron of his garments and put them on Eleazar his son.
And Aaron shall be gathered to his people and shall die there."
NUMBERS 20:25–26 ESV

Neither Moses nor Aaron were going to be allowed to enter the Promised Land. But before they were gathered to their people, the Lord made sure there was a line of succession to carry on His work. In Aaron's case, his oldest (living) son Eleazar would take his garments and take over his duties as the high priest.

As much as God might use any particular generation, He always has a plan of succession to continue His work. Often, it is continued through a generational bloodline. When you think about the spiritual work you've done to prepare your own children, would you say they are ready to continue what you've taught them after you are gone? If not, what do you need to be teaching them right now to prepare them? If you don't have any children, do you have any nieces or nephews you could invest in? How about teaching children at church?

The work of the kingdom should never stop with any given generation. The next one should always be able to build on what the previous one accomplished in the strength of the Lord.

Lord, help me to make training the next generation a priority.

DON'T LOSE HEART

"God brought them out of Egypt; for them he is
as strong as a wild ox. No curse can touch Jacob;
no magic has any power against Israel."
NUMBERS 23:22–23 NLT

As Israel set up an encampment near Moab, Balak, Moab's king, was filled with terror, thinking Israel might attack. Trying to get out in front of an offensive, he turned to Balaam, wanting him to curse Israel. But Balak's efforts were in vain. Ever since He brought them out of Egypt, God had been faithful to His people, and He would be faithful to them as they took the Promised Land. No magic has any power against Israel.

In a postmodern culture, it's easy to lose hope. Darkness is settling over the land and it seeks to infiltrate every home via television, tablets, computers, and phones. But God will be faithful to this generation of believers, just as He was faithful to all previous generations. Don't lose heart. During some of Israel's darkest hours, God intervened in a mighty way.

Live an intentional life for Christ. Have regular family devotions. Pray around the dinner table. Engage in spiritual conversations with your family. Read good Christian books. Listen to Christian radio. And call on the God of Abraham, Isaac, and Jacob to protect your family.

Father, fill me with hope as I seek to lead
my family in the fear of the Lord.

A COVENANT OF PEACE

*"So tell him that I am making a Covenant-of-Peace with him
[Phinehas son of Eleazar]. He and his descendants are joined
in a covenant of eternal priesthood, because he was zealous
for his God and made atonement for the People of Israel."*

NUMBERS 25:12–13 MSG

Numbers 25 chronicles a dark period in Israel's history. Men of Israel engaged in an orgy with Moabite women. To make matters worse, the ritual was mixed with the worship of false gods. God was furious and commanded Moses to kill the guilty men. Phinehas, the son of Eleazar, finally put a stop to the plague, prompting God to form a covenant of peace with him and his descendants—one that would cover some 950 years, according to Bible commentator Adam Clarke.

Your past may include sinful actions that would make you blush if they were ever brought to light. Sin demands justice. You came to that understanding and clung to Christ who offered you a covenant of peace with God. You were joined to an eternal priesthood at that moment because you were zealous for the righteousness of Christ. Now continue to walk in a manner that is worthy of your Redeemer.

*Lord, I'm in no position to judge the men of Israel I read about in
today's passage. I deserve Your wrath. Thank You for sending
Jesus to take my punishment as the ultimate covenant of peace.*

PROMISE KEEPING

"This is the thing which the LORD has commanded: If a man makes a vow to the LORD, or swears an oath to bind himself by some agreement, he shall not break his word; he shall do according to all that proceeds out of his mouth."

NUMBERS 30:1–2 NKJV

As you work your way through the Pentateuch, you'll see that believers in the Old Testament could make a Nazirite vow, a vow of abstinence, a vow of giving to the poor, and more. These vows were voluntary, but once they were made, they were binding between God and man. You'd do well to keep in mind what Ecclesiastes 5:5 (NKJV) says: "Better not to vow than to vow and not pay."

New Testament believers do not make vows in the sense that believers did in the old covenant. In Matthew 5:33–35 (NKJV), Jesus said, "You have heard that it was said to those of old, 'You shall not swear falsely, but shall perform your oaths to the Lord.' But I say to you, do not swear at all."

With that said, your word is your bond. If you make a promise to somebody, make every effort to follow through on your promise, no matter how difficult it is. Failing to do so will harm your witness for Christ.

Lord, may I only make promises I can keep.

FIGHTING ALONGSIDE OTHERS

Moses said, "If you do what you say, take up arms before
GOD for battle and together go across the Jordan ready, before
GOD, to fight until GOD has cleaned his enemies out of the land,
then when the land is secure you will have fulfilled your duty to
GOD and Israel. Then this land will be yours to keep before GOD."
NUMBERS 32:20–22 MSG

As the tribes of Reuben and Gad arrived at the land east of the Jordan, they liked what they saw. They had room for their huge herds of livestock, so they approached Moses and Eleazar to see if they could keep this portion of land for their inheritance. After much discussion, Moses agreed, reminding the two tribes that they would still need to help the other tribes fight their enemies.

The Christian life is one of being sensitive to the spiritual battles other believers face and being willing to show up and fight alongside them. It might mean getting involved in some sticky situations. It might mean being available twenty-four hours a day. Or it might mean using resources for others that you had planned to use for your family. But this is the call of the believer. Have you been faithful to answer it?

Lord, make me more sensitive to the spiritual needs of
the believers You've placed around me. And may I always
be willing to do and give more in service to them.

REMEMBERING GOD'S FAITHFULNESS

*At the LORD's command Moses
recorded the stages in their journey.*
NUMBERS 33:2 NIV

I n today's reading, you reviewed a long list of dozens of stops Israel made—from the moment they left Ramses to the moment they arrived at the Promised Land.

Why might God have command Moses to make such a list? God often instructed His people to build memorials to remember His faithfulness. Maybe His instructions to Moses here are for the same reason. He'd taken Israel out of bondage in Egypt and led them through the desert for forty years, delivering them to the Promised Land. Talk about a model of faithfulness! And since humans are prone to forget, maybe He wanted His faithfulness to be chronicled for all time.

When you tell the next generation about God's faithfulness in your family, how detailed do you get? Do you know the testimonies of previous generations in your family? If not, why not start by preserving your own in written, video, or audio format? Then encourage your children to do the same as they pass their spiritual history on, always remembering to highlight God's faithfulness.

Once you are done, maybe you could even start a similar class at church to help the families in your congregation do the same.

*Lord, may my family never forget Your
faithfulness to us throughout the ages.*

CITIES OF REFUGE THEN AND NOW

"The accused must stay in the city of refuge until the
death of the high priest; only after the death of the
high priest may they return to their own property."
NUMBERS 35:28 NIV

Today you won't find any traditional cities of refuge, but you will find the foundational principles almost everywhere. These principles can be seen in the world's many laws limiting the punishment of those found guilty of manslaughter.

Manslaughter is much different from murder. Both involve causing someone's death, but the first is accidental.

The most important biblical principle—complete forgiveness and protection upon the death of the high priest—is clearly seen in your Lord and Savior, Jesus Christ.

Since His ascension, Jesus is exalted forever at God the Father's right hand (Acts 2:33; 5:31; 7:55–56; Romans 8:34; Ephesians 1:20; Colossians 3:1; Hebrews 1:3; 8:1; 10:12; 12:2). There Jesus ever lives to pray and intercede for you (Romans 8:34; Hebrews 7:25; 9:24; 1 John 2:1).

How terrible to be guilty of accidentally killing a fellow human being. How wonderful to be protected judicially, and completely forgiven and protected spiritually by the Lord. What a great High Priest!

Lord, You want me seek refuge in Your Son, Jesus Christ.
Thank You so much that He is my Lord and Savior.

GETTING INTO DEUTERONOMY

*But forty years after the Israelites left Egypt, on the first day
of the eleventh month, Moses addressed the people of Israel,
telling them everything the LORD had commanded him to say.*
DEUTERONOMY 1:3 NLT

This fifth book of Moses contains his last words inspired by the Lord.
Even a quick glance suggests Moses was still going strong right up
until the end!

In this compelling sermon series, Moses reiterates the Lord's covenant
with a new generation of Israelites and urges them to claim His blessings
diligently. How? By first obeying God's commands faithfully—unlike the
previous generation.

In this fast-paced book, Moses reviews the nation's history over the
past forty years (chapters 1–3) and challenges the people to set a new
course (chapters 4–33). What a sermon it is!

Before sunset, Moses climbs Mount Nebo, surveys the Promised Land
from a distance, and goes to be with the Lord in paradise (chapter 34).

Famous passages in Deuteronomy include:

- warning against adding to or subtracting from God's commands
  (4:2)
- Ten Commandments repeated (5:6–21)
- warning against false prophets (13:1–5)
- prophecy of the Prophet to come (18:15–19)
- blessings and curses (28:1–68)

*Lord, You want me to keep going strong for You right up until the end of
my days on this earth. May I always read and review Your Word.*

SEEKING GOD HUMBLY AND WHOLEHEARTEDLY

But if from there you seek the LORD your God,
you will find him if you seek him with all
your heart and with all your soul.
DEUTERONOMY 4:29 NIV

What's important for you to know about seeking God?

1. Before Creation, God decided to seek worshippers who in turn would seek Him, humble themselves, acknowledge and confess and repent of their sins, seek His forgiveness, actively obey His commands, and love Him with all their heart, soul, strength, and mind (see Deuteronomy 4:29; 1 Chronicles 28:9; 2 Chronicles 15:12; Psalms 63:1 and 119:2; Isaiah 55:6 and 65:1; Jeremiah 29:13; and Zephaniah 2:3; see also Luke 19:10; John 4:23; Acts 17:27; and Hebrews 11:6).

2. To seek God wholeheartedly isn't always a personal matter. It's also important to seek God's blessing and favor on your community, city, and nation (see 2 Chronicles 7:14; Jeremiah 29:7 and 50:4; Hosea 10:12; and Zephaniah 2:3 and 8:21–22).

3. To seek God wholeheartedly is to seek His forgiveness, favor, approval, presence, protection, and other blessings. (See 1 Chronicles 16:10–11 and Psalms 9:10; 22:26; 24:6; 34:10; 40:16; 69:32; and 70:4. Also see Proverbs 14:32; Lamentations 3:25; Hosea 3:5; Amos 5:14; and Hebrews 11:6.)

On Saturday, you'll learn more about seeking God. Between now and then, make this your prayer:

Lord, You want me to seek You wholeheartedly.
Thank You for forgiving my sins—and for so much more.

EMBRACING GOD'S BOUNDARIES OF BLESSING

"Not with our fathers did the LORD make this covenant,
but with us, who are all of us here alive today."
DEUTERONOMY 5:3 ESV

How do you view the Ten Commandments? No, not the classic movie, but the real thing found in Exodus 20 and Deuteronomy 5.

Culturally, people often view the Ten Commandments as God's idealistic yet impossible demands for His people long, long ago. Then, as now, people want to do their own thing, their own way, without anyone or anything interfering with their choices.

If only people could see the Ten Commandments as God's boundaries of blessing. After all, each of the Ten Commandments protects God's people from serious error, terrible harm, unbearable heartache, and severe loss. Invest tens of thousands of dollars worshipping false gods? Bad idea. Work long hours seven days a week to get ahead? Another bad idea. Take a former neighbor to court on false charges and commit perjury? Super bad idea.

After nearly thirty-five hundred years, God's Ten Commandments are more relevant than ever. Each and every one continues to offer God's rich blessings.

Lord, You want me to never tire of enjoying what
You mean for my good. Thank You for the way
You designed the Ten Commandments.

DON'T IGNORE GOD'S WORD

*"Man does not live by bread alone, but man lives by
every word that comes from the mouth of the LORD."*
DEUTERONOMY 8:3 ESV

I f hundreds of millions of men honor what the Lord says, another four billion have access to God's Word but ignore it. Why should you care either way?

First, the Lord never speaks in vain, so you'd best heed His every word. Your spiritual sustenance always takes priority over the physical.

Second, you cannot add even the smallest subatomic particle of truth to the Lord's infinite and eternal knowledge, understanding, wisdom, and ways. No wonder Isaiah 55:8–9 (NIV) says, " 'For my thoughts are not your thoughts, neither are your ways my ways,' declares the LORD. 'As the heavens are higher than the earth, so are my ways higher than your ways and my thoughts than your thoughts.' "

Third, any time someone thinks he knows better than the Lord, he is acting like a fool and is in grave danger. Quoting Enoch, Jude 1:14–15 (NLT) says, "Listen! The Lord is coming. . .to execute judgment on the people of the world. He will convict every person of all the ungodly things they have done and for all the insults that ungodly sinners have spoken against him."

*Lord, You want me to heed Your every word.
I'm committed to doing that again today.*

SEEKING GOD'S FORGIVENESS AND BLESSING

You must seek the LORD your God at the place of worship
he himself will choose from among all the tribes—
the place where his name will be honored.
DEUTERONOMY 12:5 NLT

As promised, here are four more important facts about seeking God:
1. The ancient Israelites would seek God by going to the Tabernacle—and later the Temple in Jerusalem—to confess their sins, offer sacrifices, pray, and then feast together as a family, often with invited guests (see 1 Chronicles 22:19; 2 Chronicles 11:16; Psalm 27:4; and Malachi 3:1).

2. Jesus linked seeking God with seeking His kingdom purposes and His will to be done here on earth. (See the Lord's prayers in Matthew 3:2; 4:17; 6:9–13; and 7:10. Also see Mark 1:15 and Luke 11:2–4; 11:20; and 21:31.)

3. Jesus taught that seeking God isn't something you try once or twice. Instead, it requires commitment, diligence, endurance, and perseverance (see Matthew 7:7–8 and Luke 11:9–10).

4. Jesus is standing at the door of your heart—to enjoy an ongoing relationship with you. He says He wants to come in to celebrate and feast with you (see Revelation 3:20).

Lord, You want me to open my heart to You
every day. Yes, I open the door to You right now!

THREE MEGA-THEMES

*Follow justice and justice alone, so that you may live
and possess the land the Lord your God is giving you.*
Deuteronomy 16:20 niv

———◆———

Today's key verse comes near the midpoint of this great book. In it, Moses refers to two of his three favorite mega-themes. These mega-themes begin right away in Deuteronomy and continue to the end.

The three mega-themes are most succinctly stated after the sixth of Ten Commandments: "so that you may [1] live long and [2] that it may go well with you [3] in the land the Lord your God is giving you" (5:16 niv). They're echoed again at the end of that chapter: "Then you will [1] live long and [2] prosperous lives [3] in the land you are about to enter and occupy" (5:33 nlt). These three mega-themes appear dozens of times throughout the book, with [2] repeated the most, with all three appearing close together again in 11:8–9, and with Moses missing out on [3].

It's important to note that Moses is addressing the ancient Israelites. In the New Testament, only [1] is repeated (against the backdrop of possible martyrdom) and both [2] and [3] are moved to heaven (and then to the new heavens and earth). Then again, see Hebrews 11:13–16.

*Lord, You want me to stop looking around at life here
on earth. Instead, I will lift up my eyes to You today.*

HOME, SWEET HOME

When the LORD your God has destroyed the nations
whose land he is giving you, and when you have driven
them out and settled in their towns and houses. . .
DEUTERONOMY 19:1–2 NIV

I n recent days, Moses has commanded the Israelites to write the Lord's commandments "on the doorframes of your houses and on your gates" (Deuteronomy 6:9 and 11:20).

Men often look at this twice-given exhortation and wonder, "Did Moses mean they were to literally write the Lord's commands at the entrances of their homes?"

Until today's reading, most men have missed the fact that, at this point, the Israelites didn't have houses or gates! They hadn't had either for a generation, and wouldn't have for some time still.

Not every command applicable to believers today necessarily applies to you. That's the case if you don't own a home yet, if you aren't married, or if you don't have children. It's also true if you aren't sick, if you don't have unconfessed sins, or if you aren't elderly yet.

Just be sure to obey the commands applicable to you, now and in the future!

Lord, You want me review Your commands at
each new step and new stage of life. I want to
follow You wholeheartedly at every turn.

MAKING VOWS

*If you make a vow to the LORD your God, do not be slow to pay it,
for the LORD your God will certainly demand it of you and you will
be guilty of sin. But if you refrain from making a vow, you will not be
guilty. Whatever your lips utter you must be sure to do, because you
made your vow freely to the LORD your God with your own mouth.*
DEUTERONOMY 23:21–23 NIV

This is the second time Moses talks about vows in this book. The first time was back in 12:6–26. Of course, he also talked a lot about vows in Leviticus (related to promised offerings) and especially in Numbers (pertaining to Nazirites in chapter 6 and pertaining to men and women within a family in chapter 30).

As always, the important question to consider is: "What is an informed New Testament understanding of making vows to the Lord?"

1. Don't use vows when speaking to others. That's the explicit teaching of Jesus in the Sermon on the Mount (Matthew 5:33–37).

2. Make vows to the Lord cautiously and carefully after much consideration. That's the example of the apostles (Acts 18:18 and 21:22–24) and David (repeated in Psalms) and echoes the counsel of Solomon (Ecclesiastes 5:1–6). This can include swearing to tell the truth in a court of law.

*Lord, You want me to refrain from using vows to
affirm the truth of what I've promised to anyone but You.*

WHAT MIGHT HAVE BEEN

The LORD your God commands you this day to
follow these decrees and laws; carefully observe
them with all your heart and with all your soul.
DEUTERONOMY 26:16 NIV

M oses is calling the ancient Israelites to live up to the Lord God's commands and promises.

Their response? "You have declared this day that the LORD is your God and that you will walk in obedience to him, that you will keep his decrees, commands and laws—that you will listen to him" (verse 17). Impressive!

The Lord's incredible promises? First, that the Israelites will be His people and His greatly treasured possession. Second, "He has declared that he will set you in praise, fame and honor high above all the nations he has made" (verse 19). Third, that they will be a people holy and set apart to the Lord. Amazing!

Yet the rest of the Old Testament (Hebrew scriptures) tells a much different story.

Lord, You want me to start well and—much more importantly—
to live faithfully and finish well. I will stop assuming all that will
just happen automatically. I hear Your warnings loud and clear.

THE ONLY SANE CHOICE?

The sights you see will drive you mad.
DEUTERONOMY 28:34 NIV

———————◆———————

Today's two-chapter Bible reading sounds strange to modern ears. Yet Joshua and the twelve tribes of Israel followed the instructions about blessings and cursings in precise detail (Joshua 8:30–35).

The area, Shechem, is full of patriarchal history. In a sense, it was coming "home." Shechem's history includes Abraham building a memorial altar in Genesis 12:6–7 and Jacob (later renamed Israel) building another in Genesis 33:18–19. It also includes Jacob (Israel) exhorting his family to rid themselves of foreign idols in Genesis 35:2–4 and suffering through terrible tragedies involving his children in Genesis chapters 34 and 37. The place, therefore, speaks of real-life blessings and cursings on the earliest Israelites.

Shechem's geographical setting is between two mountains. Mount Ebel stands 3,080 feet tall north of Shechem, and Mount Gerizim stands 2,890 feet tall to the south. The two mountains offer a noteworthy contrast between blessings and cursings. Who, you might ask, would choose the latter? Only someone who is (or will be) insane. This isn't mere history. It still happens today.

Lord, You want me to make the only sane
choice. I gladly do so again today.

OBEY, LOVE, TURN

*The LORD your God will circumcise your hearts and
the hearts of your descendants, so that you may love
him with all your heart and with all your soul, and live.*

DEUTERONOMY 30:6 NIV

In Deuteronomy 30, Moses calls the Israelites (and by extension, you and other believers) to make a wholehearted commitment to the Lord God.

In verse 2, you're called to *obey* the Lord with your all. You don't just give lip service to the Lord God, maker of heaven and earth. Instead, you obey Him. In verse 6, you're called to *love* the Lord with your all. Moses echoes what he said in 10:16 and foreshadows what Paul goes on to say in Romans 2:29.

In verse 10, you're called to *turn to* the Lord with your all. This is after turning away from any and all known sin. In verses 11–14, you see the *possibility* and *proximity* of this call to wholehearted commitment to the Lord God.

In verses 15–18, you're given two options: *life or death.* In verses 19–20, you receive the final challenge to choose life and wholeheartedly commit yourself to the Lord God.

*Lord, You want me to choose You wholeheartedly every day
of my life. You don't want me to merely survive, but to thrive.*

MOSES DIES HOMELESS

*So Moses, the servant of the Lord, died there
in the land of Moab, just as the Lord had said.*
Deuteronomy 34:5 nlt

We often forget that Moses was homeless after fleeing Egypt, and homeless again for the last forty years of his life as he led God's people through the wilderness. The latter occurred after two transformative experiences.

First, Moses cried out to the Lord on behalf of His people and wrote down that poetic, heartfelt prayer (Psalm 90:13–16). Second, God appeared to Moses, told him to return to Egypt, and promised he would be the answer to his own prayer (Exodus 3:1–10). Sure enough, the Lord used Moses to bring about a great deliverance of God's people from their oppressors.

While homeless in the wilderness, Moses said that to "love your neighbor as yourself" means giving to the homeless and poor regularly. He also gave practical instructions on how to do that. First, by inviting the poor and needy to join your family for every holiday feast (Deuteronomy 10:18–19). Second, by sharing some of your wealth with the destitute as part of your tithes and offerings (Deuteronomy 14:28–29).

The next time you see a homeless person, or discover a neighbor's needs, or suspect someone at church requires help, think of Moses. Think of Moses and then open your wallet and bless them in the name of the Lord.

Lord, You want me to bless the homeless. I'll do that today.

HEEDING A COURAGEOUS WOMAN'S EXAMPLE

"When we heard of it, our hearts melted in fear and everyone's courage failed because of you, for the LORD your God is God in heaven above and on the earth below."

JOSHUA 2:11 NIV

After arriving at the Jordan River, Joshua secretly sends across two trusted spies. He sends them to one city, and only one, careful not to repeat the disaster that befell the nation forty years earlier. Once inside the imposing walled city, the spies soon realize they are the most wanted men in Jericho. Humanly speaking, they are doomed!

They *are* doomed—except for an unexpected and surprising ally. Rahab's remarkable faith is clearly expressed in verses 9–11. Do not miss her closing statement of faith above.

In complete contrast with her people, Rahab turns away from her sins, turns steadfastly toward the Lord God of heaven and earth, and trusts His purposes and protection for her family.

Never forget that Rahab does so at the risk of losing her own life. You can imagine she does so after many desperate and fervent pleas that the Lord spare the lives of her beloved parents, siblings, and their families.

Instead of dying, Rahab's blood is spared and later comingled with the lineage of the promised Messiah (Matthew 1:5).

What remarkable faith, indeed!

Lord, You want me to be inspired by courageous women. Thank You for Rahab.

LISTENING TO THE LORD

Joshua fell facedown to the ground in reverence, and asked him,
"What message does my Lord have for his servant?"
JOSHUA 5:14 NIV

A pastor failed to show up for work two days in a row. He also didn't cancel several important appointments. Something was clearly wrong.

A church elder took the matter to the Lord in earnest prayer. Finally, he boldly asked God to tell him what was happening. He'll never forget what God said: "Your pastor friend hasn't consummated his marriage yet." He had never heard of such a thing. Besides, the pastor and his wife had been married six months. Still, the elder believed God, kept listening, and carefully noted everything. Afterward, he messaged his pastor and invited him to lunch the next day.

After the host seated them and the waiter took their orders, the elder looked at his friend empathetically. Then he said, "I want to tell you what God told me yesterday evening. He told me that you and your wife haven't consummated your marriage."

The pastor wept for five minutes. When he finished and looked back up, the elder quietly asked, "Do you want to know what else God told me?" Today, that pastor and his wife have a thriving marriage and family and fruitful ministry. The Lord God alone gets all the glory!

Lord, You want me to listen and obey.
Please help me do both.

STONES FOR REMEMBERING

As the Israelites watched, Joshua copied onto the stones
of the altar the instructions Moses had given them.
JOSHUA 8:32 NLT

While they are quite a bit smaller than those described above, a writer in Oregon also collects stones and rocks. Some remind him of the places where his children and grandchildren live. Others remind him of favorite places he and his wife have visited in their travels.

One surprisingly large agate is a reminder that God wants men to listen and learn from the wide variety of individuals they meet along the way. What joy there is in meeting fellow believers and not-yet-Christians being drawn to the Savior. After all, what is the greatest miracle and the cause of greatest joy in heaven? The miracle of every sinner who humbly repents (Luke 15:7).

In the Gospels, Jesus compares Himself to solid rock on which a man can confidently build his house and all its rooms. The apostle Paul goes on to say: "For no one can lay any foundation other than the one already laid, which is Jesus Christ" (1 Corinthians 3:11 NIV).

There's more about "Stones for Remembering" to consider another day.

Lord, You want me to build my life on Jesus Christ.
That's my desire as well!

EXPERIENCING GOD'S POWER ANEW

*On the day the LORD gave the Amorites over to Israel,
Joshua said to the LORD in the presence of Israel: "Sun,
stand still over Gibeon, and you, moon, over the Valley
of Aijalon." So the sun stood still, and the moon stopped,
till the nation avenged itself on its enemies, as it is written
in the Book of Jashar. The sun stopped in the middle
of the sky and delayed going down about a full day.
There has never been a day like it before or since.*

JOSHUA 10:12–14 NIV

Like Saint Patrick, and like Joshua, you can experience God's power when the Holy Spirit leads you to pray for the Lord's will and glory. This is exactly what Joshua does publicly in verse 12, and he garners a spectacular miracle in verses 13–14.

Like Joshua, a righteous man obeys the Lord wholeheartedly and receives supernatural answers to prayer. Many prayed and an angel released the apostle Peter from prison twice (Acts 5:17–20 and 12:6–11). The apostle Paul received many supernatural answers to prayer (for example, in Acts 13:9–12; 14:8–10; and 16:16–18). In the words of James: "Therefore confess your sins to each other and pray for each other so that you may be healed. The prayer of a righteous person is powerful and effective" (5:16).

May you know this experientially for the rest of your days.

*Lord, You want me to ask You for miracles.
What miracle should I pray for today?*

TOUGH QUESTIONS ABOUT JOSHUA

So Joshua took the entire land, just as the LORD had directed
Moses, and he gave it as an inheritance to Israel according to
their tribal divisions. Then the land had rest from war.
JOSHUA 11:23 NIV

The toughest question asked about the book of Joshua is, "Did these events really take place?" Yes.

The second toughest question is, "Did God really order the obliteration of the people in all these cities and kingdoms?" Yes, again. It's been six hundred years since a former idol worshipper from Ur believed the Lord, and He "credited it to him as righteousness" (Genesis 15:6 NIV). It's been 430 years since the Lord announced the time and place of judgment for rejecting the Lord. Rahab is not given four hours or days to repentant or die. And her people, and neighboring cities and kingdoms, are not given four weeks or months. "The Lord is patient" is an understatement of immense proportions.

The third toughest question is, "How could an all-powerful and loving God wipe them all out?" Precisely because the Lord is all-powerful and loving. . .and much more. Even with the whole Bible in hand, it is difficult to comprehend God's infinite mercy, grace, and forgiveness. It's rarer to grasp His eternal joy and peace. But that doesn't change who God is!

Lord, You want me to find real answers to the
toughest questions in You and in Your Word. I do.

ARE YOU LIKE CALEB?

*"So here I am today, eighty-five years old! I am still as
strong today as the day Moses sent me out; I'm just
as vigorous to go out to battle now as I was then."*
JOSHUA 14:10–11 NIV

Caleb was a man who seized adventure and challenge just as vigorously in his old age as he had in his youth. More importantly, Caleb renewed his strength and ability by continually trusting and obeying the Lord wholeheartedly.

Joshua and Caleb were the only senior citizens left among the Israelites. After spying the land the first time, they alone believed God's promises and power to defeat the Canaanites and give them the land. Because of their faith, they alone were spared when everyone else over twenty years of age was sentenced to die in the wilderness wanderings.

More than forty years later, Caleb's faith in the power of God still burned bright. When he saw the great mountains and walled cities a second time, he knew they still were no match for his God. The Lord had promised the land to the Israelites and Moses had promised these particular mountains to Caleb. Age didn't matter when it came to trusting God. The Lord was with him and Caleb knew he could conquer any obstacle. You can too.

*Lord, You want me to look to the future, not the past.
You want me to take courage no matter how big the challenge.*

TRUST AND OBEY. . .AND WAIT

*[The five women] said, "The LORD commanded Moses to
give us a grant of land along with the men of our tribe."*
JOSHUA 17:4 NLT

The book of Joshua records only half a dozen occasions when people speak to him. Today's Bible reading describes the third and fourth occasions.

Joshua is happy to converse with the five daughters of Zelophehad, who clearly and compellingly recite the promise the Lord gave them (Joshua 17:3–6 and Numbers 27:1–11).

Conversely, Joshua is unhappy to converse with the tribal leaders of Ephraim and West Manasseh, who bicker and complain (Joshua 17:14–18) while leaning on the reputation of their mighty patriarch.

Without question, the patriarch Joseph is one of the Bible's greatest heroes of the faith. What can we learn from him? First, like Joseph's youthful dreams, we can have a vision of present spiritual blessings and future triumph through Jesus Christ our Lord (Romans 8:18 and Colossians 3:1–4). Second, like Joseph, we can remain steadfastly confident that God can turn anything around and bring good into our lives and the lives of others (Romans 8:28). Third, Joseph's life demonstrates that nothing can separate us from God's love (Romans 8:38–39).

You may have to wait out extremely difficult circumstances. Then again—like Joseph, Joshua, and other biblical heroes—you can always trust and obey the Lord.

Lord, You want me to always trust and obey You. I will today.

NO INHERITANCE FOR LEVI?

[The leaders of the tribe of Levi] said, "The LORD commanded Moses to give us towns to live in and pasturelands for our livestock."
JOSHUA 21:2 NLT

In obedience to what Moses commanded (Numbers 35), Joshua assigns six cities of refuge and forty-two additional cities for the Levites to share.

What's important to know about these Levitical cities?

These assignments are shared, not exclusive. For instance, Bezer, a city of refuge, is inhabited by both Reubenites (Joshua 20:8) and Levites (Joshua 21:36).

Unlike other Israelite tribes, Levi does not receive its own territory or cities for four primary reasons. First, the patriarch Jacob said they would be scattered throughout the Promised Land (Genesis 49:7). Second, the Levites serve the Lord and receive the tithes of the other tribes (Numbers 18:21 and 18:24; Deuteronomy 18:1; and Joshua 13:14). Third, the Lord said He is their inheritance (Deuteronomy 10:9; Joshua 13:14 and 13:33). Fourth, one of the Levitical clans directly descends from Aaron (Joshua 21:4).

After the exodus, Aaron served as the new nation's high priest for nearly four decades. Like his direct descendants, Aaron had days of incredible faith and obedience—and days of spectacular disbelief and disobedience. Don't follow his bad example!

Lord, You want me to trust and obey You.
I reject disbelief and disobedience.

ARE YOU LIKE JOSHUA?

*"You know with all your heart and soul that not one
of all the good promises the LORD your God gave you has
failed. Every promise has been fulfilled; not one has failed."*
JOSHUA 23:14 NIV

Joshua was a strong man of faith if ever there was one. From his youth as an assistant to Moses, to his clandestine exploration of the Promised Land, Joshua had showed himself faithful in service, brave in battle, and mighty in faith.

As the new leader of Israel after Moses' death, Joshua had many compelling reasons to be afraid. Like a good soldier, however, Joshua said "yes!" to the orders of his Commander to "Be strong. Take courage. Know my word. Obey my commands. Do not be afraid. And do not forget that I am with you!" (see Joshua 1:2–9).

While obeying God's orders, Joshua proceeded to conquer the Promised Land, proving that all God's great promises will come to pass. Later, he could confidently tell God's people, "Not one of all the LORD's good promises to Israel failed; every one was fulfilled" (Joshua 21:45).

Now at the end of his life, Joshua held out the same challenge to the Israelites to "be strong. Obey God's word. And don't forget that the Lord is with you to fight for you!" (see Joshua 23:6–11).

*Lord, You want me to continuously seek You,
live in Your presence, trust Your promises,
and meet every challenge. Yes, I will today.*

GETTING INTO JUDGES

*After that whole generation had been gathered
to their ancestors, another generation grew up who
knew neither the LORD nor what he had done for Israel.*

JUDGES 2:10 NIV

———◆———

This second book of Israelite history is full of *cycles.*
After Joshua's death, most of the Israelite tribes were slow to obey the Lord (chapter 1), and in fact many of the people began chasing after foreign gods (2:1–13). As a result, the Lord allowed other kingdoms to come in and severely oppress the nation of Israel—to drive them to their knees and back to God (2:14–3:6).

Because Israel was so apt to chase foreign gods—and so slow to repent and truly obey the Lord—for three hundred years the nation repeatedly went in cycles. They went from (1) spiritual rebellion to (2) political oppression to (3) national repentance to (4) God raising up a judge to deliver them, to another cycle of (1) spiritual rebellion, etc. (3:7–16:31).

The book ends with appendices describing two of the most graphic examples of Israel's spiritual rebellion during its first three hundred years in the Promised Land (chapters 17–21).

Before that? Stories about the most famous judges, including Deborah, Gideon, Jephthah, and Samson.

*Lord, You want me to heed the clear warning of the
book of Judges. I will not rebel against You this week.*

ARE YOU LIKE DEBORAH?

Now Deborah, a prophet, the wife of Lappidoth,
was leading Israel at that time.
JUDGES 4:4 NIV

During the time of the Judges, Israel had its own Joan of Arc and Rosa Parks in the person of a woman named Deborah. Strong men shook in fear, but Deborah gathered people to her and offered God's comfort and counsel. When God's message came to attack Israel's enemies, she didn't hesitate to issue His command to the man He had chosen. And when the day of battle dawned, she helped Barak lead the charge.

Deborah was not a glory seeker. She was ready to step up, however, to any task God gave her. If God called her to settle disputes or proclaim His Word or mobilize soldiers, she did it. She did whatever God called her to do—for His glory and for the deliverance of His people.

Deborah demonstrated a determination to obey God immediately and face difficulties courageously. Whether listening to disputes, marching into battle, or singing a victory song, she always urged the Israelites to put their trust in God.

Ordinary people living ordinary lives of obedience to God can inspire others to great deeds. What step is God calling you to take?

Lord, You want me to obey You and inspire others to
great deeds. Who do You want me to inspire today?

ARE YOU LIKE GIDEON?

The angel of the LORD appeared to him and said to him, "The LORD is with you, O mighty man of valor." And Gideon said to him, "Please, my lord, if the LORD is with us, why then has all this happened to us?"
JUDGES 6:12–13 ESV

If anyone had small mustard seed faith, it was Gideon. The Lord had to coax Gideon step by step out of hiding and into becoming the mighty hero He wanted him to be.

Gideon wanted to be sure the Lord was speaking to him. When God proved Himself, Gideon worshipped Him and destroyed his family's pagan Baal altar and Asherah pole. Soon afterward, the Spirit of the Lord filled Gideon. After another confirmation from the Lord, he was ready to set forth!

Then God gave Gideon one final sign he hadn't requested. A detailed dream recounted by an enemy soldier confirmed that Gideon could obey God in full confidence—the battle would be theirs! Sure enough, the Lord's promises came true.

Rescuing Israel in the strength the Lord had given him, Gideon the mighty hero learned what it meant that the Lord was with him.

Gideon had only a few if any pages of scripture, but you have the whole Bible. What's keeping your faith from growing?

Lord, You want me to obey Your Word's clear-cut commands for believers today. Give me wisdom and courage!

ABIMELEK'S VIOLENCE AND VIOLENT END

Then all the citizens of Shechem and Beth Millo
gathered beside the great tree at the pillar
in Shechem to crown Abimelek king.

JUDGES 9:6 NIV

In Judges 8:22–23, Gideon refuses to become the first king of Israel. After Gideon's death, however, Abimelek (the son of Gideon's concubine in Shechem), decides *he* wants to be king. After publicly slaughtering all but one of Gideon's other seventy sons, Abimelek and his hometown's citizens are publicly cursed by Gideon's traumatized yet bold youngest son, Jotham.

Jotham says, in effect: "After all my father Gideon did, risking his life to deliver you from the raiding Midianites, you have repaid him in a horrific manner. You have done this to make one of your own a so-called king, but he's no such thing. Therefore, I pronounce this curse: you and Abimelek will destroy each other."

The next three verses say Jotham safely got away, Abimelek ruled over (vs. judged) Israel for three years, and then God saw that Jotham's curse came true with violent force.

World history is replete with rulers whose violent reigns ended with their own deaths. Their violent deaths, like Abimelek's, prove that "all who draw the sword will die by the sword" (Matthew 26:52 NIV).

Lord, You want me to abhor violence. I do.

ARE YOU UNLIKE JEPHTHAH?

Jephthah made a vow to the LORD. He said, "If you give me victory over the Ammonites, I will give to the LORD whatever comes out of my house to meet me when I return in triumph."
JUDGES 11:30–31 NLT

Although soldiers are known to plead with God from foxholes, the Lord isn't interested in bargaining. He is more delighted with a heartfelt prayer than a hasty promise.

Jephthah had the Spirit of the Lord upon him as he gathered the armies together to meet the enemy. God had given him all he needed for victory. Still, Jephthah felt compelled to make a hasty promise to the Lord—a vow that only ensured his own grief, not the battle's outcome.

As soon as the victorious Jephthah saw the face of his daughter, his only child, his heart broke. Most likely, Jephthah's daughter did not lose her life, but both she and her father lost something very precious. She was deprived of marriage, children, and the social acceptance they gave. He lost grandchildren and posterity.

Years later, Solomon warned, "Don't make rash promises. . .before God" (Ecclesiastes 5:2 NLT). Even wiser? Jesus said to count the cost before making a commitment (Luke 14:28), make sure your "yes" is "yes" (Matthew 5:37), and obey God out of love and worship—no strings attached.

Lord, You want me to never make a rash vow. I won't.

WHAT'S IN A LOOK?

*Then the Philistines seized him, gouged out his eyes
and took him down to Gaza. Binding him with bronze
shackles, they set him to grinding grain in the prison.*
JUDGES 16:21 NIV

As a young man, Samson's eyes got him into trouble. He saw a beautiful young woman and wanted to marry her even though she was a Philistine. At the end of the wedding week, however, Samson's wife betrayed him and Samson took out his rage by slaughtering thirty Philistine men and burning thousands of acres of crops.

The older he got, the more Samson's eyes got him into trouble. By the opening verse of Judges 16, Samson spends the night with a Philistine prostitute. It's unclear if she betrayed Samson, but he took out his rage by ripping out the city's gate.

Three verses later, Samson starts cohabiting with a Philistine woman named Delilah. She keeps betraying Samson, who just doesn't see how much trouble he's in. At the moment of truth, poetic justice deprives the world's strongest man of his roaming eyes.

No wonder the apostles warn against *the world* (culture and society trying to press you into its mold), *the flesh* (our own carnal and self-destructive desires), and *the devil* (Satan, the archenemy of your soul). You can't successfully battle those three in your own strength. Even if you're the strongest man in the world.

*Lord, You want me to have pure eyes.
Wash, cleanse, and purify mine.*

PICK-AND-CHOOSE REALITY
DOESN'T WORK

Now a man named Micah from the hill country of Ephraim said to his mother, "The eleven hundred shekels of silver that were taken from you and about which I heard you utter a curse—I have that silver with me; I took it." Then his mother said, "The LORD bless you, my son!"
JUDGES 17:1–2 NIV

The opening paragraphs of today's Bible reading present a plethora of errors committed by a biblical illiterate, pseudoreligious, and loosely governed people.

Judges 17 begins with massive theft against one's own family and continues with a curse against the unknown thief, who fears that curse and confesses his deed. And that's just the first verse and a half!

The next two and a half verses continue with pious references to the Lord, blessings void of reality, corrupted parental nurturing, misdirected and wholly pagan religious actions, blatant and unabashed idolatry, syncretism of religious practices and beliefs, corruption of the arts (for idol making), wealth associated with God's blessing, false repentance, pseudoforgiveness, and misguided vows and almsgiving.

Verses 5 and 6 show corrupted religion becomes a matter of personal preference and practice, with generation after generation affected by letting their conscience be their guide. Worst of all? They're satisfied and content in the midst of all this wreckage!

Lord, You want me to hold fast to what is true and abhor pick-and-choose reality. It's no reality at all.

WHY ALL THE R-RATED STORIES?

*"I took my concubine, cut her into pieces and sent one
piece to each region of Israel's inheritance, because they
committed this lewd and outrageous act in Israel."*
JUDGES 20:6 NIV

The first seven books of the Bible all contain stories that make good men wince. Murder. Rape. Slaughter. Incest. Pillaging. Prostitution. Annihilation. Gang Rape. Mutilation. The short book of Ruth (tomorrow) is the first Bible book that's only PG-13. Then it's back to more sex and violence at every turn from 1 Samuel to 2 Chronicles. The two short books after that dial it back to PG-13, but Esther. . .well, you get the idea. Sex and violence and more sex and violence.

Two of the most disturbing stories are found in yesterday and today's Bible readings. The book of Judges repeatedly shocks, and the appendices drive home the utter terror of these bookends: "In those days Israel had no king; everyone did as they saw fit" (Judges 17:6 and 21:25 NIV).

In this case, the ancient moral of the story is obvious. The contemporary moral is no less terrifying: if you do whatever seems right in your own eyes, there is no limit to how depraved you can be. Why is the Bible so honest? For very good reasons, indeed.

*Lord, I didn't enjoy today's Bible reading.
Maybe that was the point.*

ARE YOU LIKE RUTH?

"Where you go I will go, and where you stay I will stay.
Your people will be my people and your God my God."
RUTH 1:16 NIV

Ruth wouldn't have laughed at the best comedian's mother-in-law jokes. Even though her widowed mother-in-law, Naomi, was a distraught old woman, Ruth emphatically declared her commitment to her. Ruth chose to do so not because of family obligation, but out of a conscious decision to leave her own pagan culture and embrace the love and community of her Jewish mother-in-law's Lord God, maker of heaven and earth.

Ruth first shared her loyal care simply by her presence as they walked the long roads back to Bethlehem. Once they arrived, Ruth immediately began working to provide for Naomi. God allowed her to work in the fields of Boaz, a relative of Naomi's. Ruth's loyal care for Naomi immediately aroused Boaz's interest and revived Naomi's own discouraged heart. In turn, Naomi began to care for Ruth, doing her part to bring about a secure marriage and home for her with Boaz.

Ruth chose to care for her mother-in-law and found herself cared for by the God of Israel. Boaz and Naomi were blessed by Ruth's loyal love and the world has been blessed by her descendants—King David and, ultimately, the Lord Jesus Christ (Matthew 1:5).

Lord, You want me to care loyally for
someone in my family. Who, Lord?

ARE YOU LIKE SAMUEL?

All Israel from Dan to Beersheba recognized that
Samuel was attested as a prophet of the Lord.
1 Samuel 3:20 niv

Four-year-old Cole knew God. And he knew that when disease took his life, he would be with God. So he told everyone he knew that they needed to know God too. After his funeral, Cole's uncle and aunt went searching for God and found him in Jesus Christ. All because of four-year-old Cole.

There is no age discrimination with God. He will use anyone who loves and obeys Him. He used a four-year-old to bring the message of salvation to his family. He also used the young boy Samuel to bring a message of coming judgment to a sinning priest. When God roused him, Samuel was sleeping near the ark of the covenant. Once he knew the voice of God, there was no turning back from obeying Him.

That wholehearted, childlike commitment to God never left Samuel. From his youngest days to his old age, he was God's man, always available to be used for God's glory. Do not let anyone look down on God's ability to use someone because they are young (1 Timothy 4:12). What's more, never retire from glorifying and serving God because you are old (Psalm 63:4).

Lord, You want me to trust You no matter what my age.
I want to live for You for the rest of my life.

ARE YOU UNLIKE ELI?

Now Eli, who was very old, heard about everything his sons were doing to all Israel and how they slept with the women who served at the entrance to the tent of meeting.

1 SAMUEL 2:22 NIV

———◆———

J esus' teaching that you are to love the Lord your God more than your own father and mother, spouse, and children (Matthew 10:37 and Luke 14:26) seems strange. Strange, that is, until you see someone who loves family more than God.

Eli was a man who, for all his priestly duties and privileges, had reduced God in his heart. On the throne of Eli's life was his own comfort. His affections were set on the prosperity to be had from the Tabernacle offerings, and on the calm to be enjoyed when his sons were not provoked. Perhaps saddest of all? When Eli is confronted with the reality of pending judgment, he doesn't seem to care. He reveals himself as a man who had let God slip to last place in his affections.

Thankfully, Jesus affirmed that loving God "with all your heart, all your soul, all your mind, and all your strength" (Mark 12:30 NLT) doesn't preclude loving others or yourself (12:31). On what have you set your affections? Whom do you value most? Yourself? Your loved ones? Or the Lord God?

———

Lord, You don't want me to devalue You in my heart and affections. You have all my love.

STONES OF HELP

*Then Samuel took a stone and set it up. . .and called its
name Ebenezer, saying, "Thus far the LORD has helped us."*
1 SAMUEL 7:12 NKJV

The Hebrew word we call *Ebenezer* means "stone of help" and appears three times in 1 Samuel—in 4:1, 5:1, and the verse quoted above. It also appears in the beloved nineteenth-century hymn "Come, Thou Fount of Every Blessing." Notice how the first verse focuses on the glories of our Savior in heaven, and the second on the Lord's help amid the sorrows of life here below. What fitting words to read aloud quietly the day after Good Friday and before Easter Sunday.

"Come, Thou Fount of every blessing, Tune my heart to sing Thy grace; Streams of mercy, never ceasing, Call for songs of loudest praise. Teach me some melodious sonnet, Sung by flaming tongues above. Praise the mount, I'm fixed upon it, Mount of Thy redeeming love.

"Sorrowing I shall be in spirit, Till released from flesh and sin, Yet from what I do inherit, Here Thy praises I'll begin; Here I raise my Ebenezer; Here by Thy great help I've come; And I hope, by Thy good pleasure, Safely to arrive at home."

*Lord, You want me to look to You for help every day until I'm with
You in heaven. Thank You so much for all Your help thus far.*

PRAY FOR OTHERS FAITHFULLY

*"As for me, far be it from me that I should sin
against the LORD by failing to pray for you."*
1 SAMUEL 12:23 NIV

In the midst of national upheaval, the prophet Samuel assures the people that he will never stop praying for them. Samuel himself was a miraculous answer to his mother's prayers (1 Samuel 1:1–20). He knew the power of a righteous person's prayers.

As a young man, and well into middle age, one writer always knew that several older friends prayed for him daily. Years later, the Lord gave him the gift of loving to pray for others daily in specific, detailed ways.

Few things are more exciting than when God answers your prayers with specificity—even though only you and He know what you have been praying. That's why you should pray more often and more boldly!

After all, the Lord's providential work in your life, and His many answers to your specific prayers, increase your faith and trust in Him.

*Lord, You want men to be courageous in their prayers.
Please give me the gift and joy of praying for others daily.*

ARE YOU LIKE JONATHAN?

Jonathan said to his young armor-bearer, "Come,
let's go over to the outpost of those uncircumcised men.
Perhaps the LORD will act in our behalf. Nothing can
hinder the LORD from saving, whether by many or by few."

1 SAMUEL 14:6 NIV

Jonathan never said, "I'm just one person. What can God do through me?" Bold for God and dependent on Him alone, Jonathan attempted difficult tasks for God's glory. He always sought God's will before taking risks, of course, and he didn't go it alone. Then again, Jonathan didn't put his trust in his armor-bearer, whom he instructed to climb up behind (not ahead) of him.

No wonder Jonathan was drawn to David as a committed friend for life. The cliff climber met the giant slayer. The first man went up the side of a mountain on his hands and feet to fight a well-armed contingency. The other man took five small stones and slung one at a Philistine giant's head. Both knew what it was to trust God's power in the face of overwhelming odds.

Have you ever had that experience? Are you bold enough to do so again?

Lord, You want me to trust Your power to do Your
will Your way. I trust You wholeheartedly today.

ARE YOU UNLIKE SAUL?

*Samuel said to him, "The LORD has torn the kingdom of
Israel from you today and has given it to one of
your neighbors—to one better than you."*
1 SAMUEL 15:28 NIV

Saul had it all. Good looks, height, charm, and leadership ability. He was chosen by God, touched by His Spirit, and given the opportunity to be Israel's first and greatest king.

When Saul's own insistent disobedience against the Lord dashed any opportunity for an enduring dynasty, however, jealous bitterness began to brew in the king's heart. Jealousy ate at Saul's tormented mind. Like a man unhinged, he was driven to chase David in the wilderness, bent on destroying the man God had chosen as his replacement.

In his jealous rage, Saul eventually viewed his own soldiers as conspirators against his happiness and saw God's priests as traitors. His jealousy mushroomed into a terrible cloud of destruction. Saul murdered hundreds of innocent people but never caught David. In the end, Saul fell victim to his own sword.

Years later, David's son Solomon wrote, "Anger is cruel, and wrath is like a flood, but jealousy is even more dangerous" (Proverbs 27:4 NLT).

*Lord, You want me to abhor jealousy and flee from it.
You know the jealousy in my heart. I forsake it today.*

ARE YOU LIKE DAVID?

David said to the Philistine, "You come against me with sword and spear and javelin, but I come against you in the name of the LORD Almighty, the God of the armies of Israel, whom you have defied."
1 SAMUEL 17:45 NIV

Today's Bible reading has always been a favorite. . .for good reason! Imagine David leaving his sheep and going to check on the welfare of his brothers (at his dad's request), only to hear Goliath bellow out his challenge for the eightieth time (1 Samuel 17:16) in defiance of the Lord God of Israel.

Being a youth of courage (17:34–37) and faith (17:37; 17:45, and more), David couldn't stand there and listen to this overstuffed Philistine curse what David esteemed most. He was a man of action and—incredible as it must have seemed—volunteered to take on the brute.

At first, Goliath was amused at David's boldness. Then he became angry and cursed him. Finally, Goliath was "very must astonished when David hit him with a stone" because "such a thing had never entered his head before" (Dean Rivers, *Conundrums*, 1921).

David's response to Goliath is a challenge to every man who follows the Lord today.

Lord, You want me to be a man of faith, courage, and action. When faced with trials and temptations, may I be all three.

HOW CAN MEN BE SO EVIL?

Saul sought to pin David to the wall with the spear,
but he eluded Saul, so that he struck the spear into
the wall. And David fled and escaped that night.

1 Samuel 19:10 esv

Sadly, King Saul was not the first, and certainly not the last, ruler to descend into grave suspicion, growing madness, extreme violence, and worse.

Edward Gibbon's *The Decline and Fall of the Roman Empire* describes the turning point in Emperor Commodus's character. Instead of celebrating his escape from assassination, Commodus descends into grave suspicion, growing madness, and extreme violence. The son of an acclaimed and well-respected emperor, Commodus was the opposite. He led a reign of terror that would have slit Rome's throat except for a second assassination attempt that succeeded in the wee hours of the new year AD 193.

How can men be so evil? In King Saul's case, he turned away from God and lost His presence in his life. He then distrusted God all the more and gave into his base instincts. A man doesn't have to rise to greatness before committing great sins. All such sins begin in the mind not focused on God and His Word.

Lord, You want me to abhor evil in all its forms.
I reject my suspicions of others.

DAVID WAS HOMELESS

So David and his men, about six hundred in number,
left Keilah and kept moving from place to place.
1 SAMUEL 23:13 NIV

Many Bible heroes experienced homelessness. Moses. Ruth. Even Jesus. David too was homeless for years while on the run from King Saul. Yet in every psalm David penned during those trying times, he reaffirmed his faith in the Lord. Later, David penned more psalms saying God delights in raising up the humble and righteous to positions of honor.

First, God will cause them to inherit the land and enjoy great peace (Psalm 37:11). Likewise, the Lord will grant them blessings and prosperity (Psalm 65:9–13).

Second, God's people may have to go through much adversity, but eventually they will enjoy great abundance (Psalm 66:10–12). He withholds no good thing from those whose walk is blameless (Psalm 84:11). He bestows honor upon them (Psalm 113:7–9) and crowns them with salvation (Psalm 149:4).

David himself experienced this. At one point, he asked the Lord, "Give me a sign of your goodness" (Psalm 86:17 NIV). Then, at just the right moment, God made David the nation's new king, and he and his people enjoyed unprecedented prosperity and peace.

Lord, You want me to be humble and righteous.
You take delight in seeing both in my life.

ARE YOU LIKE ABIGAIL?

"My lord will not have on his conscience the staggering burden
of needless bloodshed or of having avenged himself."
1 SAMUEL 25:31 NIV

———————

If Abigail held public office today, she probably would be suited best for secretary of state.

Living with an ill-tempered husband, Abigail had plenty of opportunity to sharpen her conflict resolution skills. When Abigail heard that David and his men were on their way to take revenge on her husband and household, it probably wasn't the first time she had to think fast to keep her household safe.

Fortunately, Abigail wasn't just a quick thinker but also a wise communicator. She knew when to speak and when to keep quiet. Most importantly, she knew how to speak to the heart of a man of God (see Galatians 6:1 and James 5:19–20). David dropped his vow of vengeance immediately when confronted with Abigail's appeal.

What if Bathsheba had responded to David as Abigail had? Bathsheba's simple, "Don't do it, David," might have diverted him from another sinful course that took the life of Bathsheba's godly and courageous husband, Uriah.

A good and courageous man appeals to his fellow men for their good and God's glory.

Lord, You want me to appeal to other believers to resist
sinful choices and continue to live for You. Give me
wisdom to make one such appeal today.

BIBLICAL DEFINITION OF "ANOINTED"

But David said to Abishai, "Don't destroy him! Who can lay
a hand on the LORD's anointed and be guiltless?"
1 SAMUEL 26:9 NIV

What or who is "the LORD's anointed"? Like many biblical questions, we're often tempted to raise our hands, wave them eagerly, smile big and answer, "Jesus!"

In Exodus, Moses received the Lord's instructions about anointing Aaron, his sons, and other Levites as well as the furniture and fixtures within the tabernacle. In Leviticus, Moses carried out those instructions.

In Judges, Gideon's youngest son, Jotham, talked about other nations anointing their kings. In 1 Samuel 2:10 (NIV), Hannah ends her prayer of thanksgiving with this declaration: the Most High Lord "will give strength to his king and exalt the horn of his anointed." This foreshadows the anointing of the first two kings of Israel, Saul and David, which happens in 1 Samuel 10:1 and 16:13.

So significant is "the LORD's anointed" that David spared Saul's life in 1 Samuel 24 and again here in 1 Samuel 26. This is true even though Saul earlier had scores of anointed priests slaughtered in 1 Samuel 22. Saul's terrible wickedness did not give David any justification to execute judgment. The Lord Himself will take care of that.

Best of all? In the end, the Lord Himself became the "Anointed One"— later translated "Messiah" and still later "Christ."

Lord, You want me to reverence and worship Jesus,
the ultimate Anointed One. I do!

DID DAVID MAKE A NEW COMMAND?

"Who will listen to what you say? The share of the man
who stayed with the supplies is to be the same as that
of him who went down to the battle. All will share alike."
1 Samuel 30:24 niv

The Bible contains more than 31,100 verses. So, when a question comes up that we can't answer in the immediate context, it's helpful to look elsewhere. So, what about the verse and question above? Sorry, no, but David did something else much more important.

Four hundred years earlier, Moses commanded, "Divide the spoils equally between the soldiers who took part in the battle and the rest of the community" (Numbers 31:27 niv).

A generation later, Joshua commanded, "Return to your homes with your great wealth—with large herds of livestock, with silver, gold, bronze and iron, and a great quantity of clothing—and divide the plunder from your enemies with your fellow Israelites" (Joshua 22:8 niv).

So, what important something did David do? He knew the five books of Moses and the book of Joshua, took their commands to heart, and (mostly) obeyed them.

Lord, You want me to know Your commands for believers today,
to take them to heart, and to obey them. That's why I'm reading
this daily devotional. Thanks for today's encouragement.

DAVID LAMENTS THE FALLEN

"How the mighty have fallen!"
2 SAMUEL 1:19 ESV, NIV, NKJV

Hundreds of contemporary English sayings find their origins in English Bibles.

Today people sometimes say, "How the mighty have fallen," to gloat over the downfall of others socially, politically, or financially. Athletically, it's often used to emphasize the dramatically negative turn of events for a once-great sports team or player.

Biblically, "How the mighty have fallen" speaks of something far different, of deep sorrow and lament after the death of royalty in battle. In particular, it expresses David's grief poetically, and runs from top to bottom of his lament in 2 Samuel 1:19–27. The phrase appears in every odd-numbered verse except the lament's middle stanza—its focal point (verse 23)—where Saul and Jonathan's names appear for the first time.

A thousand years later, Paul warned, "So, if you think you are standing firm, be careful that you don't fall!" (1 Corinthians 10:12 NIV).

May "How the mighty have fallen" never be said of you. If it is, may you enjoy rich experiences of God's marvelous, amazing mercy and grace.

Lord, You want me to care less about what
others think and most about what You think.

MURDER IN A CITY OF REFUGE

Now when Abner returned to Hebron, Joab took him
aside into an inner chamber, as if to speak with him
privately. And there, to avenge the blood of his brother
Asahel, Joab stabbed him in the stomach, and he died.
2 SAMUEL 3:27 NIV

The devotionals for March 1 and March 21 talked about the six cities of refuge. Hebron was one of those cities. In such cities, someone could not be slain by a blood avenger without a trial. Unlike King David, Joab had no use for God's law and violated it in every turn this day.

In the United States, someone who dies may not be buried for days or even weeks. In most of the world now and down through the ages, a dead body is buried right away, typically in the same place where the person dies. That was the case after Abner's death. You can still see his tomb today not far from the Cave of the Patriarchs. The tomb is featured in the writings of many visitors down through the centuries.

David wept at the grave of Abner, leading the rest of the people to do the same. Instead of saying "How the mighty have fallen" in battle, David lamented the treacherous way Abner was slain in a city of refuge.

Lord, You want me to recoil at Joab's treachery. May I never
be guilty of high-handed disregard for You and Your Word.

WORSHIP GOD EXUBERANTLY

Wearing a linen ephod, David was dancing before the LORD
with all his might, while he and all Israel were bringing up
the ark of the LORD with shouts and the sound of trumpets.
2 SAMUEL 6:14–15 NIV

You can imagine a thirteen-year-old's surprise when he opened his first Bible and discovered his name attached to many of the psalms. You can imagine his further surprise when he started reading his Bible cover to cover and discovered the saga of David's life.

Granted, it was a mixed blessing. He smiled and cheered when he read the David and Goliath story and discovered he shared the name of a biblical hero. Then again, he winced and shook his head when he read the David and Bathsheba and Uriah story and realized David had broken half of the Ten Commandments (but sincerely repented some months later).

Mostly the thirteen-year-old loved discovering how exuberantly David loved to worship God. This was true all through David's life—as a young man, on the run from Saul, as the triumphant king over Judah and Israel, and even into old age.

How good that you can thank the Lord God daily for His sovereignty (greatness), providence (guidance and goodness), holiness (glory), love (graciousness), and mystery ("God alone knows"). Do that every day with an uplifted heart full of joy and praise.

Lord, You want me to worship You exuberantly.
Stir my heart to do just that today.

DOES GOD WANT YOU TO SUCCEED?

The LORD gave David victory wherever he went.
2 SAMUEL 8:6 AND 8:14 NIV

———————◆———————

D o you want to be successful? If so, great! If not, what are your other options?

God made Abraham very successful. God granted Abraham's servant success (Genesis 24). A few generations later, God made Joseph extremely successful. Four centuries later, Moses talked about God's desire to make His people successful and prosperous. Six centuries later, God made David extremely successful (1 Samuel 18:5, 14, 15, and 30). The list goes on and on.

Is God willing to make *you* successful? It depends.

In Joshua 1:7–8, God promises you will be prosperous and successful if you study His Word, meditate on it daily, and faithfully obey His commands.

In Psalm 1:1–3, God promises that anyone who delights in obeying His Word and meditates on it daily will prosper and succeed in whatever he does. Many similar verses follow throughout the Psalms and the book of Proverbs.

Why would God make such extravagant promises? Not because He wants you to be rich and famous! No, that's missing the point completely.

Lord, You want me to reimagine what success means in my life. I see it starts with taking You at Your Word.

WRITING NEW SCRIPTS ABOUT WOMEN

Late one afternoon, after his midday rest, David got out of bed and was walking on the roof of the palace. As he looked out over the city, he noticed a woman of unusual beauty taking a bath.

2 SAMUEL 11:2 NLT

I n public, is it a sin to *see* a beautiful woman? No, it's not. Is it a sin to *notice*, keep looking, and then lust after that beautiful woman? Yes, of course it is. It all comes down to scripting.

You've heard about the Hollywood scriptwriters behind blockbuster movies. You've also heard the scripts being recited by every unwanted robocall you get. What you're not used to doing, however, is writing your own scripts for predictable life situations. Then again, if you're not writing your own scripts, who is?

In public, when you *see* a beautiful woman, why not recite a counterintuitive script of thanksgiving to God? That script could say, "Lord, thank You for the beauty with which you make woman." Okay, that wording is a bit clunky, but maybe that's the point—to take your thoughts captive for Christ. It works!

Lord, You know I see beautiful women in public. Each time I do, I will thank You for the beauty with which You make woman.

ARE YOU UNLIKE AMNON?

He refused to listen to her, and since he was stronger
than she, he raped her. Then Amnon hated her with
intense hatred. In fact, he hated her more than he had
loved her. Amnon said to her, "Get up and get out!"
2 SAMUEL 13:14–15 NIV

In biblical times, men didn't have to deal with pornography. Then again, wrestling with powerful sexual desires was nothing new to them.

Amnon was a man driven by selfish, dark desires. True love gives and pleases. Lust consumes and destroys. Amnon wanted Tamar, but not as a cherished wife. Instead, he wanted her for what he could experience in the moment. Having gained the sexual experience he craved, he found the taste bitter and repulsive.

Amnon was not simply another sexual addict. Like any other man, he had a choice to forsake lust and pursue love. Even in the midst of his passion, he still could have chosen the way of love by heeding Tamar's pleas of reason. Instead, he chose the cruel path of rape. As a result, Amnon left Tamar desolate and made himself a target of an enraged brother's revenge.

The pursuit of dark lust always leads to destructive ends. Broken lives and broken spirits lie strewn in its path. In the end, it never delivers what it promises.

Lord, You want me to experience true sexual
satisfaction only within marriage. I agree.

ARE YOU UNLIKE ABSALOM?

*Absalom behaved in this way toward all the
Israelites who came to the king asking for justice,
and so he stole the hearts of the people of Israel.*

2 SAMUEL 15:6 NIV

In many ways, Absalom was the perfect politician. But Absalom pursued what he wanted in all the wrong ways—for all the wrong reasons. He kept going his way, not God's way, to right the wrongs in his life and to gain the justice and power he thought he deserved.

When Amnon angered Absalom, God's way called for Absalom to seek justice and show mercy. Instead, Absalom pursued violent revenge. Then, when his father David verbally pardoned Absalom for murdering his brother, God's way said to seek full reconciliation. Instead, Absalom schemed and manipulated to win the public's favor and overthrow his still grieving father.

Absalom had what it took to be a national leader—good political sense, excellent counsel, fine leadership. But he grabbed power for himself instead of seeking God's best. And the hand that grabbed for more and more came up empty. Only when your hands are outstretched and open before God, and seeking His glory, can He fill them up with privilege and power and blessing.

*Lord, You want me to seek Your glory, not my own.
What do You want me to stop doing?*

WHERE IS YOUR FOCUS?

[Joab] took three javelins in his hand and plunged them into
Absalom's heart while Absalom was still alive in the oak tree.
2 Samuel 18:14 niv

This isn't the first time Joab directly disobeyed God and his king. Both times, April 14 and today, Joab murders a man in cold blood.

How could a man be so wicked? For starters, pride and anger.

In *Confessions of an Angry Man*, Brent Hofer says words that should haunt every man. Without divine and professional help, there's no limit to how much wickedness a prideful and angry man could do someday.

Of course, pride and anger are only two in a long list of things that make a man cold blooded. To pride and anger, James adds false religiosity, lack of love for all men, dead faith, a tongue lit on fire by hell, bitter envy, selfish ambition, and. . .well, you get the idea.

Paul adds: "Get rid of all bitterness, rage and anger, brawling and slander, along with every form of malice" (Ephesians 4:31 niv) and "rid yourselves of all such things as these: anger, rage, malice, slander, and filthy language from your lips" (Colossians 3:8 niv).

All such cold-blooded sins begin in the mind not focused on God and His Word.

Lord, You want me to abhor evil in all its forms.
I will focus on You and Your Word today.

LISTENING TO A WISE WOMAN

Then a wise woman cried out from the city, "Hear, hear!
Please say to Joab, 'Come nearby, that I may speak with you.'"
2 SAMUEL 20:16 NKJV

At almost every turn throughout the Bible, the Lord features outstanding women, including women of exceptional intelligence and wisdom.

Today's Bible reading is no exception. The story takes place in the distinguished city of Abel, known for its wise men and women. Not surprisingly, 2 Samuel 20:16–22 begins and ends by calling the hero a wise woman, that is, a woman who speaks and acts wisely.

Unlike God and His Word, men down through the ages have disparaged the intelligence of women. Actually, men have disparaged women in every way possible. It's abhorrent and appalling, disgusting and evil, foul and gross, hideous and horrendous, nasty and noxious, obnoxious and obscene, odious and offensive, rancid and repugnant, repulsive and revolting, shameful and sickening.

No man with a high view of the Lord God, maker of heaven and earth, can have a low view of God's final creation, woman. The Lord called her "very good" in every way. That doesn't mean women are superior to men, but in no way are they inferior.

Lord, You want me to change my view
of women. I hear that loud and clear.

DAVID'S FELLOW GIANT KILLERS

These four were descendants of Rapha in Gath,
and they fell at the hands of David and his men.
2 SAMUEL 21:22 NIV

When young David faced Goliath, why did he take five smooth stones? An old quip says because Goliath had four brothers. Well, the Bible doesn't exactly say they were all brothers, but they were all descendants of the Rephaim in Gath, one of the five largest Philistine cities.

So, who were these big brutes taken down by four of David's mighty men?

- Ishbi-Benob, killed by Abishai brother of Joab
- Saph, killed by Sibbekai the Hushathite
- Lahmi brother of Goliath (1 Chronicles 20:5), killed by Elhanan from Bethlehem
- Unnamed brute, killed by Jonathan, son of David's brother Shimeah

Some skeptics laugh at the idea of giants nine feet or taller. They apparently haven't consulted the authoritative *Guinness Book of World Records* or Wikipedia's "List of Tallest People." The former lists Robert Wadlow at 8 feet, 11.1 inches. The latter lists two men from Russia and England at 9 feet, 3 inches and a Neolithic man estimated to have been 11 feet, 6 inches (as reported in France's *La Nature*).

Lord, You want me to take You at Your Word even
when it comes to Goliath and his kin. I believe.

DAVID WROTE GOD-INSPIRED WORDS

"The Spirit of the LORD spoke through me;
his word was on my tongue."
2 SAMUEL 23:2 NIV

Barbour Publishing's *The 5-Minute Bible Study for Men* lists six insights regarding God's inspiration of the Bible. Here are the last two:

Jesus Christ fully supported all of scripture. See Matthew 5:17–19. Jesus confirmed its historical accuracy, down to the tense of a verb (Mark 12:26). He declared that scripture is permanent (Matthew 5:17–18), is inspired by the Holy Spirit (Mark 12:36), contains enough information to support our faith (Luke 16:29–31), is unbreakable (John 10:35), and agrees with His teachings (John 5:46–47 and Luke 24:27, 44).

The New Testament writers viewed both testaments as the Word of God. Peter affirmed that the Holy Spirit inspired the Old Testament (Acts 4:25). He compared the commandments of Jesus Christ, which the apostles taught, with the words the holy prophets spoke (2 Peter 3:2). He declared that the Gospel that was preached to them was the Word of the Lord (1 Peter 1:23, 25). Peter also recognized Paul's writings as part of scripture (2 Peter 3:15–16). In turn, Paul repeatedly confirmed that he preached God's Word, not his own message.

Lord, You want me to accept all scripture as God-inspired. I do.

A KING RIDING A MULE

[David] said to them: "Take your lord's servants
with you and have Solomon my son mount my
own mule and take him down to Gihon."
1 KINGS 1:33 NIV

Isn't God's appointed king supposed to ride a valiant warrior horse? No, in biblical history. Yes in biblical prophecy yet to be fulfilled.

David rode on a mule. Solomon rode his father's mule.

David's greatest descendant, the Messiah, would ride a mule. Listen to Zechariah 9:9 (NIV): "Rejoice greatly, Daughter Zion! Shout, Daughter Jerusalem! See, your king comes to you, righteous and victorious, lowly and riding on a donkey, on a colt, the foal of a donkey." Jesus fulfilled that prophecy in every way as seen in Matthew 21 and John 12.

Then again, in Revelation 19, John pictures Jesus in His second coming. Verse 11 (NIV) introduces the scene: "I saw heaven standing open and there before me was a white horse, whose rider is called Faithful and True. With justice he judges and wages war."

Isn't God's anointed King of kings and Lord of lords supposed to ride a valiant warrior horse? Yes, indeed!

Lord, You want me to look forward always to the return of Jesus.
He is my King, Lord, and Savior now and always.

EVERY MAN UNDER HIS FIG TREE

*Judah and Israel lived in safety, from Dan even
to Beersheba, every man under his vine and
under his fig tree, all the days of Solomon.*

1 KINGS 4:25 ESV

What's up with the Bible and fig trees? More than you might suppose! In the Old Testament, God's blessings of peace and prosperity included the imagery of every man under his own fig tree. You see this in Deuteronomy 8:8 shortly before the Israelites entered the Promised Land. You see this again in 1 Kings 4:25 and 10:27 (and 2 Chronicles 1:15 and 9:27) during the reign of Solomon.

Then again, the Lord uses unfruitful and dead fig trees as metaphors of His judgments against the rebellious nation of Israel. You see this in Isaiah 9:10 and 34:4; Jeremiah 5:17 and 8:13; Hosea 2:12 and 9:10; Joel 1:7 and 1:12; Amos 4:9; Habakkuk 3:17; and Haggai 2:19.

This plethora of prophecies sets the stage for one of Jesus Christ's last and most misunderstood miracles, the cursing of the fig tree in Matthew 21:18–22 and Mark 11:12–14 and 11:20–25. Both picture the Lord's judgments against rebellious Israel and compel His followers to offer authentic, faith-filled, and God-focused prayers always.

*Lord, You want me to see figs and fig trees as You
see them. They're compelling metaphors, indeed.*

SOLOMON BUILT THE TEMPLE

So Solomon built the temple and completed it.
1 KINGS 6:14 NIV

———————◆———————

When the Bible repeatedly says "Solomon built the temple," it doesn't mean he did any of the physical work. Why then, does the Bible say that *Solomon* built it?

First, did Solomon use the divinely inspired and very detailed architectural plans for every part of the incredibly beautiful and transcendent temple? Yes.

Second, did Solomon use the extravagantly expensive stockpiles of gold and other materials specially earmarked for the temple and its furnishings? Yes.

Third, did Solomon seek to obey the Lord and his father David at every turn? Yes.

Fourth, would the temple have been built precisely as instructed to glorify the Lord God if Solomon had been against it? No.

Fifth, does the Bible clearly recognize the 150,000+ workforce that did all of the labor precisely as instructed? Yes.

Finally, do men still talk about the new house they're building, even if they're doing only some or none of the physical work? Yes.

———————————————————————

Lord, You want me to see what You're saying in every
word and verse by looking carefully at the immediate
and broader context of what You say in scripture. I will.

THE GOSPEL ACCORDING TO SOLOMON

*Then Solomon stood before the altar of the LORD in front of
the whole assembly of Israel, spread out his hands toward
heaven and said: "LORD, the God of Israel, there is no
God like you in heaven above or on earth below."*
1 KINGS 8:22–23 NIV

In 1 Kings 8:22–53, Solomon presents both the good and bad news of the Gospel in eight points. All eight points can be found in the inspired sermons of the apostles Peter and Paul (Acts) and in their equally inspired writings (from Romans to 2 Peter).

First, the Lord is God alone. Second, the Lord's name alone is to be worshipped, honored, and glorified. Third, the Lord is holy, mighty, and just. He is a God who keeps His word, who blesses those who follow Him, and who judges those who disobey His commands and go astray.

Fourth, all have sinned (1 Kings 8:46). Fifth, by turning to the Lord in repentance and confessing His name in prayer, there is forgiveness. Sixth, to reject the Lord is to bring condemnation on one's head. Seventh, God is ready, in times of extremity, to hear men's prayers and forgive them.

Eighth, God is a deliverer, a Savior who wants to make men into His people, and into His servants, blessed by Him forever.

*Lord, You want every man to believe and live
out the Gospel. Thank You for saving me.*

SOLOMON'S BIGGEST SIN

Now King Solomon loved many foreign women.
1 KINGS 11:1 NLT

Everyone knows about Solomon's biggest sin: loving an unending string of foreign wives. Unlike his father, Solomon's sin was deeply rooted, blatant, prolific, all-consuming, and unconfessed—to the very end.

The man renowned for his wisdom and wealth ended up leaving a kingdom about to collapse, and set in motion wicked, destructive practices for which both the kingdoms of Israel and Judah would be destroyed and exiled. So fearful was Solomon's biggest sin—and resultant misery—that it struck fear in men long after the Babylonian captivity (Nehemiah 13:25–26).

By comparing today's key verse with 1 Kings 3:1 and 14:21 and 14:31, it becomes apparent that Solomon loved foreign women *before* he became king, and married one or more before forming a marriage alliance with Pharaoh by marrying his daughter. Solomon's son Rehoboam, who reigned after Solomon's death, was born of an Ammonite woman about a year prior to Solomon taking the throne.

Solomon's biggest sin began in his youth, and ran its full course unabated even though twice God had appeared to him, exhorting Solomon to obey His commands. What sin, perhaps long entrenched and scarcely recognized, still embraces men's hearts today?

Lord, I repent of the "foreign wives" I love. I don't want them drawing me away from You. I turn away from them, and turn back to You. Forgive me, free me, and release me from their grip.

ARE YOU UNLIKE REHOBOAM?

*Rehoboam rejected the advice the elders gave
him and consulted the young men who had
grown up with him and were serving him.*
1 KINGS 12:8 NIV

Solomon's wisdom was a gift from God. Genetics had nothing to do with it, as his son Rehoboam found out soon after his father's death. Rehoboam's first official act as king? Rejecting wise counsel!

Wisdom asks, Does this plan call for a short-term sacrifice for a long-term benefit? Will this plan benefit others? Is this counsel peace-loving? Does this advice appeal to my pride or to my generosity?

In the end, God's will to take a large part of the nation from Solomon's son was fulfilled. Then again, that's no excuse for Rehoboam's blunder. You can always choose to do what is right. And God can easily make His plan come to pass without your foolish schemes and outright sins. Rehoboam's biggest sin? No heart for God, no fear of God, and no beginning of wisdom. All that was left was a mushy mind heeding foolish counsel and reaping terrible consequences.

Unlike Rehoboam, ignore the clamoring voices of bad advice. Instead, listen only to those who direct you to heed God's Word.

*Lord, You want me to heed Rehoboam's terrible example.
I will do the opposite of what he did today!*

ARE YOU SENT BY THE LORD?

*So when Ahijah heard the sound of her footsteps at the
door, he said, "Come in, wife of Jeroboam. Why this
pretense? I have been sent to you with bad news."*
1 Kings 14:6 niv

The Bible is full of irony, and today's key verse is an example. Wicked King Jeroboam's wife comes and goes, but the blind prophet Ahijah is *sent* by God—even though he doesn't leave his house!

This seems suggestive of part of what Jesus meant in John 20:21 (niv) when He said, "As the Father has sent me, I am sending you." Perhaps the emphasis, when the Lord sends someone, isn't so much on coming and going, but on doing what He commands. . .being a *sent* man.

This seems borne out by many other statements by Jesus from Matthew 4:19 to John 13:20 and statements by the apostles themselves from Acts 8:14 to 1 Thessalonians 3:2 and 3:5.

Like Ahijah, are you willing to obey the Lord's clear-cut commands to declare His inspired, biblical message points to others?

*Lord, You want me to live as a man sent by God—
in my home, in my workplace, and in other spheres
of my life. Where I am, I'll live as sent by You!*

WILL YOU ACCEPT GOD'S PROVISION FOR YOUR PROBLEMS?

So she did as Elijah said, and she and Elijah and her family continued to eat for many days. There was always enough flour and olive oil left in the containers, just as the LORD had promised through Elijah.
1 KINGS 17:15–16 NLT

What did the widow have in mind as a solution to her need for food? Perhaps she was so full of despair over her family's needs that she couldn't think of a way out. Did she expect Elijah to help her? In her moment of desperation, Elijah offered a solution that required faith to trust God each day. Would the containers continue to be full each day? Would God come through?

Perhaps you are seeking God's provision right now, but are you ready to receive what He offers? What if God sends just what you need for today? Will it be enough?

The solution God sends may still require living by faith, trusting that He will show up at the start of yet another day. Praying for "daily bread" each day may get old. It may appear less than ideal in the moment, but it will benefit your faith over the long term. Your ability to endure challenges and uncertainty will grow as you learn to trust God day in and day out.

God, I trust that You can provide what I need for today and that my faith will grow as You care for me.

DO YOU NEED AN OUTSIDE PERSPECTIVE?

"I have not made trouble for Israel," Elijah replied. "But you and your father's family have. You have abandoned the LORD's commands and have followed the Baals."

1 KINGS 18:18 NIV

Ahab was more than ready to transfer the blame for his troubles onto Elijah. Rather than examining his actions and taking ownership for the ways he had abandoned God's laws, it was much easier for him to point the finger at the messenger.

When you're going through a difficult or uncertain time, it's quite difficult to step back and see the highs and lows with clarity. An outside perspective, like Elijah's, can cut to the chase in an instant, offering a point of view that cuts through any doubt, debate, or attempts to minimize your actions.

Relying on someone else for wisdom and guidance isn't easy. It can be a vulnerable space where you need to trust that another has your best interests in mind. That's why it's so easy to blame the messenger instead. Yet God's mercy is plentiful and His patience defies all expectations. If you can take that step of faith and seek the help of a trusted friend or mentor, see matters as they truly are, and act accordingly, you can find new freedom and life where you otherwise would have been stuck.

Lord, help me to see my life with clarity and to listen to those who can help me see the truth.

HOW ENVY STEALS WHAT YOU HAVE

*And Ahab went into his house vexed and sullen because of
what Naboth the Jezreelite had said to him, for he had said,
"I will not give you the inheritance of my fathers." And he lay
down on his bed and turned away his face and would eat no food.*

1 KINGS 21:4 ESV

It's easy to see how a king could look ridiculous as he pouts and laments a field he can't buy. While he had no shortage of fields and wealth in his kingdom, Ahab let his desire for land destroy his contentment and even drive him to condone the owner's murder.

Such a scene appears over the top today, but it illustrates the real problem of envy, which steals your enjoyment of what you have. When you are focused on what others have, or on what you can't have, you essentially lose sight of what you *do* have. Your enjoyment of God's blessings is blocked by the dark clouds of envy.

If left unchecked, envy can take hold and push people to take actions they never would have considered at first. While today's reading sits on the more extreme end of the spectrum, it remains a true illustration of how much damage envy can do to you and to the people around you.

*Lord, help me to enjoy the blessings
You have given me with gratitude.*

DO YOU WELCOME A REBUKE?

*The king of Israel replied to Jehoshaphat, "There is one
more man who could consult the LORD for us, but I hate him.
He never prophesies anything but trouble for me! His name
is Micaiah son of Imlah." Jehoshaphat replied, "That's not the
way a king should talk! Let's hear what he has to say."*

1 KINGS 22:8 NLT

It's human nature to only want good news, and the king of Israel routinely turned to people who only said what he wanted to hear. This wasn't just disastrous for him. It spelled disaster for everyone in his family and for all who depended on his leadership. By valuing his own wisdom and refusing to ignore the warnings from God's messengers, he lost his hold on the position and power he had valued so highly.

How do you respond to a friend's rebuke or to a warning from a trusted mentor? Are you willing to accept it and to rethink your course? The warning that comes from God may not be what you want to hear, but it can be the very message that saves you and those around you from ruin. That means sometimes searching out people who will say what you don't want to hear. You'll need to seek views beyond those you typically consider. It may be uncomfortable, but it may be exactly what you need to hear.

*Lord, give me ears to hear even the
bad news I don't want to receive.*

BLESSING AND MINISTRY COME THROUGH FAITHFULNESS

Elijah said to Elisha, "Stay here; the LORD has sent me to Bethel."
But Elisha said, "As surely as the LORD lives and as you live,
I will not leave you." So they went down to Bethel.

2 KINGS 2:2 NIV

Even after Elijah ordered him to stay behind, Elisha remained faithful to his master and chose to travel with him into the unknown on Elijah's last day on earth. He faced the uncertainty of the moment and received a rich blessing and ministry because he took the harder path of faithfulness. As he watched Elijah ascend to heaven, he received a double portion of his spirit, which he used to guide, defend, and bless God's people in the coming years.

Standing by someone in a time of loss or uncertainty can feel disruptive and devastating. Yet, as you stand with those who mourn or who stand on the brink of a major change, you will find blessings and even God's life in those moments. You may gain wisdom and insight that would have come to you in no other way—and which prepares you to minister to others in deeper ways.

As you consider your relationships today, take special note of those going through a transition. Are there ways you can show up and remain with them? Can you help them endure their trial and uncertainty until the end?

Lord, help me to see those in need of
my presence and comfort today.

THERE WILL NEVER BE
ENOUGH WITHOUT GOD

But his servant said, "How can I set this before a hundred men?" So he repeated, "Give them to the men, that they may eat, for thus says the LORD, 'They shall eat and have some left.'" So he set it before them. And they ate and had some left, according to the word of the LORD.

2 KINGS 4:43–44 ESV

Even though the bread on hand wasn't sufficient to feed the multitude present, Elisha put his trust in God's care and provision. He believed in God's promise rather than the facts of the moment before him. As it turned out, he quickly went from insufficient food for those in need to an overabundance of food.

When John D. Rockefeller, one of the wealthiest individuals to ever walk the planet, was asked, "How much money is enough money?" he famously replied, "Just a little bit more." Even when there's an abundance, it's human nature to doubt, fear, and worry about the future.

Consider an area of your life where you fear falling short or not having enough. How can you entrust that situation to God? Perhaps you will feel prompted to seek additional help, but what if God is asking you to step forward with what you have, trusting that He can multiply whatever you offer?

Lord, on this National Day of Prayer, I trust in Your abundance to care for my needs and the needs of others.

HOW DOUBT DEPRIVES GOD'S PEOPLE OF BLESSING

The officer assisting the king said to the man of God,
"That couldn't happen even if the LORD opened the windows
of heaven!" But Elisha replied, "You will see it happen with
your own eyes, but you won't be able to eat any of it!"
2 KINGS 7:2 NLT

The officer didn't believe God could save his people, and it's hard to blame him. The city was surrounded and the odds were not in his army's favor. Yet, Elisha assured a deliverance the officer believed to be impossible. While the officer's fate is quite extreme, there is a far-reaching lesson for today as well. Failing to trust in God will rob you of the joy of deliverance.

What are you worried about today? Is there something big and important that demands your full attention? These are the kinds of things to trust to God's care, looking up to the horizon for His deliverance and provision.

It's not easy to trust God with your most important, if not most frightening, challenges, but you will grow in faith as you see Him provide time and time again. The hope of yesterday's deliverance can help you persevere and endure in the face of tomorrow's worries.

Lord, I look to You for my help and provision.

THE THREAT OF A DIVIDED HEART

*Yet Jehu was not careful to keep the law of the LORD, the God
of Israel, with all his heart. He did not turn away from the
sins of Jeroboam, which he had caused Israel to commit.*

2 KINGS 10:31 NIV

It's tempting to think of Jehu as a king with an unprecedented opportunity for a clean start. He removed a violent and disobedient king. He waged war against the idols of the land. He had a loyal band of supporters. And yet, he failed to follow through on his reforms. Over time, his failures caught up with him, dividing his heart and sending his reforms off course.

When you've made a lot of progress in your life, it's easy to drop your guard and lose the discipline that had been so helpful in the first place. Why go overboard in getting everything just right? In the case of today's reading, a little bit of failure goes a long way.

Your heart will determine the course of your life. If you have a seed of rebellion or distraction in place, it may not take long for it to begin growing, taking root, and sending you in a completely different direction. Take a moment today to examine your heart for anything you're holding back from God. Consider how you can be thorough and spiritually whole in your commitments to Him.

*Father, examine my heart and heal any divisions
or diversions that could keep me from You.*

ENDURANCE THROUGH WISE COUNSEL

And Jehoash did what was right in the eyes of the LORD all
his days, because Jehoiada the priest instructed him.
2 KINGS 12:2 ESV

The history of the kings of Judah is not a pretty picture for the most part. One king after another either goes after his own desires and aspirations or makes needed reforms without following through in some of the most important areas of religious worship. Jehoash was wise to lean heavily on Jehoiada the priest. After all, insanity is doing the same thing over and over again, expecting different results.

Seeking a mentor or the counsel of wise friends and leaders may run against the grain of today's culture, which is full of seemingly bootstrapping, self-made men. Who wants to lean on someone else in order to succeed when you can get all the credit on your own?

As it turns out, one of the most highly revered and godly kings in the history of Israel and Judah endured where so many else had failed because he had the right person guiding his decisions. Community and mutual support are essential for the spiritual life. You will need someone who can offer wise counsel in a trying time or help you avoid common mistakes. This will help you live a long life of faithfulness to God and service to others.

Lord, as I celebrate my mother's influence today,
may I also have caring guides in my spiritual
life who can help my faith endure.

WHOSE EXAMPLE WILL YOU FOLLOW?

Amaziah did what was pleasing in the LORD's sight, but not like his ancestor David. Instead, he followed the example of his father, Joash. Amaziah did not destroy the pagan shrines, and the people still offered sacrifices and burned incense there.

2 KINGS 14:3–4 NLT

Amaziah could have done worse. Unlike the majority of the kings of Israel and Judah, he followed many of God's laws and led his people without any of the horrible injustices or failures of his predecessors. Nevertheless, he only set his standards as high as his father, not his ancestor David, whose heart was fully committed to the Lord.

Having the right kind of mentor or example to follow can make all the difference in a man's life. If you are following someone whose commitment to obedience or living by faith is minimal, you'll have little in the way of instruction or in modeling a God-honoring life for you. Leaders or mentors who cut corners won't show you how to pursue the best path forward.

Is there someone in your life who has high standards or leads by a powerful example? While such a person may seem a tough act to follow, he is exactly the kind of person who will stretch your faith and show you the path toward a deeper reverence for God.

Lord, help me to find people who will guide me toward You and toward a life of faith.

YOU BECOME WHAT YOU DO

*They rejected his decrees and the covenant he had
made with their ancestors and the statutes he had warned
them to keep. They followed worthless idols and themselves
became worthless. They imitated the nations around them
although the Lord had ordered them, "Do not do as they do."*
2 Kings 17:15 niv

Consider what you have done in the past twenty-four hours. What stands out to you? Could you list a few things from the past week as well? What you do will shape you in one way or another. The more you immerse yourself in spiritual practices and in the story of scripture, the more those things will shape you. The more you immerse yourself in the values of our culture, the more they will direct and influence you.

God's desire for His people is to guide them toward His rest, peace, and justice—often described by the word *shalom*. Yet, by making more time for other priorities and influences, God's hope for His people can be lost, if not drowned out. One act of disobedience or one choice to follow your own plan may seem small in isolation, but accumulated over time, the consequences can be dire, shaping you and leading you in ways you may have never imagined.

There is hope for you as one of God's people, but enjoying that hope and the peace that comes with it depends on faithfulness to the path God has set before you.

*Lord, grant me the wisdom to follow Your
commandments and to remain attentive to You.*

WHAT HAVE OTHERS SAID ABOUT GOD?

Isaiah said to them, "Say to your master, 'Thus says the LORD:
Do not be afraid because of the words that you have heard, with
which the servants of the king of Assyria have reviled me. Behold,
I will put a spirit in him, so that he shall hear a rumor and return to
his own land, and I will make him fall by the sword in his own land.' "
2 KINGS 19:6–7 ESV

Who do you listen to when you make your decisions and live by faith? Do you listen to those in power who overestimate their influence? Do you focus on those who predict doom and despair? Isaiah reminds the king to spend more time focusing on what God is capable of doing. But can you blame the king for being afraid?

Whether you are facing steep odds or fear the worst in a situation, take time to consider how God is with you throughout your challenges. There's no guarantee that you'll get what you hope for, but if you trust in God's loving presence, you will know God's comfort.

Rather than looking at everything that could go wrong, offer your future to God with open hands, allowing Him to work toward your best interests. Over time, you may find that He has been with you all along, guiding and directing your steps.

Lord, I trust that You are able to guide and
direct my steps in fearful and uncertain times.

WHAT WILL YOUR LEGACY BE?

*Then Hezekiah said to Isaiah, "This message you have given
me from the LORD is good." For the king was thinking, "At
least there will be peace and security during my lifetime."*
2 KINGS 20:19 NLT

A common theme throughout the Old Testament is passing along the
stories and laws of God to future generations. Hezekiah ended his
otherwise commendable rule with a tragic failure that set the stage for
disaster for future generations. Rather than leaving behind a legacy of
care for future generations, he only concerned himself with his own
comfort and safety, leaving a blemish on his kingship.

How can you leave a legacy of faith and love for God? Future
generations will benefit from the choices you make today. Beyond leaving
an inheritance, you leave a godly legacy by trusting in God and loving Him
with your heart, mind, soul, and strength. Rather than seeking to just
get by with the comfortable choice or avoiding responsibility for your
actions, each time you open yourself to God's influence is an opportunity
to shape future generations.

You may make mistakes and there will be consequences, but beware
of the mistake of Hezekiah, who didn't resolve to repent or make things
right. Consider how you can correct your wrongs not only for your own
sake but for those who follow in your steps.

*Lord, help me to leave a legacy of wisdom and
repentance for the sake of future generations.*

IT'S NEVER TOO LATE TO REPENT

"Because your heart was responsive and you humbled yourself
before the Lord when you heard what I have spoken against
this place and its people—that they would become a curse
and be laid waste—and because you tore your robes and wept
in my presence, I also have heard you, declares the Lord."
2 Kings 22:19 niv

Although Josiah feared disaster because of God's judgment, he took prompt action to repent of his people's sins and to grieve the ways his people had angered God. The Lord was eager to hear their prayer and relented His anger immediately.

You may have failed in some pretty dramatic and public ways. You may think you're a phony. You may worry about letting people down with your poor choices. However, you can't lose God's love and concern. Even the most stubborn sinners found rich mercy and forgiveness when they changed their ways. Jesus went so far as to suggest that God throws a party for one repentant sinner!

Today is the day to examine your failures, your shame, or your weaknesses and to bring them to God. There is nothing beyond God's mercy, and if you trust Him with your paths, you can change how you see yourself. The good news is that God has never changed the way He sees you, viewing you as a beloved child He longs to see return home.

Lord, I receive Your mercy and
forgiveness as I confess my sins today.

HOW WILL YOU FINISH?

*So Jehoiachin put off his prison garments. And every day
of his life he dined regularly at the king's table, and for his
allowance, a regular allowance was given him by the king,
according to his daily needs, as long as he lived.*
2 KINGS 25:29–30 ESV

If you thought that the story of Jehoiachin ended with him being led off in chains to exile, you may have missed the story's final chapter. While living in a foreign land, the king showed compassion on him and provided for him, giving him a peaceful ending to a tragic and failure-ridden life.

Some people lead lives that run in the right direction, making sound, responsible choices. . .until a point where they break apart, have an affair, abandon their responsibilities, or turn away from God. Starting on the right path isn't a guarantee of a good finish. But a major detour—or ten—does not disqualify anyone from a strong finish.

Where are you right now? Are you on the right path, uncertain, or stuck on a detour? Regardless, turning to God and seeking the help of friends and mentors can help you stay the course, figure out your questions, or get you back on track. If there is hope for a king who was treated like a criminal at one point in his life, then there surely is hope for you in God's mercy!

*Lord, help me to finish strong, to continue depending on You,
and to bring You glory as I finish my course in this life.*

GOD SHOWS MERCY TO SAVE HIS PEOPLE

Later Judah had twin sons from Tamar, his widowed daughter-in-law.
Their names were Perez and Zerah. So Judah had five sons in all.
1 CHRONICLES 2:4 NLT

I f you were going to make a list of people who demonstrate how to live a holy life, Judah may not be at the top of it. Having first deceived his daughter-in-law and then sleeping with her because he thought she was a prostitute, Judah could have run his life right off the rails. Yet, he wasn't defined by his failures earlier in his life, and God's blessings settled on his children and their descendants. Far from minimizing Judah's sins, the Lord desired to bring salvation to His people, and Judah's family became exhibit A of God's kindness.

God desires to save you as well, to show you mercy and bless you and your family with His presence. There is no hope for anyone to find God apart from His mercy and saving acts. Even when you've fallen far short of the ideal that you may imagine for your life, you are never disqualified from God's mercy. The only qualification you need for God's mercy is a humble need for it! By coming to Him with your great need, you prepare yourself to receive His great salvation.

Perhaps the people of the Bible appear larger than life in retrospect, but the accounts left behind remind us that they needed God's mercy and love because they often failed and gave into their passions—just like us.

Lord, I trust in Your mercy and love.

HOW ARE YOU FILLING YOUR NEEDS?

*But they were unfaithful to the God of their ancestors
and prostituted themselves to the gods of the peoples
of the land, whom God had destroyed before them.*

1 CHRONICLES 5:25 NIV

The language of the Bible doesn't pull any punches when it describes unfaithfulness to God. The people of Israel are described as prostitutes seeking the provision offered by other gods to meet their needs. An idol or false god wasn't just a matter of religious observance. It met a need, such as more rain for the farms in a land that lacked other irrigation options. An idol was a means to fill a need, to pay the bills, or to make the pain go away.

You may not have a statue you bow in front of in a temple or an altar on a hillside dedicated to a god that promises rain, fertility, or peace. But there are plenty of other wrong ways to meet your needs, to take care of your problems, and to dull the pain and fear of life. Whatever you rely on rather than God will fast become an idol that will make more demands on your life and claim your allegiance. Over time, you can find that you can rely on your own means (and idols)—or you can surrender your future to God alone. You can't keep up that kind of division forever.

Today may be the moment to make a choice once and for all.

*Lord, teach me to trust in You completely,
with an undivided heart.*

WHY DO BAD THINGS HAPPEN?

*So Saul died for his breach of faith. He broke faith with
the LORD in that he did not keep the command of the LORD,
and also consulted a medium, seeking guidance.*
1 CHRONICLES 10:13 ESV

The writers of scripture often sought to explain the reasons for trage-dies, and in the case of Saul's death, and the death of his son Jonathan, a national tragedy called for reflection. Why had such a heroic figure, chosen by God to lead Israel, fallen so far that he died on the battlefield and lost so much territory to his enemies? Had God abandoned Saul and the people of Israel?

It's not always possible to trace a tragedy directly to disobedience, but it would be foolish to skip self-examination in a time of difficulty or struggle. Such introspection may help reveal how your conduct or decisions have contributed to a tragedy or challenge. While it's likely that most people haven't consulted a medium like Saul, resisting God's commands is another matter that you can surely relate to in your own life. A stubborn streak, a hasty decision, or an action that harms yourself or others can send you into trouble fast. The sooner you repent and get back on course, the better.

The sorrow that leads to repentance is far better than the sorrow after a time of loss or suffering that results from your choices.

*Lord, reveal the ways I am resisting You so that
I can live in obedience to Your commands.*

A BRIEF REMINDER THAT YOU'RE NOT GOD

So the Three broke through the Philistine lines, drew some
water from the well by the gate in Bethlehem, and brought
it back to David. But David refused to drink it. Instead,
he poured it out as an offering to the LORD.
1 CHRONICLES 11:18 NLT

David was more homesick than in desperate need of water, and his three most trusted soldiers demonstrated their devotion by drawing water from the well in his hometown, which had been occupied by the Philistines. Their sacrifice could have been extremely costly, and by pouring the water on the land, David recognized that his life was not worth such an incredible sacrifice or devotion. David remembered that he wasn't worthy of the devotion that belongs to God alone.

It feels good when others appreciate and value you. You probably wouldn't complain if a friend went to the trouble of bringing you a cup of coffee or tea. Yet, where do you draw the line in desiring the admiration and respect of others? At what point do you cross over from wanting to be recognized to *demanding* reverence or honor that no person can rightly claim as his own?

Mind you, respect and devotion may be well earned. David's soldiers loved him for the right reasons. But today's reading is a brief, welcome reminder that the admiration of others can become a trap. Sometimes your character is revealed by the kind of praise you won't receive.

Lord, help me to serve others humbly, giving You the glory.

WHAT ARE YOU SEARCHING FOR?

Sing to him, sing praise to him; tell of all his wonderful acts.
Glory in his holy name; let the hearts of those who seek the LORD
rejoice. Look to the LORD and his strength; seek his face always.
1 CHRONICLES 16:9–11 NIV

What are you searching for today? Are you focused on something in particular? What you're searching for is probably linked with solving something or fulfilling a particular need. It may be a promotion, a new technology device, a way to handle a difficult relationship, or an improvement to your home—if not a new home altogether! Each of these things is tied to accomplishing something, but they aren't necessarily reliable or adequate for the task. Are there any other options?

Seeking the Lord may not provide any direct solutions to your problems right away, but as God's presence shapes you and the Spirit guides you, you will find renewed strength and sufficient wisdom to face what had seemed impossible. Even better, by seeking the Lord first, you'll experience the joy of God's provision and can sing God's praises. It's not an easy first step to take, but once you've tasted the goodness of God, singing His praises will no doubt be more restorative than worrying about tomorrow.

Lord, today I seek Your presence and wisdom, trusting in You alone.

GOD'S PEOPLE LEAD WITH JUSTICE AND EQUALITY

Then he put garrisons in Edom, and all the Edomites became David's servants. And the LORD gave victory to David wherever he went. So David reigned over all Israel, and he administered justice and equity to all his people.
1 CHRONICLES 18:13–14 ESV

Justice and equity go hand in hand throughout the Old Testament accounts of Israel and Judah's kings. Behind a king's commitment to worship God alone in the temple, justice and equity often stand as the measures of a king's domestic policy. Rather than evaluating a leader's programs, buildings, or economy, God wants leaders who will ensure the just laws of the land are enforced fairly and who will treat everyone based on the same standard without playing favorites.

What would you consider a success for yourself when you have a position of influence or a leadership role? Perhaps a good starting point, one based on God's standards for leaders, is whether you have been fair in your treatment of others and whether you have faithfully obeyed God's commands. That isn't necessarily a guarantee of continued success or acclaim, but if you hope to lead according to God's standards, modeling yourself after the man said to have a heart modeled after God's own is a good place to start!

Lord, help me to use my influence to serve others with justice and equity in all situations.

HOLINESS PREPARES FOR SERVICE

*"Now seek the Lord your God with all your heart and soul.
Build the sanctuary of the Lord God so that you can bring
the Ark of the Lord's Covenant and the holy vessels of
God into the Temple built to honor the Lord's name."*
1 Chronicles 22:19 NLT

The daily decisions Solomon made to follow God, or to follow his own plans, had everything to do with his ability to serve God and His people. If he sought God with all of his heart and soul, he would be prepared to build God's temple and to lead God's people in worship. The consequences for his daily decisions were extremely serious.

You may not have as much on the line as Solomon, but your ability to discern God's leadership in your life, to obey God's commands, and to serve others has everything to do with your inner life. If you abandon your soul through immersion in busy projects and one more thing to do, you'll lose the inner capacity to hear God and will lack the spiritual resources others will need. If your heart is turned toward what you desire, you'll likely miss the opportunities God has prepared for you.

If you care for your soul and direct your desires toward God, then you will be prepared to act on His behalf, and many will benefit from your obedience.

*Lord, guard my soul and direct my
heart toward what You desire.*

THE TRAP OF PRIDE

David did not take the number of the men twenty years old or less,
because the LORD had promised to make Israel as numerous as the
stars in the sky. Joab son of Zeruiah began to count the men but did not
finish. God's wrath came on Israel on account of this numbering, and the
number was not entered in the book of the annals of King David.
1 CHRONICLES 27:23–24 NIV

After enjoying incredible success, King David wanted to look at some numbers to find out just how successful he had been. Putting down such an impressive number would clearly set him apart from everyone who followed him.

Have you been tempted to count something that demonstrates your accomplishments to everyone in your circles? That temptation may be a helpful clue about the parts of your life you are clinging to and that you have prioritized over God or serving His people. It is enough to be faithful and to trust the final numbers with God. While it may be appealing to tally your accomplishments for all to see, the praise and esteem that matters the most comes from God.

This may require swallowing your pride, but you could find that such measurements are quite toxic for your soul. If only God knows what you've accomplished, then your glory will come from Him alone.

Lord, help me to let go of my desire to be recognized and
admired for my accomplishments by anyone but You.

FAMOUS LAST WORDS

"And you, Solomon my son, know the God of your father and serve him with a whole heart and with a willing mind, for the LORD searches all hearts and understands every plan and thought. If you seek him, he will be found by you, but if you forsake him, he will cast you off forever."

1 CHRONICLES 28:9 ESV

After a lifetime of serving God, David finally distilled his lessons into a powerful charge for Solomon. While Solomon could hide himself behind his palace walls and powerful title, he couldn't hide himself from God. God would perceive the sincerity of his actions and search his secret thoughts.

Today's promise is a simple one. Seek and you will find. Jesus assured His listeners of as much. Yet, it's not just what you seek out that God looks at. God sees your thoughts, desires, and inner motivations. There is nothing to hide before God.

Perhaps that is unsettling for you, but it's also an opportunity. If you have not gotten your heart right before God, now is your opportunity to confess your faults. God won't be surprised anyway! As you begin to seek God anew, you can have confidence that He will not hide from you. That doesn't mean God will show up at the times or in the ways you desire or expect. Rather, it means that God is always near, whether or not you are aware of Him.

Lord, search my heart and sustain me as I seek You today.

HOW CAN YOU BECOME
A BLESSING TO OTHERS?

*"Give me the wisdom and knowledge to lead them properly,
for who could possibly govern this great people of yours?"*
2 CHRONICLES 1:10 NLT

———————————

O ut of everything Solomon could have asked of God, he sought something that would bring the most benefit to the people he ruled. Given a chance to receive a blessing from God, he sought a way to bless others.

Perhaps one way to think about your spiritual growth today is to seek ways you can grow in your ability to bless others. Rather than seeking financial security just for yourself, ask God to grow your generosity so that you can help others become secure. Rather than asking for safety for just yourself, ask God to show you people in your community who are vulnerable. As you seek to bless others richly, you may find that God also takes care of your needs as well.

If you are facing a challenge that appears beyond your abilities, now is a great time to lean on God, trusting in His provision. Turning your focus toward the ways you can bless others, rather than the ways you may fail, can change your prayers so that you trust fully in God's resources for you.

*Lord, turn my eyes away from what I lack, and help
me to see how You can bless others through me.*

GOD IS VIGILANT FOR YOUR PRAYERS

*"May your eyes be open toward this temple day and night,
this place of which you said you would put your Name there.
May you hear the prayer your servant prays toward this place."*
2 CHRONICLES 6:20 NIV

———————

The way you worship may look a little different from the days of the temple, when the people turned toward the building regardless of their location when they prayed. Such a practice may not be necessary today, but the same mind-set holds true: God is attentive to the prayers of His people, both day and night.

It may be difficult to find a good time to pray, but since God is vigilant for you at all times, you can seek Him in the middle of the night, on your way to work, or sitting in the pew at church. There's no better time than another to pray, and you can trust that God is present and aware of your needs before you even ask. As you are present for God, you can enjoy the peace of His presence and love.

Just as Solomon prayed with confidence for the new temple, you can rest assured that God treasures your silence and your words. God is present and is willing to intervene in your life for your good.

*Lord, I trust that You hear my prayers and that
You will respond with love and mercy.*

HOW CAN YOU WIN PRAISE FOR GOD?

"Blessed be the LORD your God, who has delighted in you and set you on his throne as king for the LORD your God! Because your God loved Israel and would establish them forever, he has made you king over them, that you may execute justice and righteousness."

2 CHRONICLES 9:8 ESV

No one is going to feel better about themselves by making a comparison with King Solomon's wisdom and wealth, especially when the Queen of Sheba heaps praise on him. Solomon is clearly an outlier in his fame and fortune, but his dependence on God won him the glory and praise.

How can you grow in your dependence on God and trust Him to provide for you? Are you seeking wisdom, insight, or compassion that you can use to bless others? Are there unique gifts you can trace back to God's intervention in your life?

Whatever you bring to others, consider how God can empower you to bless others and to demonstrate His goodness. You may not be able to wow a powerful political leader, but you may call attention to God's mercy by showing mercy to others. At other times you may share hard-won wisdom by trusting your ways to God. Your life can become a testimony of God's presence for a world that is looking for signs of His life.

Lord, grant me wisdom so that I can help others and bring glory to You.

DRAWING A BULL'S-EYE
AROUND YOUR ARROW

Jeroboam appointed his own priests to serve at the pagan shrines,
where they worshiped the goat and calf idols he had made.
2 CHRONICLES 11:15 NLT

Facing a divided kingdom and the possibility that his subjects would leave for his rival's land in order to worship, Jeroboam came up with a "good enough" solution by creating his own idols and appointing his own priests rather than worshipping in the temple and with the priests God had appointed. You could say he drew a bull's-eye around wherever his arrow landed, choosing the easiest solution rather than seeking a way to remain faithful to God despite the threat to his kingdom.

The easy way out may save some headaches today. A few compromises may smooth over a conversation or three. Yet, the "good enough" option will eventually lead you astray from God's purpose and could even cause others to make similar mistakes.

Consider your temptations to compromise, the ways you have cut corners, or the times you could be tempted to settle in the future. How can you entrust these situations to God? Are worries about your future, your relationships, or your finances leading you toward a shortcut? These are what you can bring to God in prayer today, seeking His guidance so that you can pursue His best for you and your family.

Lord, deliver me from my fears and my
compromises so that I can follow where You lead.

GOD DESIRES TO BE FOUND

For a long time Israel was without the true God, without a priest to teach and without the law. But in their distress they turned to the Lord, the God of Israel, and sought him, and he was found by them.
2 CHRONICLES 15:3–4 NIV

Jesus echoed a long line of prophets when He promised His followers that they could seek and find God by faith. The prophet Azariah promised the people of Israel that despite their unfaithfulness and rejection of God, they could still find Him in their moment of distress. Although God lets His people walk away if they choose, He also desires that His people find Him.

When you pray and nothing seems to happen, do you sometimes worry that God is playing games with you or is even becoming passive-aggressive? It can be hard to believe that you will find God when He doesn't show up in any of the ways you're expecting.

However, if you can surrender your expectations and pray with faith, you may find that God has already shown up in your life in ways you hadn't before noticed or that you aren't aware of in the present. God is already present, but sometimes it may take your perception a little time to catch up.

Lord, help me to find You when I seek You with my whole heart.

GOD DEMANDS FAIR JUDGMENTS

"Now then, let the fear of the LORD be upon you.
Be careful what you do, for there is no injustice with
the LORD our God, or partiality or taking bribes."
2 CHRONICLES 19:7 ESV

As Jehoshaphat established his reign in the land of Judah, he took particular pains to appoint judges who could not be swayed by bribes or biased toward certain parties. He even went as far as reminding his judges that they should fear God, remaining aware of His justice in their own judgments.

You may not have the same responsibility as these judges, but it's good advice to remain aware of God's presence and justice when making decisions or relating to others. As God watches over His people, He demands fairness in their dealings to the point that those who cheat their neighbors should fear His response.

God is already searching your heart and knows what's behind your motivation and choices, and the stakes are even higher for judgments and decisions that could harm your neighbors. You better believe that God will take notice! That is why He requires that we apply wisdom and compassion toward others in every situation.

Lord, grant me wisdom and compassion
in my dealings with others.

THE HIGH STAKES FOR OBEDIENCE

Then the Spirit of God came upon Zechariah son of Jehoiada the priest.
He stood before the people and said, "This is what God says: Why do you
disobey the LORD's commands and keep yourselves from prospering?
You have abandoned the LORD, and now he has abandoned you!"

2 CHRONICLES 24:20 NLT

While it's impossible to give a clear-cut diagnosis for everyone who feels far from God or is suffering through adversity, Zechariah offers a helpful starting point. Consider if you have abandoned God or disobeyed His commands. Jesus Himself assured His disciples that illness is not always punishment from God for sin, but that doesn't rule it out as a consequence of disobedience. God will permit everyone who chooses their own way to pursue their own course, taking what comes of it.

God will permit you to strike off in your own direction, much like the Prodigal Son, but don't blame Him when you end up eating pig slop. Following God's path is hardly smooth sailing. Jesus promised adversity and even persecution at times. However, obedient sons and daughters of God will have the benefit of God's presence comforting them in their trials and adversity.

Although the stakes in your daily choices are high, God's mercy reaches even higher, beyond what you can imagine.

Lord, thank You for Your commandments and for Your promises of mercy
when I turn to You. Please help me to remain on Your path always.

TRAINING IN GODLY LIVING

Uzziah was sixteen years old when he became king and reigned for fifty-two years in Jerusalem. . . . He was a loyal seeker of God. He was well trained by his pastor and teacher Zechariah to live in reverent obedience before God, and for as long as Zechariah lived, Uzziah lived a godly life.
2 Chronicles 26:3–5 msg

God asks you to endure for the sake of His name and *with His help*. He sends people to help when you think you walk alone. Some resist or even refuse the help, but God knows two are better than one.

Uzziah became Judah's king at the age of sixteen. Maybe you can't imagine a teen becoming a nation's ruler, but this young man remained king for more than half a century. He became a good king because he didn't endure alone. Zechariah, a preacher by trade, came to the rescue. He became the king's mentor. This friendship resulted in a king who was noted for his godly life. Uzziah had help.

If you're following God but trying to do it alone, you would do well to begin following Uzziah's example. Find someone who has followed God longer than you have, and learn, grow, and serve together. Get some training in godly living and you'll find it's much easier to endure the next hard day.

Father, You want me to grow in You. When You walk with me, I have companionship. Godly friendships give me added encouragement to keep walking with You.

BREAK THE CYCLE

"Do not be like your ancestors and relatives who abandoned
the Lord, the God of their ancestors. . . . Do not be stubborn,
as they were, but submit yourselves to the Lord. Come to his
Temple, which he has set apart as holy forever. Worship the
Lord your God so that his fierce anger will turn away from you."
2 CHRONICLES 30:7–8 NLT

Thousands of people turned their backs on God. One good king stood between the Promised Land and exile. King Hezekiah ordered the temple repaired and reopened. The people needed a place to worship—and a time to celebrate the long-neglected Passover. The people needed to remember the God who rescues.

Some people failed to remember God. Many others had mounted a collective rebellion against Him. Hezekiah was doing everything he could to foster an environment where God was welcome. God blessed Hezekiah for his faithfulness.

Maybe you didn't have the greatest example of godly living as a child. Maybe you didn't have a clear picture of how to be that example. You can plead with others to engage in a new and faithful endurance like King Hezekiah: "Do not be like your ancestors and relatives who abandoned the Lord. . . . Do not be stubborn, as they were, but submit yourselves to the Lord. . . . Worship the Lord your God." Yeah, do that.

Lord, if someone doesn't come from a family that honored You,
he can still set an example for his children. Let me be that example.

BEHAVIOR MODIFICATION?

[The chief priest said], "Since the people began to bring the
offerings into the house of the LORD, we have had enough to
eat and have plenty left, for the LORD has blessed His people;
and what is left is this great abundance."

2 CHRONICLES 31:10 NKJV

The example of King Hezekiah led the people to return to worshipping God and following His command to give. The priests couldn't do their job because they needed resources. The people began giving. God knew they couldn't endure forever, but He blessed the people and they gave more than enough.

Had revival come to Judah? It looked more like *behavior modification*. The hearts of the people were connected to popular opinion, but their national pride changed their actions only as long as they kept up their personal pep rallies.

Perseverance is more than self-discipline and personal resolve. This won't be enough to endure difficulty, pressure, and temptation. You do what you believe God wants you to do, yet trouble still comes, life remains difficult, and you wonder why obedience is so important.

Faith endurance is always about working alongside the One who does the most work. . .much more than you can. Understand that a relationship with Him is worth infinitely more than trying to do good on your own.

God, take my desire to do the right thing and add Your willingness
to help. Allow me to really follow instead of existing in a
world of good intentions but failed outcomes.

INSTRUCTIONS OVERLOOKED

Go, inquire of the Lord for me and for those who are left in
Israel and in Judah about the words of the book that is found.
For great is the Lord's wrath that is poured out on us because
our fathers have not kept the word of the Lord.

2 CHRONICLES 34:21 AMPC

It wasn't the first time a king asked for repairs to God's temple. Nor was it the first time God saw evil in the hearts of His people. Another good king stepped up and proclaimed that God's house was open once more. Josiah was eight years old when he became king. He was eager to make God famous among the people.

King Josiah had heard God stories, but hadn't read them for himself. Very few had. When God's words were found in the abandoned temple, the king had them read. Josiah was brokenhearted. He could hear how far the people had strayed from what God had actually commanded. Josiah knew why God was angry.

God has given instructions for right living. How many of those instructions are overlooked, rejected, or left unread and unknown? God wants you to endure. He will help, and He wants you to be fully aware of what you're enduring. How meaningful is the act of enduring if you don't know what you've endured?

Father, help me know what I'm enduring so I can
be grateful for Your help. When I know what
You want, help me do what You've asked.

HIS STEADFAST, ENDURING LOVE

"For he is good, for his steadfast love
endures forever toward Israel."
EZRA 3:11 ESV

It was a melody lost to time. The song was short but powerful. *God is good and His love for Israel endures forever.*

Years had passed, and people who endured captivity for most of their lives had returned to the land of promise—and a song was born.

The temple once more had been neglected and needed repair. This was a pattern for people who had been distracted by anything that was not God.

There are times when God allows you to be held captive as a result of choices that lead you away from following His footsteps. The endurance of that which holds you captive often means you're reintroduced to or recall the God who has endured your waywardness.

Sometimes, when you get your own way, you're faced with the truth that God's way was right from the beginning. Think about the sinful choices you've made. Do they lead you closer or further away from God? When you miss the companionship of your Maker, it's best to recall His faithfulness and say, "He is good. . .His steadfast love endures forever."

Lord, You are good, and Your love is more enduring than my
choice to sin. I fail, and my sin can draw me away from Your side.
Instead of pursuing even more sin, let me endure Your love.
It helps my mouth form the words "I'm sorry."

THE PURPOSE MESH

*So these people started beating down the morale of the people of
Judah, harassing them as they built. They even hired propagandists
to sap their resolve. They kept this up for about fifteen years.*
EZRA 4:4–5 MSG

The city of Jerusalem looked nothing like its former glory. The walls
were in shambles and the temple had been overlooked for decades.
There was a lot to do, and those who stepped up to build needed help.

That's when imposters stepped in and offered assistance. They may
have picked up debris or handed workers a tool when needed, but their
tongues were agents of emotional warfare. They used their words in a
way that attempted to make the workers believe they were foolish for
rebuilding in a place that should be defined by its ruins and not potential
future. Why? Because they were against the only option that included
God's plan for the city.

The rebuilding wasn't just a weekend warrior project. The language
of defeat was delivered to workers for fifteen years.

God has a plan for your life. He has a purpose that meshes well with
your skills and interests. When you do what He asks, you may find people
gathering who try to talk you out of enduring the things that result in His
work being done through your life.

*God, I can endure when You walk with me, encourage me,
and remind me that it's You I follow and not the opinions of others.*

STUDY. OBEY. TEACH.

*The gracious hand of his God was on [Ezra]. This was because
Ezra had determined to study and obey the Law of the LORD and
to teach those decrees and regulations to the people of Israel.*
EZRA 7:9–10 NLT

Ezra was a priest—and a disciple who made disciples. He asked for God's help in learning what He had asked His people to do. Ezra taught others. He wasn't trying to become an expert in Bible trivia. He learned. He shared. God blessed him.

Ezra didn't have a running total on how much time he spent in prayer or Bible study. His desire was knowing God more. Tracking time was less important than learning. Learning was less about pride than a relationship with God.

Wouldn't it be great to have it said of you, "The gracious hand of God was upon _____. This is because _____ had determined to study and obey the law of the Lord and to teach those decrees and regulations"?

Most people fail to understand that walking with Jesus includes being a student. Many never accept that role so they never become teachers. They accept a lack of knowledge while society keeps looking for real answers that can be known—because God teaches.

*Father, help me study and then obey what I learn. Help me share
what I know with those willing to listen. Give me a heart for
You and an opportunity to share You every chance I get.*

OVERWHELMING SADNESS

When I heard this thing, I tore my garment and
my robe, and plucked out some of the hair of
my head and beard, and sat down astonished.
EZRA 9:3 NKJV

Ezra was a dedicated student of God's Word. He'd learned what God wanted, loved, and said to avoid. When Ezra saw that the people were violating God's revolutionary rules, he mirrored God's broken heart. He tore his clothes to show his profound grief. He pulled out some of his hair, showing his frustration. He sat down astonished because this news had left him undone.

How do you react to sin? Does it leave you visibly shaken? Are you left speechless?

Ezra heard the truth, saw the sin, and made it known that sadness overwhelmed him. He caught a glimpse of what it must have been like for God to endure the outright defiance of people He had rescued over and over again.

Maybe you could start by grieving over your own sin first. What would it be like to get to the place where you were genuinely undone by the reality of your sin? Have you endured sin for so long that grief seems ridiculous? Ezra didn't think so. God's not immune from a broken heart either.

Lord, my sin doesn't amuse You. You don't overlook it, and You don't
forgive my sin until I admit that You're right and I am wrong.
May I be undone by the sin that separates people from You.

GRIEF

When I heard these things, I sat down and wept.
For some days I mourned and fasted and
prayed before the God of heaven.
NEHEMIAH 1:4 NIV

The people of Israel and Judah would soon be returning home after a long exile. But what would they come home to? Ezra saw the disrepair of Jerusalem, but another man also learned of Jerusalem's condition. Nehemiah worked for King Artaxerxes, who oversaw the exiled.

The verse above describes Nehemiah's response. He couldn't keep the grief from etching his features when he visited the king. Artaxerxes saw the grief and asked Nehemiah what he wanted.

This response answered a prayer. Nehemiah told the king everything he knew and about his interest in seeing the restoration of Jerusalem's city walls. He asked for help—and the king gave him everything he needed.

Sometimes God will ask you to endure a time of sadness. This can lead to healing, but it can also lead to a resolve to do something about the thing that caused the grief.

It is natural to feel loss over a friend or family member, a job, or a health issue. Grief is a companion in each instance. It means something to you because it seems unfair, but when you work through the pain, you may find yourself more compassionate toward those who face similar grief.

God, help me accept grief as a way for You
to teach me, soften my heart, and lead me
to a place where I can help others.

THE MOST VULNERABLE

*I said to them, We, according to our ability, have bought back our
Jewish brethren who were sold to the nations; but will you even sell
your brethren, that they may be sold to us? Then they were silent.*
NEHEMIAH 5:8 AMPC

Nehemiah spoke with authority. Some people had been sold into slavery
when they couldn't pay their bills. Nehemiah was part of a group
that had actively been buying Hebrew slaves from other countries and
setting them free. Some local Hebrews were selling other Jews, expecting
Nehemiah to pay the price to redeem them. They used the generosity of
one group to get a slave payment for those who couldn't pay their bills.

Nehemiah did some public shaming to get them to stop. Zechariah
7:9 says, "Thus has the Lord of hosts spoken: Execute true judgment
and show mercy and kindness and tender compassion, every man to his
brother" (AMPC).

Human trafficking doesn't fit God's view of how mankind should
treat mankind.

You might be called to endure an injustice and offer forgiveness, but
you might be asked to step up, stand up, and speak up against the injustice
someone else faces. The most vulnerable have the least opportunity to
help themselves. When they ask God for help, He might send you.

*Father, give me a heart that identifies with those
who hurt, a voice used to comfort others, and a
will to help when it's just the right thing to do.*

JOY AND FRESH STRENGTH

"This day is holy to our Lord. And do not be grieved,
for the joy of the LORD is your strength."
NEHEMIAH 8:10 ESV

The wall was finally rebuilt in Jerusalem. It felt like a city once more—no longer a trash heap. The people had come face-to-face with bad behavior and turned a corner in God's direction. Then Ezra read God's law. The people wept.

It was a time to celebrate God's goodness and not the sinful behaviors of mankind. The day wasn't dedicated to grief, but to joyful remembering. It was in recalling the faithfulness of God that the people discovered their strength came from God alone.

You may have lived through more than most. Some things may seem too horrible to even talk about. You may even be dealing with how to get past your past. There will be times when God asks you to stop grieving for a time because when you find reason to praise God, you'll find strength that's somehow infused with joy. You get to choose where you focus your attention.

Praise is a time set apart (holy) to and for God. Grief may lead you to a place of praise, but praise will lead to joy, and that's the source of fresh strength.

Lord, help me take my eyes off myself and my
past long enough to focus on You and remember
that You guard my future. In that place I am safe.

SAY YES AND MEAN IT

They solemnly promised to carefully follow all the commands,
regulations, and decrees of the LORD our Lord.
NEHEMIAH 10:29 NLT

It was a promise that would be broken. The people of God believed they could follow the commands, regulations, and decrees of God. They were willing to recognize Him as Lord. But long after Jerusalem's wall was rebuilt and the people settled into daily living, the promise became less remembered. The praise faded. Worship came to a halt. God's law became suggestions instead of commands.

You, or someone you know, may have made a promise to God in the midst of desperation. Living for God seemed the best choice. If God could take you from a no-win situation to a place that made sense, then following Him seemed a great choice. But once the desperation diminished, the promise faded into compromise.

A solemn promise only means something when God makes it. Humans routinely take oaths and break them. Maybe that's why God said to forget oaths and simply say yes and mean it—or say no with similar conviction. God endures your inability to fulfill your promises. He just wants you to keep turning in His direction every time you fail to live up to your promise to follow His commands.

God, I don't know anyone who hasn't turned his back on
a promise. I want to live up to my promises, but I fail. May I
make my choice to follow You with a daily "yes"—and mean it.

CELEBRATE

That day they offered great sacrifices, an exuberant celebration
because God had filled them with great joy. The women
and children raised their happy voices with all the rest.
Jerusalem's jubilation was heard far and wide.
NEHEMIAH 12:43 MSG

Graduation days are meant to be celebrated. Weddings are happy occasions to join in a joyful union. But these celebration-worthy events can disrupt plans you had already made. You could have finished a home-improvement project, tackled some extra work, or enjoyed time on a lake. You set aside the *daily* to experience the *rare and remembered*.

This was what it was like when the Jerusalem wall was dedicated. People came from all over the region. Some relocated to live in the city. The streets were filled with people instead of debris. Impromptu choirs were heard throughout the city and the people were thinking about the miracle that had come to town.

This public works project was taken care of by people who didn't seem qualified or fully equipped to manage a project many opposed. But on this day, they celebrated something that could only happen when God steps into the circumstances of man and makes the impossible *actual*.

He does the same for you. And because God answers prayers, raise your voice in praise and make people aware of His good work. Celebrate!

Father, You are good—better than my best moments.
You're willing to guide me when I've lost my way.
Make my praise a celebration.

THE BANNER READ LOVED

So the king and Haman sat down to drink,
but the city of Shushan was perplexed.
ESTHER 3:15 NKJV

F lag Day is a visible representation of the American spirit. It invites people to remember the freedoms all Americans enjoy.

In a time when the Israelites were scattered, it was hard to celebrate their nation's heritage. Most people couldn't understand a reason to celebrate a country that had been overtaken.

Jealousy led a high-ranking official in King Ahasuerus's kingdom to draft a rule subjecting the people of Israel to genocide. Haman considered the Jew Mordecai an enemy, so he persuaded the king to destroy *all* Jews. The king agreed. He didn't realize his own queen was a Jew. Haman was happy to have the decision on the books. While Haman celebrated, anxiety spread like a disease among the Jews.

There's always bad news to endure. It may seem small and only touch you. It might seem large and touch most people you know.

Freedom seems to be slipping from your grasp, and the very thing you don't want to experience is happening. Good news! You're not defenseless. You're not forsaken or forgotten, and you never need to forfeit your trust in God.

His banner over you reads LOVED. Endure a little longer—help is on the way.

Lord, I don't understand why some people celebrate
the misery of others. But You don't do that—and You
never have. Help me endure while I wait for You.

IMPOSSIBLE. DIFFICULT. DONE.

*Then the king asked, "What is it, Queen Esther? What is your request?
Even up to half the kingdom, it will be given you."*
Esther 5:3 niv

———◆———

Queen Esther was faced with a full-blown anxiety attack. Her cousin Mordecai had suggested she visit King Ahasuerus to intervene for the Jewish people. This wasn't done. The king decided when he would see the queen. If she went to see him and he was angry, she could be killed. If she didn't try, then the Jewish people were on the fast track to annihilation.

It's hard to endure the unknown. Dealt with incorrectly, it can lead to debilitating fear.

Face the unknown and keep walking. Rely on your faith in God, trust in His power to rescue, and believe that with Him, you can face any dark valley fearlessly.

Missionary Hudson Taylor once said, "There are three stages to every great work of God; first it is impossible, then it is difficult, then it is done." God's work in you is just as great. It always begins as something that seems impossible. And when you cooperate with Him, it gets done.

Because Queen Esther endured the unknown, God used her willingness to save His people from death. God can lead your life circumstances too.

*God, the unknown can be frightening. Give me an enduring faith
that trusts Your life map for me. Help me move from impossible
and difficult to the place where You say, "It is finished."*

A QUEEN'S VOICE

For how can I endure to see the evil that shall come upon my people?
Or how can I endure to see the destruction of my kindred?
ESTHER 8:6 AMPC

Queen Esther's unscheduled visit to the king made him aware of the injustice of Haman. It revealed a plot to wipe out an entire people group. It opened a dialogue that seemed to bring the royal couple closer. There was a second unscheduled visit, and the king wanted to hear what Esther had to say.

The law couldn't be altered, but the king wrote a new law allowing the Jews to defend themselves when the unfair law took effect.

Because Queen Esther couldn't endure the loss of her people, she endured the unknown by being bold enough to seek justice from the king. She couldn't endure evil coming to her people without a challenge. God gave her the courage to bridge the gap between lawlessness and His answer.

Have you ever determined that it was impossible to endure evil and destruction among people you know—including your own family? Have you sought justice for the oppressed? Have you used prayer to ask God to help the defenseless? Have you ever been righteously angry on behalf of those who are hurt without cause?

Father, You answer prayers that have actually been prayed. Help
me stand up for others who hurt. Help me see others as more than
a cause. They are made in Your image—and they need Your help.

FAITH IN A GOOD GOD

There was a man in the land of Uz whose name was Job,
and that man was blameless and upright, one who
feared God and turned away from evil.
JOB 1:1 ESV

Job persevered when he was told to give up. He hung on when he was told off. He trusted God when told he'd been abandoned. The advice he received could have led to rebellion. This same man was described as blameless, upright, God-fearing, and one who resisted evil.

Job faced personal endurance because he *was* faithful to God. Satan didn't believe anyone could be as faithful as God described Job, so he was allowed to test Job, and this book of endurance follows Job's story.

Sometimes the need to endure is based on choices you've made. Sometimes endurance is a test because of the choices of others. Some endurance challenges have their root elsewhere. You don't have to spend as much time discovering why you must endure. This thinking focuses on the past and diminishes the available energy to walk toward your future.

A marathon isn't filled with people who cannot endure. A positive workforce isn't populated by people who give up easily. For Christians, it's faith in a good God that welcomes a positive outcome at the end of an endurance.

Lord, maybe it's less important for me to discover why I endure
and remember that this journey means I can walk closer to
the One who endures with me. Let's persevere together.

UNIQUE SUFFERING

"If my misery could be weighed, if you could pile
the whole bitter load on the scales, it would
be heavier than all the sand of the sea!"
JOB 6:1 MSG

Have you ever had one of those *no-one-understands* kind of days? Weeks? Months? People can say insensitive things when they self-diagnose your misery.

If you think it's possible to know exactly what someone is going through, then one read through the book of Job should provide enough evidence that you never know the full story. Because you don't know, you can't understand. There's just too much that is unique to the person suffering.

Maybe you know Job's story. You have the benefit of knowing what he didn't and seeing what his well-meaning friends never could. But you might feel as if you've both been there and done that when you read, "If my misery could be weighed, if you could pile the whole bitter load on the scales, it would be heavier than all the sand of the sea!"

Call it a heavy heart, an overwhelmed spirit, or an oppressive load, but while everyone experiences this phenomenon, no one's equipped to face it the same way. All men feel and deal with pain differently. Walk a mile in someone's shoes instead of criticizing the way they limp.

God, why is it so easy for me to be a know-it-all?
Why is it easier to criticize than encourage?
When I see a friend hurting, help me hurt with them.

DON'T KICK. DON'T PUSH.

"People who are at ease mock those in trouble.
They give a push to people who are stumbling."
JOB 12:5 NLT

It's easy to analyze why other people struggle. You have answers to questions they never asked. You offer unsolicited opinions. You mean well, but your words can inflict additional wounds.

Toss phrases around like, "If you just made better choices," or "If you ask me," or even "I thought this would happen." When you do, don't be surprised when conversation is cut short or a strain in your friendship develops.

Job's trial was unique. His friends assumed he'd offended God and a massive struggle was his divine paycheck. Job defended his own innocence, but while he was down, his friends kicked a little harder and pushed when he stumbled.

The earliest days of their visit were different. They just sat with Job and kept quiet. There's benefit to simply being a friend who listens and refuses to attempt to fix things unless help is requested.

Friends should never be left to endure alone, but they also don't need your personally drafted five-step recovery plan. Pray for those who must endure. Listen to them as they express their pain. Allow God to speak to them in *your* silence.

Father, because I don't want to see friends hurt, it's possible
I will say things I think will help but won't. Give me the
wisdom to let You speak while I wait with my friend.

THE PROBLEM WITH TONGUE CLUCKERS

"I also could speak as you do, if your soul were in my soul's place. I could heap up words against you, and shake my head at you; but I would strengthen you with my mouth, and the comfort of my lips would relieve your grief."

JOB 16:4–5 NKJV

Tomorrow's the first day of summer. Thoughts turn to beaches, mountains, road trips, and pools. Plants grow best this time of year. This is a time to be refreshed. Job may have longed for the benefits of summer, but he felt locked in a forever winter with three unwelcome guests.

Job's friends wouldn't give him the benefit of their many doubts. They were certain Job's sin was the building blocks of his personal calamity. They wouldn't let him vent without reprimand or ask questions without replies that amounted to a collective "Knock it off."

When Job was given a moment to speak, he tried to place his shoes on different feet. If his friends were struggling—if they were in his place—he would encourage, comfort, and help them find relief. He wouldn't shake his head, cluck his tongue, and tell them they were wrong for feeling pain.

Take Job's ideas. Try them out. Encourage, comfort, and relieve a friend's pain. They're experiencing winter—bring summer with you.

God, I've experienced winter in my spirit, and it's a lonely place to exist. Help me remember this when I see pain in the path of a friend.

BIG ENOUGH TO LISTEN

*"My feet have closely followed his steps; I have kept to his way without
turning aside. I have not departed from the commands of his lips;
I have treasured the words of his mouth more than my daily bread."*

JOB 23:11–12 NIV

You can almost hear the astonishment of Job's friends when he declared his innocence. They might have been thinking that his divine correction was just about to be upgraded. It was clear they didn't believe Job continued to follow God—maybe he hadn't for a long time.

Job told the truth—*they called him a liar*. Job asked God why—*they were offended that he wouldn't just take correction quietly*. Job told them they would say rude things—*they said rude things*.

Pain can cause you to say what you don't mean, but it can also bring clear truth from a broken heart heard by a God who can lead you beyond the pain. He's big enough to listen to your "why" questions. You probably won't have an immediate understanding—you may *never* know—but sometimes you need to talk through the things you struggle with most and let God deliver comfort while you continue to endure.

Don't give up. Don't entertain the idea of rejecting God. Don't be afraid to be honest with Him. Perhaps the hardest part of endurance is bearing with the misunderstandings of the well meaning.

*Lord, people can say some cruel things. When people don't know
what they're talking about, help me to remember that You do.*

RESTORATION VS. CONDEMNATION

Behold, even the moon has no brightness [compared to God's glory] and the stars are not pure in His sight—How much less man, who is a maggot! And a son of man, who is a worm!

JOB 25:5–6 AMPC

There are three typical reasons people face hardship. The first is an event in which everyone around you endures *generally*. This could be something like a flood or other natural disaster. The second is enduring because of poor personal choices. You endure the consequences of the choices you make or are affected by the negative choices of others. The third is enduring the ridicule of people who stand opposed to your faith.

Job fit a rare fourth way—he endured circumstances that had nothing to do with a personal sin or sin someone committed against him. It was a test that Job's friends didn't understand—and *neither did Job*. One friend seemed to suggest that Job was little more than a maggot or worm.

It's hard to know how to handle people who judge your circumstances and find it reason enough to condemn. Aren't you glad God knows your heart and understands your circumstances? God's desire is restoration instead of condemnation (see Romans 8:1).

Ask God to help you see those who suffer through His eyes of compassion. Allow love to replace judgment.

Father, help me admit when I don't understand what someone is going through. May I never be accused of standing between their pain and Your hope.

A LITTLE LONGER

"I will get my knowledge from afar and ascribe
righteousness to my Maker. For truly my words are
not false; one who is perfect in knowledge is with you."
JOB 36:3–4 ESV

Two days from now, the book of Psalms will provide the inspiration for these daily readings. Today's verse reads a little like a psalm. But these verses weren't written by King David. They delivered no compassion—and only limited understanding.

The words of Job's companion sounded true, but they didn't represent God. He thought he knew it all, but he hadn't welcomed God to his speech making. God would soon be speaking, and His words would be remarkably different.

Not everyone who says they speak for God really do. Well-meaning people don't always know God's plan for your life or why bad things happen. What you can know is that humans aren't perfect, *but God is*. His Word leaves guesswork behind. Listen to the advice of others, but only act on wisdom you learn from God.

God said in Isaiah 46:10 (ESV), "My counsel shall stand, and I will accomplish all my purpose." Job would need God's counsel—it would change his future. The best counsel will always be found in the pages that continue past Genesis 1:1. Endure a little longer—God is in control.

God, if I want perfect wisdom, then the final word will
need to come from You. Your wisdom is my best guide.
Your hope leads me through endurance.

TOO MANY WORDS

[God said] "I've had it with you and your two friends.
I'm fed up! You haven't been honest either with me
or about me—not the way my friend Job has."
JOB 42:7 MSG

Job was at the end of his endurance test. He had questioned God, and Job quickly saw that no matter how hard things were, his difficulties were insignificant when he was face-to-face with the God who made everything, knows everything, and controls everything.

Once God spoke of all that He controls and how He provides, Job realized he'd gone too far. In Job 40:3–5 (MSG), Job answered: "I'm speechless, in awe—words fail me. I should never have opened my mouth! I've talked too much, way too much. I'm ready to shut up and listen."

This may have been the best response in the book of Job. He had spoken, and when God answered, there was no need for clarification. And as much as Job's friends were certain they spoke the truth, God called them out for dishonesty.

Awe is the perfect way to respond to God, even when you struggle to endure another day. He knows. He cares. He comforts. When seeking answers seems like a game of hide-and-seek, remember that God can be known and that He's always seeking you.

Lord, may I seek Your words long enough that my
questions cease and my praise begins. May my
words fail me when Your words comfort me.

IT'S NOT A PROBLEM

I lay down and slept, yet I woke up in safety,
for the LORD was watching over me.
PSALM 3:5 NLT

Insomnia is nothing new. Waking up when everyone else sleeps is an age-old problem with an age-old source: *anxiety.*

King David knew that if God was taking care of things, then he didn't need to survive another night of worry. For Christians, if the worst thing about going to sleep is that you may never wake up, then the good news is you get to realize your heavenly citizenship. You might nurture worry in a way that causes protests every time you put it down. Worry wants you to hold it, cherish it, and give it every moment of your attention. Maybe it's worry's persistence that makes you think you can't live without it.

Worry isn't a baby, but it acts like one. Yet a king with significant responsibilities could say that God was watching over him so he could sleep and then wake up in safety.

Release the things that concern you, because you serve a God who can take your worry and watch over your life. If you're tired, weary, and yet very restless, it could be that you've taken responsibility for worry God said is not your problem. Give it to Him.

Father, take my worry. I don't need it, and You won't keep it entertained. You take care of me. What's left to worry about?

THE ENDURANCE CHOICES

I will love You, O LORD, my strength. The LORD is my rock and my fortress
and my deliverer; my God, my strength, in whom I will trust; my shield
and the horn of my salvation, my stronghold. I will call upon the LORD,
who is worthy to be praised; so shall I be saved from my enemies.

PSALM 18:1–3 NKJV

Is it easier to endure alone or with help? Is it easier to endure if you feel exposed or protected? Is it easier to endure if you feel abandoned or rescued? When you have to stand, do you want to step into quicksand or onto solid rock?

You could endure alone and exposed while feeling abandoned. But if you recognize the strength of God, you have access to help, protection, and rescue. The great men of faith trusted God when they faced difficulty. You should too.

Endurance isn't a test you must take alone. God is available and is described as strength, salvation, and a stronghold. Call on Him, give Him praise, and find rescue when you need it most. Doing life alone may sound rugged, individualistic, and the pinnacle of self-reliance. But unexpected and undesirable things happen when you struggle alone. You've simply decided to try to do what you can't do—*without* help.

God, I can think You are more impressed with me when
I endure alone, but instead You patiently wait to be
invited to my crisis. Welcome to my crisis. Help!

ABSOLUTE WISDOM

*The law of the Lord is perfect, refreshing the soul. The statutes
of the Lord are trustworthy, making wise the simple.*
PSALM 19:7 NIV

———◆———

You don't have to endure wrong thinking. You don't need to think you'll always be foolish. You don't even have to attend any school building to wise up. God's Word is absolute wisdom.

God's laws are perfect and trustworthy. His plans? *Worth following.* His love? *Incomparable.*

There are many things that seem like burdens you must endure. You carry a load just like every other human being. It can be hard, lonely, and relentless. God can bless you in the midst of struggle while He asks you to pass along your anxiety and worry because of things you must endure. But He also never withholds wisdom. He wants you to ask Him for wisdom, and He promises that His Word—the Bible—contains all the wisdom you'll need.

Follow His commands, and even when they don't make sense to you, they make a crooked life path straight. Become familiar with His statutes, and know that what you learn helps you understand God better. Verse 11 (NIV) talks about God's commands when it says, "By them your servant is warned; in keeping them there is great reward."

═══════════════════════════

*Lord, I don't have to endure personal foolishness. I can know
what You want because You've given me a blueprint to
Your way. Help me read. Help me discover wisdom.*

NEVER ENDURE SIN

Have mercy and be gracious unto me, O Lord, for I am in trouble; with grief my eye is weakened, also my inner self and my body. For my life is spent with sorrow and my years with sighing; my strength has failed because of my iniquity, and even my bones have wasted away.

PSALM 31:9–10 AMPC

———————✦———————

There is a heavy price for sin. You have likely lived through its consequences. Poor choices lead to personal loss, destroyed families, and loss of respect. If you could take back a moment of weakness, you would—*but you can't.*

God even says that sin always leads to death. That could be physical, but it could also be a spiritual separation from Him until you turn away from sin.

When you sin, when you know you're in trouble, when it seems like you've handed over the last bit of life left, and when the most profound act you can think of is to sigh, then do what King David did. Admit your guilt and ask for mercy. When you've endured all you can without God's blessing, the wisest thing you can do is walk back to Him—*a reformed prodigal.*

God doesn't bring up your past—*He forgives.* He doesn't condemn—*He loves.* He doesn't treat you like a criminal—*you're an adopted son.*

Father, I'm not sure why, but sin always makes me want to hide from You. I can get defiant, angry, and defensive. Help me admit what I've done and come back to You.

MOMENTS OF SIN

For I am ready to fall, and my pain is ever before me. I confess my iniquity; I am sorry for my sin. But my foes are vigorous, they are mighty, and many are those who hate me wrongfully. Those who render me evil for good accuse me because I follow after good.
PSALM 38:17–20 ESV

King David was either on the verge of a miracle or collapse. He returned to God and admitted his wrong. You learned yesterday that God is merciful and gracious, but the consequences of your sin can mean you may need to endure the loss of trust among those you broke trust with. You may discover the hurt you caused others is something they aren't ready to let go of. You may even discover that anger leads others to keep their distance from you.

You may endure more than you think is fair. Why? Sin breaks what God gave to you unbroken—and you're never the only person who must endure its aftermath. Maybe that's one of the reasons God warns so strongly against it. God gave you commands to keep relationships in good shape. Choosing sin always damages relationships. Some relationships don't return easily. Don't allow this time of endurance to bring you to the point of giving up.

God, when I sin, I can run to You. Give me the strength to endure the hurt I've caused others. Help me make things right and rebuild trust.

DIGNITY FOR THE DOWNCAST

Dignify those who are down on their luck;
you'll feel good—that's what GOD does.
PSALM 41:1 MSG

Being at the bottom looking up is no fun, but it can be the start of a climb. Delving down among the downcast seems hard, but it's an opportunity for a rescue mission.

Resolve to take what you know about endurance and help someone else endure. Don't step on others when they're down—help them up whenever you can. You might be thinking this only applies to places like soup kitchens and homeless shelters. While those can be on your list, you might have a friend, neighbor, or family member who could use a friend as they move through their own unique difficulty.

Helping others is all about showing the same love God's shown you. It's not judgmental, but it doesn't mean you deny sin and its impact. The greatest help you can offer is by inviting God to come with you—letting the words from His book come from your mouth. Let His grace, love, and mercy be evident in how you respond to the struggler. As odd as it may sound, you can reduce the intensity of your own struggle by helping someone else through theirs.

Lord, may my actions be a mirror that introduces Your love to the downcast. My story includes endurance, and everyone I can help has a similar story. Everyone struggles. With Your help, let me help.

GIVE GOD YOUR WORRIES

Cast your cares on the LORD and he will sustain you;
he will never let the righteous be shaken.
PSALM 55:22 NIV

Someone once defined life as "one crisis after another." Whether you agree with that probably depends on your own definition of the word *crisis*. But there's no doubt that we all go through difficult times in this life. Jesus stated it well when He said, "In this world you will have trouble" (John 16:33 NIV). But we believers should feel grateful that Jesus followed His warning that we'll have trouble in this life with this comforting promise: "But take heart! I have overcome the world."

One of the Bible's most comforting themes is that God cares about us and for us. He knows about our struggles and He cares. Better yet, He strengthens us and encourages us—if only we'll give Him all our cares and worries.

What worries you most in this life? Issues with your family? Your financial situation? Your health or the health of someone you love? Give it to God. Nothing is too small that He doesn't care about it. . .or too big for Him to handle.

Father in heaven, I have so many worries and concerns weighing on me
right now. Please humble me, and help me to leave these things to You.
Thank You for caring for me—and for the things You've given me to do.

OUR PLACE OF REFUGE

Have mercy on me, my God, have mercy on me,
for in you I take refuge. I will take refuge in the
shadow of your wings until the disaster has passed.
PSALM 57:1 NIV

David wrote Psalm 57 during a time of extreme stress. He knew that King Saul, whose days as Israel's first monarch were numbered, was in hot pursuit, intending to kill him because God was with him and had anointed him to replace Saul.

Very few of us will ever find ourselves in a situation where someone literally wants to murder us. But that doesn't mean we're immune to situations that bring us extreme stress or anxiety. It's during those times when we need to run to the refuge our God promises to be for us. He is our source of comfort, peace, encouragement, safety, and help in our times of extreme need.

Like David, we'll go through times when our lives feel like one big disaster. But no matter how severe the situation may seem, we can always run to God, who will give us a place of refuge—just like the refuge a mother hen gives her chicks by gathering them under her wings.

My loving Father in heaven, thank You for being Jehovah Sabaoth, my protector God. I thank You that I can always run to You when things get rough, knowing that I can count on You to get me through any disaster.

WHEN YOU FEEL LIKE YOU'RE SINKING

Save me, O God, for the waters have come up to my neck.
I sink in the miry depths, where there is no foothold.
I have come into the deep waters; the floods engulf me.
PSALM 69:1–2 NIV

Can you remember a time when it seemed like life was treating you unfairly, when it seemed as though someone was mistreating you or slandering you without cause? In Psalm 69, David's words convey those very feelings.

David felt as though he was sinking in deep waters, but he started his prayer with four vitally important words for any man going through what feels like an impossible situation: "Save me, O God!"

There must have been some place within David that wondered if he was going to drown—figuratively anyway. But in the very midst of his distress, he remembered that his God was his only hope for deliverance.

When you're in a place of human impossibility, a place where you feel like life is dragging you down for good, you're in a place where God can do amazing things for you. Just remember those four important words: "Save me, O God!"

Lord of all, I'm no stranger to the feelings today's verse conveys.
I sometimes feel like the cares of this world will swallow me up.
And they would too, if not for Your promise to deliver me
and preserve me through the most stressful of times.

YOUR DEEPEST DESIRE

Whom have I in heaven but you? And earth has nothing
I desire besides you. My flesh and my heart may fail, but
God is the strength of my heart and my portion forever.
PSALM 73:25–26 NIV

Augustine of Hippo, the fourth/fifth-century church leader, once prayed, "Lord, bring me a sweetness surpassing all the seductive delights that I once pursued. Enable me to love You with all my strength that I may clasp Your hand with all my heart."

That's a great request for any of us to make of God, isn't it? It's Augustine's confession that he wanted—*needed*—to love God the way the psalmist did.

If we're honest with ourselves, we may have to confess that we don't always love and desire God the way we should. We may read Psalm 73 and think, *Why can't I love God and feel that incredible sense of devotion to Him?*

The good news is that we can. Just as a needy man once told Jesus, "I do believe; help me overcome my unbelief!" (Mark 9:24 NIV), we can come to God our Father and earnestly pray, "I love You and desire You, Lord. Help me to love and desire You more."

That's the kind of prayer God loves to hear. . .and answer!

God of love, so many things in this life compete for my attention
and my affections. Please help me to remember that You
should be the first object of my affection and devotion.

LOVING JUSTICE

"How long will you defend the unjust and show partiality to the
wicked? Defend the weak and the fatherless; uphold the cause
of the poor and the oppressed. Rescue the weak and the needy;
deliver them from the hand of the wicked."

PSALM 82:2–4 NIV

Psalm 82 is different from most of the other 149 psalms in that the psalmist, Asaph, has written in the form of a prophecy—specifically one against powerful, influential leaders who failed to act justly toward the most vulnerable in Israel at the time. Instead of defending the weak and the fatherless, the poor and the oppressed, they showed favoritism to those in power.

If we're not careful, we can find ourselves doing the very same thing. But God calls each of us to avoid being "respecters of persons" and understand that we are to love and care for all people, including those Jesus called "the least of these."

God loves the poor, disadvantaged, and the vulnerable—and He wants to love them *through us*. What can you do today to show God's love to someone who desperately needs to see it in action?

God of justice, so many people in today's world are forgotten,
exploited, and mistreated that it drains my emotions just
thinking about them. I know You want me to make a difference,
if only in my own sphere of influence. Remind me to pray and to
speak up or take action when I see wrong being done to others.

CONFIDENCE

Listen closely to my prayer, O LORD; hear my urgent cry. I will call to you whenever I'm in trouble, and you will answer me.
PSALM 86:6–7 NLT

You can usually tell when a child is part of a loving, caring home by observing one thing: confidence. That child just *knows* that Mom and Dad care about him and that they will joyfully meet his needs, even before he says anything about them. The child also knows that his parents will defend and protect him against any perils this world throws his way.

Love always gives and protects. It's just what love does. That's what a good parent's love looks like. . .and even more so with our heavenly Father's love for us. That's partly why the apostle John wrote, "This is the confidence we have in approaching God: that if we ask anything according to his will, he hears us" (1 John 5:14 NIV), and why another New Testament writer wrote, "Let us then approach God's throne of grace with confidence, so that we may receive mercy and find grace to help us in our time of need" (Hebrews 4:16 NIV).

Are you confident in God's love for you and in His desire to provide for you and to protect you when you need it?

God in heaven, I want to always approach You with humility but also with confidence, knowing that You have promised to hear me when I need something from You.

OUR OBJECT OF TRUST

*He who dwells in the secret place of the Most High shall abide
under the shadow of the Almighty. I will say of the LORD,
"He is my refuge and my fortress; My God, in Him I will trust."*
PSALM 91:1–2 NKJV

In Western culture, men are taught from the time they are infants that they should develop and put their trust in their own abilities and strength. Most of us may not think of it in these exact words, but deep down we believe it's up to us to "pull ourselves up by our bootstraps."

It's fine to have a measure of self-confidence, but we should always remember that there is only one in whom we should feel 100 percent confident: our Father in heaven. Others may fail us sometimes, but God will not. We can fail ourselves, but we never have to worry about God letting us down.

The Bible is filled with promises about the results of trusting fully in God, of being fully reliant on Him to get us through every life situation. That includes today's encouragement to "abide [stay] under the shadow of the Almighty," where we receive protection, comfort, and encouragement.

Where do you place your trust at all times, especially when you face a life crisis?

*Father, I've learned that relying first on myself is the first step
toward burnout and ultimate failure. May I always place my
trust first in Your power and strength and not in my own abilities.*

GOD IS GOOD

For the LORD is good; His mercy is everlasting,
and His truth endures to all generations.
PSALM 100:5 NKJV

Do you ever just sit and think about how many things you have to be grateful for? You've probably heard that having a thankful attitude is good for you on many levels. And if there's one thing we all have to be grateful to God for, it's that He is. . .well, *good*!

The Bible repeatedly tells us that God is good, loving, and benevolent. Not only that, it contains many more examples of Him putting His goodness on display. The most amazing example of God's goodness is that He made a way for sinful humans to be at peace with Him. This is God's ultimate expression of goodness. But it doesn't stop there. God is good to His people in many, many ways—and that's because He Himself is good.

James wrote, "Every good and perfect gift is from above, coming down from the Father of the heavenly lights, who does not change like shifting shadows" (James 1:17 NIV). So think about how God is not just good, but *good to you*. Then take a few minutes today and thank Him for His goodness!

Benevolent, loving God, I sometimes lose sight of the fact that You are not only an all-wise, all-knowing, all-powerful Creator; You are also, in a word, "good." Remind me daily that You are good to me, not because I deserve it but because You choose to be.

HUNGERING AND THIRSTING FOR GOD

*Let them give thanks to the LORD for his unfailing love and
his wonderful deeds for mankind, for he satisfies the
thirsty and fills the hungry with good things.*
PSALM 107:8–9 NIV

When God created our bodies, He arranged it so that we would feel a hunger for nourishment and a thirst for hydration, both of which we need to survive and thrive. On a spiritual level though, He instilled in us something even more important: a hunger and thirst for Him.

Sadly, many men try to quench that thirst and satisfy that hunger for God with anything and everything but Him. They attempt to use power, money, relationships, sex, and many other things this world has to offer to find the satisfaction only God can give them.

Jesus once told His followers, "Blessed are those who hunger and thirst for righteousness, for they will be filled" (Matthew 5:6 NIV). We can take these words to mean that when we take our spiritual hunger and thirst directly to God to find satisfaction, we can be sure that He will fill our souls and bless our lives with the very best thing: Himself.

*Provider God, as much as I need physical nourishment and
hydration, I need You even more. Thank You for making me
hungry and thirsty for You—and for giving me Yourself
every day so that I can live as You've called me to live.*

HOW TRUSTWORTHY ARE YOU?

It is better to take refuge in the LORD than to trust in humans.
It is better to take refuge in the LORD than to trust in princes.
PSALM 118:8–9 NIV

If someone were to ask you how trustworthy you are on a scale of 1 to 100, how would you answer? If we're being honest, even those of us who consider ourselves generally trustworthy and dependable know we can't rate ourselves at 100, or even 99 or 98. That's simply because we're all fallen humans and therefore prone to failing other people from time to time.

This is why the writer of Psalm 118 asserted that it is better to trust in God than any human. While we all fail our friends and loved ones from time to time, and while others will certainly fail us occasionally, we never need to question God's trustworthiness or dependability—even in the most difficult of times.

Trustworthy loved ones and dependable friends are blessings from God, and we should express our gratitude for them. But we must always remember that He and He alone is worthy of our complete, unwavering trust.

God in heaven, You've given me some wonderful friends—men who have earned my trust in many ways over the years. But help me to never forget that I have only one friend I can trust 100 percent of the time in 100 percent of all circumstances. That friend is You.

AVOIDING SIN

*I seek you with all my heart; do not let me
stray from your commands. I have hidden your
word in my heart that I might not sin against you.*
PSALM 119:10–11 NIV

O n the cover of his Bible, the seventeenth-century Christian writer John Bunyan scrawled this note: "Either this book will keep you from sin, or sin will keep you from this book."

Bunyan understood the same thing about the Word of God as the writer of Psalm 119: it gives believers the power to endure temptation to sin. The Bible identifies itself as a source of tremendous power for the Christian who reads it and allows the Holy Spirit to make it come alive in his life.

If you want a good example of this kind of power, look no further than Jesus Himself.

In Matthew 4, we read of the devil relentlessly tempting the Lord, but we also read of Jesus defeating that temptation by speaking the Word of God back to the enemy (see vv. 4, 7, 10). In the end, Satan had no choice but to flee the scene of the attempted crime.

There is no more powerful weapon against sin than the words in the Bible. Believe it! And then see how God can keep you from sin when you make the Book a priority in your life.

*Lord Jesus, thank You for providing Yourself as an
example of how to endure the temptations the devil,
this world, and my own flesh throw my way.*

BUILDING GOOD THINGS

Unless the LORD builds the house, the builders labor in vain.
Unless the LORD watches over the city, the guards stand watch in vain.
PSALM 127:1 NIV

It's probably safe to say that there is at least one do-it-yourself book for just about any life endeavor. Do you want a strong marriage? There are countless publications out there devoted to married life. Do you need to repair your car but can't afford a mechanic? You can find many books about car repair. How about building a house? Again, tons of books that can help you construct one from the ground up.

At a glance, it looks like today's verse specifically addresses the importance of seeking God as you build a literal house. But there is a deeper meaning here, and it's this: God does not want us to approach our endeavors with an attitude of self-sufficiency. In fact, when we do that, we're likely to end up feeling frustrated, empty, and defeated.

God wants to build great things in your life: a strong relationship with Him, a good marriage, and a powerful ministry—just to name a few. Your part in that deal is to step back and let Him lead in the building.

God of power, remind me daily to approach everything
I do with humility, knowing that You are the source of
everything good that I receive or accomplish—at work,
in my marriage and family, and in my church.

YOU CAN'T HIDE FROM GOD

Where can I go from your Spirit?
Where can I flee from your presence?
Psalm 139:7 niv

We Americans value our privacy. Most of us don't want any person or entity monitoring or watching as we live our lives. And when someone seems to be watching us, we feel great discomfort, even to the point of lashing out and protesting, "Leave me alone!"

The Bible, however, teaches us that nothing we do truly is in private, that we have eyes on us at every moment. The eyes of our loving God are on us every moment of every day. Our God knows what we do, what we think, and where we go. He also knows when we're struggling and need His help to endure.

But God doesn't watch us constantly out of some sort of voyeurism or because He's waiting for us to mess up so He can pounce. He watches us at all times because He loves us and wants to care for our needs, because He wants to bless us for our obedience and correct us and teach us when we stray from His ways.

You can't hide yourself from the eyes of your eternally loving heavenly Father. And even if you could, you shouldn't want to!

All-seeing Father in heaven, thank You for knowing me and knowing everything I do. Help me to walk so closely with You that I'm overcome with the knowledge that You're with me always.

PREPARING FOR BATTLE

*Blessed be the LORD my Rock, who trains my
hands for war, and my fingers for battle.*
PSALM 144:1 NKJV

Somewhere, somehow, many followers of Christ today have come to believe that the Christian life is easy, quiet, and without conflict. But that's not what the Bible teaches. In fact, Jesus Himself plainly told His followers, "In this world you will have trouble," (John 16:33 NIV).

In the Old Testament and New Testament alike, the writers likened life on this earth for the believer to war. The Bible tells us that we will be at war with our flesh, with the world around us, and with spiritual forces (the devil and his demons).

Christian man, it really is a war out there! But it's a war we don't have to fight alone—even if we could.

In today's verse, David the psalmist thanks and praises his God for empowering and preparing him for war with his enemies. And our Lord does the same thing today!

In one beloved passage (Ephesians 6:10–18), the apostle Paul tells his readers how they can use the weapons of war God has given them to fight their spiritual battles.

When we let God train our hands for war and our fingers for battle, we'll reap the victory we'd never see on our own.

*Protector God, thank You for always protecting me,
arming me, and preparing me for battle here on earth.
With You on my side, I'll be a winner every time.*

GOD-GIVEN WISDOM

For the LORD grants wisdom! From his mouth come knowledge and understanding. He grants a treasure of common sense to the honest. He is a shield to those who walk with integrity.
PROVERBS 2:6–7 NLT

The Old Testament gives us a good example of wisdom when it refers to the men of Issachar as, "men who understood the times and knew what Israel should do" (1 Chronicles 12:32 NIV).

It's good to have knowledge of God's Word, but actually applying it to your life requires wisdom, which God has promised to give each and every man who asks for it in faith (see James 1:5). God uses different tools to give us wisdom, including His Holy Spirit and our experiences in our walk with Him. When we have that wisdom, we'll know what to do when we're faced with a life situation that would otherwise leave us frustrated and discouraged.

When we turn to the world for wisdom—from our political leaders, from celebrities, and (oftentimes) from spiritual leaders—we're going to flawed sources. But our heavenly Father promises that when we go to Him and ask for the wisdom we need in this life, He'll gladly give it to us.

Heavenly Father, there are so many times when life presents problems I just don't know how to solve—if I can solve them at all. Give me the wisdom I need to handle the problems You allow to come my way. . .and the strength to endure them.

FEAR OR LOVE?

*The fear of the LORD is the beginning of wisdom, and knowledge
of the Holy One is understanding. For through wisdom your
days will be many, and years will be added to your life.*
PROVERBS 9:10–11 NIV

A man who'd always enjoyed an amazing relationship with his earthly
father once said, "My father never had to punish me to make sure I
stayed in line. I loved him so much that I was afraid to do anything that
would disappoint him."

That's a pretty good illustration of the fear of God, isn't it?

When we think of the word *fear*, our minds usually go to the dread a
man might feel toward a cruel tyrant or dictator. But that's not how God
wants us to approach Him. God is good and He's the very definition of
love. He wants us to love Him so deeply and reverentially that we won't
want to do anything that displeases Him.

We hear much about the love of God these days, but not a lot about
the fear of God. But when we understand that those two things aren't
in conflict with each other, we can find joy, and the strength to endure,
that comes only when we walk with Him as He desires.

*Father in heaven, thank You that I can love You, know You, and honor
You as only You are worthy. That is the beginning of the kind of
wisdom that can lead me to a productive life lived for You.*

HUMAN PRIDE

When pride comes, then comes disgrace,
but with humility comes wisdom.
PROVERBS 11:2 NIV

When we think of the word *sin*, our minds usually move to the "biggies": murder, sexual immorality, theft, blasphemy, and others. But when you look at the message of the Bible as a whole, you'll see that at the heart of any sin we can commit is this five-letter word for something God really hates: pride.

Pride can be defined as believing you can handle your life better than God can. And while it's easy to say you trust God, it's even easier to have an attitude of pride, an attitude that says to God, "It's okay. . .I've got this."

That kind of thinking can lead you to all kinds of places in life, and none of them are good.

Even a little bit of pride can lead a man into disastrous decisions—in his walk with God, in his marriage, in his relationship with his children, in his ministry. . .the list is long and distinguished. But humility before God and others leads to good decisions and to the very best God has for you.

Lord, Your Word repeatedly warns me against the sin of pride,
which is me trusting in and depending on myself instead of You.
Lord, keep me from making a mess of my life through human pride.
Instead, help me to glorify You as I humbly seek You each day.

GIVING IT ALL TO THE LORD

*Commit to the LORD whatever you do,
and he will establish your plans.*
PROVERBS 16:3 NIV

If you're a father, you know that somewhere between infancy and toddlerhood, children (especially boys) go through that stage where they want to assert their independence from Mom and Dad. It's during this time when kids often make what any adult understands are foolish decisions—*lots* of foolish decisions.

Really, though, there's a lot of that in most of us Christian men. We speak the words of trust in God, but there is still a streak of independence in all of us that shows itself when it's time to make our plans. Rather than committing our plans to God, it's easy to charge ahead, just assuming that God is behind what we want to do.

But that's a highly risky way to live!

Today's verse tells us that it's wise to trust God enough with our plans to bring them to Him before moving forward. We can do that because we know that God is good and trustworthy. . .and that He wants the very best for us in this life.

Lord, I confess that there are times when I want to run out ahead of You, when I want to move forward with my own plans before bringing them to You. Help me to trust You enough to bring my plans to You so that You can either bless them or change them.

GETTING EVEN

Don't say, "I will get even for this wrong."
Wait for the LORD to handle the matter.
PROVERBS 20:22 NLT

You live in a fallen world filled with fallen, hurting people, so it's only a matter of time before someone does or says something to hurt or offend you. How you handle a slight, be it intentional or unintentional, will tell you a lot about your relationship with God.

That's partly why Jesus once told His followers, "You have heard that it was said, 'Love your neighbor and hate your enemy.' But I tell you, love your enemies and pray for those who persecute you, that you may be children of your Father in heaven" (Matthew 5:43–45 NIV).

When we choose to forgive those who have hurt us, we show that we are God's children. Not only that; we open ourselves up for His blessings, including a mind and heart free of anger and bitterness, both of which make us miserable and degrade our relationship with other people and with our Father in heaven.

Has someone hurt or offended you? Go to God and ask Him to bless and heal that person. Then let Him handle the matter for you.

God of mercy, sometimes I feel justified in seeking to "get even"
with those who have mistreated me or spoken unkindly to me.
Instead, let me be an example of Your grace and mercy
as I choose to walk in peace and forgiveness.

RESPONDING RIGHTLY TO EVIL

Don't fret because of evildoers; don't envy the wicked. For evil people have no future; the light of the wicked will be snuffed out.
PROVERBS 24:19–20 NLT

We've all seen situations like the following: a man leaves his wife and children to be with someone else, and he seems to be wildly happy in his "new life." A businessman engages in questionable practices, and he prospers financially from his misdeeds. Or a backbiting coworker somehow gets promoted to a higher-paying job over someone clearly more qualified.

When we see people profiting from the evil they do, it's easy to feel angry, even a little envious. When that happens, we want to cry out to God—or to anyone who will listen—"It's not fair!"

The fact that you recognize the unfairness of situations like the ones above says a lot about your sense of right and wrong. But, as today's verses point out, it's not good or helpful to dwell on your anger at the hurt evil men cause others. Instead, focus on the good things God has promised those who live right, treat others justly, and trust in God to one day make things right.

Father, I sometimes find myself feeling angry or envious of those who seem to prosper from their misdeeds. Forgive me for those feelings. Help me to focus on living the life You have for me, knowing that the rewards will be glorious, eternal ones.

BLESSINGS IN CONTENTMENT

"Two things I ask of you, LORD; do not refuse me before
I die: keep falsehood and lies far from me; give me neither
poverty nor riches, but give me only my daily bread."
PROVERBS 30:7–8 NIV

It's a sad fact that not all men—including Christian men—are content with what they have. But Solomon, who understood the folly of spending life chasing after "more," shares this bit of simple but profound wisdom: *Be content with what you have, for it is God who provides.*

If you've ever spent time around someone who isn't content with his life, you probably have come to the conclusion that few things will drag a man down to lower depths of mind and spirit than discontentment. This is the kind of man who seems to bring his gloom with him everywhere he goes, a man who believes life just isn't fair and that he's gotten a raw deal.

Nowhere in the Bible are we men discouraged from working hard to make a better life for ourselves and our families. The key, however, is knowing that God has you in the place He wants you, whether you are rich or poor.

That is what a balanced life—a *content* life—looks like.

Generous Father in heaven, forgive me for wanting "more" when that's not what You have for me right now. Help me to always be both grateful and content with all the material wealth You have given me.

WHY?

*The words of the Teacher, son of David, king in
Jerusalem: "Meaningless! Meaningless!" says the Teacher.
"Utterly meaningless! Everything is meaningless."*
ECCLESIASTES 1:1–2 NIV

Those unhappy souls who hold to the philosophy called "existential nihilism" believe that life has no real meaning, that a man—all mankind, in fact—has no purpose for existing and that he really can't know why he is here.

What a grim view of life that is!

As you read through the book of Ecclesiastes, it almost seems like its writer, Solomon, is engaging in his own brand of existential nihilism. It seems that he sees no purpose for his own existence or for anything or anyone around him.

Unless you hang in there with Ecclesiastes, you might wonder why it's in the Bible at all. Why would God include a book that essentially tells us that life and everything about it has no meaning? Such a fatalistic view of life would have no place in scripture. . .right?

But that's not where Solomon is coming from—not at all. Tomorrow, you'll see what he has to say about every man's ultimate duty and purpose in this life.

*Gracious God, thank You for giving me purpose in this life.
Thank You that my life isn't just a meaningless existence.
Thank You that You've made me for a purpose and a plan.*

MAN'S CHIEF END

Now all has been heard; here is the conclusion of the matter: Fear God and keep his commandments, for this is the duty of all mankind.
ECCLESIASTES 12:13 NIV

In AD 1646–1647, a group of English and Scottish theologians and laymen got together to write a famous document called the *Westminster Shorter Catechism*. It was written in a question-answer format, opening with the following:

Q1: "What is the chief end of man?"

A1: "Man's chief end is to glorify God, and to enjoy him forever."

This exact phrase doesn't appear anywhere in the Bible, but the message can be drawn from today's scripture verse. Solomon had written at length about the meaningless of life, but in the end (the very last two verses of Ecclesiastes) he states that every man's purpose can be summed up like this: "Fear God and keep his commandments."

As a man of God, you never have to wonder why God made you or why He saved you. You never have to allow yourself to wonder why you're here. God has made you to love Him, to live for Him, and to be the man He's created you to be.

Thank You, Lord, for creating me for these specific purposes: to love You, to honor You, and to live my life in a way that pleases You. May I pursue those purposes wholeheartedly.

GOD'S DECLARATION OF LOVE

Let him lead me to the banquet hall,
and let his banner over me be love.
SONG OF SOLOMON 2:4 NIV

If you drive around just about any city, large or small, you're likely to see banners displayed just about anywhere they can easily be seen. Banners contain all kinds of messages—including support of political candidates and encouragement for people to buy certain products or embrace certain causes.

God has raised a banner for those who follow Jesus, and it communicates loud and clear His love for us. As David wrote, God has raised this banner as a loud proclamation of His devotion to His people: "You have given a banner to those who fear You, that it may be displayed because of the truth" (Psalm 60:4 NKJV).

There is no better place to be than under God's banner of love. It is there that we find security and rest from the world around us. It's a place where we can allow God to give us strength and perseverance, even during the most trying times.

Loving Father in heaven, thank You that I can feel secure in
Your love. Remind me often that everything You've done for
me is out of a love for me that I can only begin to understand.
Help me to love others as You have loved me.

HE WANTS TO FORGIVE

*"Come now, let's settle this," says the LORD. "Though your sins
are like scarlet, I will make them as white as snow. Though
they are red like crimson, I will make them as white as wool."*
ISAIAH 1:18 NLT

It's not a pleasant experience to be in a place in life where it seems like sin is getting the best of us. It can give us a sense of hopelessness, and we can come to a point where we can't imagine God ever wanting to hear from us again.

But, as the Bible repeatedly promises, it doesn't have to be that way for the man who has trusted Jesus Christ as his Lord and Savior.

Think of it this way: If your child made a big mess of himself and desperately needed to be cleaned up, would you tell him, "Forget you! You're on your own!"? Of course not! The first thing you'd do is clean up his mess. Then comes a time of correction and teaching.

Our heavenly Father does the same thing with us when we sin—and He does it willingly and joyfully!

The Bible tells us that God hates all sin. But it also teaches that He doesn't abandon us when we fall but instead cleanses us and forgives us when we confess our wrongdoing.

---

*Heavenly Father, thank You for sending Your Son so that
my heart could be purified and made acceptable to You.
Help me to run to You when I sin, not away from You.*

HERE I AM!

Also I heard the voice of the Lord, saying: "Whom shall I send,
and who will go for Us?" Then I said, "Here am I! Send me."
ISAIAH 6:8 NKJV

D o you ever find your heart breaking over the hurting and needy
people in your neighborhood, in our nation, or around the world?
Do you ever grieve over the lostness of humanity and wonder what you
can do to reach them with the message of salvation through Jesus Christ?

If you answered "yes" to one or both of the above questions, it may
be that God is preparing you for some kind of service—just like He did
the prophet Isaiah.

God had purified Isaiah and made him ready to serve (see Isaiah
6:1–6). Now ready to speak God's message to His hard-hearted people,
Isaiah eagerly volunteered when God asked whom He should send.

God has something for you to do for His kingdom. He has given you
gifts and can enable you to do what He's calling you to do. Your part in
that is to pray, like the prophet Isaiah, "Here I am! Send me."

Lord God, I am willing, so use me in any way You want to bring others
to You and to glorify You in every way. Help keep me attuned to
opportunities to do those things every day. May my every action
and word be motivated by my love for You and for others.

GOD IS IN CONTROL

*This is what the LORD says to me with his strong hand upon me,
warning me not to follow the way of this people: "Do not call
conspiracy everything this people calls a conspiracy;
do not fear what they fear, and do not dread it."*

ISAIAH 8:11–12 NIV

After Election Day of 2020 (just eight months ago!), you probably heard more than a few pundits, political activists, comedians, and even some of your friends state that we're either back on the right track or that our days as a great nation are numbered. For many, the results of the election brought either crippling fear or unrestrained elation.

For the Christian man, however, the election results should neither shake nor confirm his belief that no matter who leads our country, God is and always will be on the throne and is still in complete control. That is why His message, "Do not fear what they fear," applies as much today as it did in Isaiah's time.

Do you ever find yourself feeling fearful for your nation's future—or even where it is today? Don't forget: God's in control. He always has been, and He always will be!

*Sovereign God, every time I read or watch the news, I can't help but think
that the world I live in is very quickly coming unraveled. Remind me
daily that no matter how bad things look, You are in complete control.*

TRUST IN FEARFUL TIMES

"Surely God is my salvation; I will trust and not be afraid.
The LORD, the LORD himself, is my strength and
my defense; he has become my salvation."

ISAIAH 12:2 NIV

Can you remember the last time you felt absolutely consumed with fear? How about a time when you were so stressed that you couldn't eat, sleep, or even think clearly?

Life has a way of putting us through fearful times. Problems in our marriages, conflicts with our kids, issues at work, and health difficulties can all can put any man in a place where he feels afraid, anxious, and stressed out.

In today's verse, the prophet Isaiah writes words telling us not to fear but to trust in God. Centuries later, the apostle Paul gave New Testament voice to this attitude when he wrote, "Do not be anxious about anything, but in every situation, by prayer and petition, with thanksgiving, present your requests to God. And the peace of God, which transcends all understanding, will guard your hearts and your minds in Christ Jesus" (Philippians 4:6–7 NIV)

When life gives you reasons to feel afraid, it can be a huge help to remember two things: God is in control *and* He promises to give you peace when you take your fears to Him.

All-powerful God, life gives me many opportunities
to feel afraid. Remind me often to trust You and You
alone as I live as You have called me to live.

BEYOND HOPE?

The LORD will strike Egypt with a plague; he will strike
them and heal them. They will turn to the LORD,
and he will respond to their pleas and heal them.
ISAIAH 19:22 NIV

I saiah 19 tells the story of how God sent a series of terrible judgments on the land of Egypt. . .and about how He would so mercifully and graciously heal many Egyptians when they finally called out to Him.

Egypt had been an enemy of Israel at different times in the two nations' histories. What's more, the Egyptians had become a proud, rebellious, idolatrous people who seemed to want nothing to do with the God of Israel.

But God did not give up on the people of Egypt. One day, He would draw many Egyptians to Himself so that they could be saved. As it turned out, a strong and growing church thrived in Egypt for more than six centuries after Christ returned to heaven.

So, what can we learn from what happened in Egypt many centuries ago? We should never see even the most indifferent of sinners as beyond hope. Instead, we should pray that God would do anything it takes to bring that person to a point of understanding his own need for salvation. When that happens, we need to be ready to speak the message.

Gracious God, I often think of certain sinners as beyond reach.
Help me to remember that You want even the worst of
sinners to turn to You for healing and forgiveness.

REPENTANCE

The Lord, the LORD Almighty, called you on that day to weep and to wail, to tear out your hair and put on sackcloth. But see, there is joy and revelry, slaughtering of cattle and killing of sheep, eating of meat and drinking of wine! "Let us eat and drink," you say, "for tomorrow we die!"
ISAIAH 22:12–13 NIV

You've probably heard or seen the acronym "YOLO," which stands for You Only Live Once. In our culture, that line of thinking is often taken as an encouragement for people to cram as much "fun" into their lives as they can before they die.

But the Bible teaches that YOLO isn't the full truth. Yes, we only live this life on earth once. But after that is a second life in eternity—with God in heaven or in a terrible place called hell. That's why the book of Hebrews warns, "And as it is appointed for men to die once, but after this the judgment" (9:27 NKJV).

And it's also why we Christian men should take stock of our lives regularly, and then turn *away* from anything we know does not please God and turn *to* those things that bring eternal rewards.

Lord God, may I never forget that I'll stand before You one day and that You will judge the things I do here on earth. Help me to rid my life of the things that don't please You, and fill my life with the things that will bring eternal reward.

A BETTER DAY COMING

The Sovereign Lord will wipe away the tears from all faces;
he will remove his people's disgrace from all the earth.
Isaiah 25:8 niv

Have you ever been going through a difficult time, and a friend tries to encourage you with a meaningless platitude like, "Just hang in there! Things will get better."

In real life, though, it sometimes seems like our difficulties will never end. But one of God's most amazing promises is that there will come a day when the kinds of earthly difficulties we face permanently become things of the past. No more pain, no more death, no more tears. . .only a joyful eternity in our heavenly Father's presence.

The apostle John echoed the message of today's scripture verse when he wrote, " 'He will wipe every tear from their eyes. There will be no more death' or mourning or crying or pain, for the old order of things has passed away" (Revelation 21:4 niv).

Living on this earth, it's hard to imagine a time when death, despair, or pain are no longer a part of our existence. But it's God's promise to His people, and it's one that can get us through our most difficult life experiences.

Loving Father, I can hardly wait for the day when I can be
with You in paradise, where there will be no more death, pain,
sickness, or despair. Until that time, help me focus on eternity
and to speak words of hope to those who most need to hear them.

PRECEPT UPON PRECEPT

"To whom will he teach knowledge, and to whom will he explain the message? Those who are weaned from the milk, those taken from the breast? For it is precept upon precept, precept upon precept, line upon line, line upon line, here a little, there a little."
ISAIAH 28:9–10 ESV

As Ephraim is threatened with judgment over its pride and drunkenness, God offers hope to those who are faithful (His remnant) in the form of a crown of glory (Isaiah 28:5)—as opposed to those who are engaged in sin, who wear a crown of pride.

Bible commentator John Gill wrote that the crown of glory is God "surrounding, adorning, and protecting his people; granting them his presence; giving them his grace, and large measures of it; causing them to live soberly, righteously, and godly."

As God's people live in such a manner, He takes them deeper, weaning them from spiritual milk, one precept at a time. When you notice the Holy Spirit's gentle nudges to drink from the Word, obey Him. This is evidence of God at work in you, and He wants you to have a deeper understanding of who He is and how you should live.

Spiritual growth occurs over a long period of time, usually a little at a time. Be faithful to study the scriptures line by line.

*Lord, teach me Your ways precept by precept
and line by line. I want to go deeper with You.*

KILLING THE FLESH

*He who walks righteously and speaks uprightly, who despises the
gain of oppressions, who shakes his hands, lest they hold a bribe,
who stops his ears from hearing of bloodshed and shuts his eyes
from looking on evil, he will dwell on the heights.*

ISAIAH 33:15–16 ESV

Galatians 5:19–21 (ESV) says "the works of the flesh are evident: sexual immorality, impurity, sensuality, idolatry, sorcery, enmity, strife, jealousy, fits of anger, rivalries, dissensions, divisions, envy, drunkenness, orgies, and things like these. I warn you, as I warned you before, that those who do such things will not inherit the kingdom of God."

The antidote to those things is the fruit of the Spirit: love, joy, peace, patience, kindness, goodness, faithfulness, gentleness, and self-control (Galatians 5:22–23). Want a good test to see if you are displaying the fruit of the Spirit? Examine today's verses and ask yourself if you're walking righteously, speaking uprightly, despising oppression, not hearing bloodshed, and not watching evil.

Not that you'll do these things perfectly. But is this your heart's desire? Do you long to shun the flesh and embrace all that is good and right? Confess your sin to God and begin the difficult work of putting your flesh to death by starving it of all it desires.

*Lord, I want to walk righteously, speak uprightly, despise
oppressions, not listen to bloodshed or watch evil. Forgive me
for sinning against You. Empower me to put my flesh to death.*

STAY ON THE NARROW PATH

*Then GOD told Isaiah, "Go and speak with Hezekiah.
Give him this Message from me, GOD, the God of your
ancestor David: 'I've heard your prayer. I have seen your
tears. Here's what I'll do: I'll add fifteen years to your life.' "*
ISAIAH 38:4–5 MSG

On average, the length of a man's life in the United States is between seventy-five and seventy-six years of age, depending on which study you believe. Second Chronicles 29:1 (MSG) says, "Hezekiah became king when he was twenty-five years old and was king in Jerusalem for twenty-nine years." So he would have been just thirty-nine years old when he got sick and nearly died. But he asked God for more time and received it.

In his commentary, Albert Barnes says this: "If the desire be to do good; to advance the kingdom of God; to benefit others; or to perfect some plan of benevolence which is begun, it is not improper to pray that God would prolong the life."

In addition to today's passage being an encouraging one about answered prayer, it's also a great reminder to stay on the narrow path as you advance in years. As you get older, what is your focus? Is your heart growing fonder about God's kingdom or is it growing colder? If it's the latter, then fan the flames.

*Lord, use however long I have left on this
earth to advance Your kingdom.*

FEAR NOT

Fear thou not; for I am with thee: be not dismayed; for I
am thy God: I will strengthen thee; yea, I will help thee; yea,
I will uphold thee with the right hand of my righteousness.
ISAIAH 41:10 KJV

God offered the comforting words from today's verse to the Jews who were in Babylonian exile. If you search for the phrase "fear thou not" or "fear not," you'll find it over and over again in the scriptures:

- "Therefore fear thou not, O my servant Jacob, saith the LORD; neither be dismayed, O Israel: for, lo, I will save thee from afar, and thy seed from the land of their captivity" (Jeremiah 30:10 KJV).
- "But the angel said unto him, Fear not, Zacharias: for thy prayer is heard; and thy wife Elisabeth shall bear thee a son" (Luke 1:13 KJV).
- "And when I saw him, I fell at his feet as dead. And he laid his right hand upon me, saying unto me, Fear not; I am the first and the last" (Revelation 1:17 KJV).

As you face uncertainty of all sorts today, what promises from God come to your mind? "Fear not," the Lord says. He's in your circumstances, and He will uphold you. Trust Him.

Lord, when my circumstances threaten to overwhelm me, may I hear
Your calming voice reminding me to fear not, for You are with me.

STAND ON HIS PROMISES

"When you pass through the waters, I will be with you; and through the rivers, they shall not overflow you. When you walk through the fire, you shall not be burned, nor shall the flame scorch you."
ISAIAH 43:2 NKJV

M any of the old spirituals that slaves sang before and during the Civil War were about God's protection and provision and the expectation of heaven. Songs such as "Swing Low, Sweet Chariot," "Wade in the Water," "Deep River," "Ezekiel Saw the Wheel," "A Balm in Gilead," "Go Down, Moses," and so many others offered hope in a seemingly hopeless situation.

Passages like the one today are rich and have carried many generations of people through difficult times. God's promises give life where death looms. You'll find many of God's promises in old hymns. Do you have any hymns committed to memory? If not, you might consider picking up a hymnal and adding a few to your arsenal for spiritual warfare or for times when you're feeling blue.

Start with a few of the classics, like "Amazing Grace," "How Great Thou Art," "It Is Well," and "Great Is Thy Faithfulness." Then progress from there, finding your own personal favorites that remind you of God's faithful provision.

Lord, thank You for the many promises You've offered Your people in the scriptures. Keep them fresh in my mind and heart as difficult times come.

THE LORD HAS REDEEMED

Go forth out of Babylon, flee from the Chaldeans! With a voice
of singing declare, tell this, cause it to go forth even to the end
of the earth; say, The Lord has redeemed His servant Jacob!
ISAIAH 48:20 AMPC

I magine finally hearing the Lord say "go forth" and "flee" your captivity, especially after being held for so long. The people of Israel were to do so with a voice of jubilation, telling anybody within earshot that the Lord had redeemed them.

It seems odd that they would need to be told how to react to being set free, doesn't it? But keep in mind that they (or their ancestors) had been in captivity for seventy years, so they probably didn't even fully believe that they were free until this very minute.

How many times and for how long did you hear the Gospel before you responded with jubilation? Jesus threw open the door of the prison that held you, but it may have taken you months or even years to fully believe the message and then act on it by walking out the prison door.

As you encounter others who are enslaved by their sin and then proclaim the Gospel to them, be faithful to share it with them over and over until they finally walk out the door.

Lord, thank You for Your everlasting patience
with humanity. We are so undeserving but so
happy You've offered us a way to be free!

GOD NEVER FORGETS YOU

*Behold, I have indelibly imprinted (tattooed a
picture of) you on the palm of each of My hands;
[O Zion] your walls are continually before Me.*
ISAIAH 49:16 AMPC

In 1973, Tony Orlando and Dawn released the chart-topping song "Tie a Yellow Ribbon Round the Ole Oak Tree." People used the practice reflected in this song title to show support for or to remember a loved one who was away from home for military service or for other reasons. It was a beautiful symbol that showed how much the missing person was loved and cherished.

In spite of God's continued promises to never forget His people, the people of Jerusalem were convinced that God had indeed forgotten them while they were in captivity (Isaiah 49:14). But He was quick to tell them He'd tattooed a picture of them on His palms. Doesn't that imagery just take your breath away? As angry as God was with His people, He never stopped thinking about them. He feels the same way about you.

Yes, you've committed dreadful sin, and you are without excuse. But God has never forgotten you. Now walk in the freedom that Christ has provided for you. And love others as much as God does.

*Lord, when I think about You loving me
as much as today's verse describes, I'm humbled.
I'm also inspired to love others more deeply.*

CERTAINLY NOT!

All we like sheep have gone astray, we have turned
every one to his own way; and the Lord has made
to light upon Him the guilt and iniquity of us all.
ISAIAH 53:6 AMPC

As a prophet, Isaiah was able to look forward some seven hundred years not only to the birth of the Messiah but also to His dreadful and glorious mission—to take on the wickedness of humanity and, therefore, suffer the full wrath of God.

Today, in the Gospel dispensation, you look backward to the cross and the work of Christ. And while your sins are indeed covered, the apostle Paul asks, "What shall we say [to all this]? Are we to remain in sin in order that God's grace (favor and mercy) may multiply and overflow? Certainly not! How can we who died to sin live in it any longer?" (Romans 6:1–2 AMPC).

Sin will remain a constant battle the rest of your life, but you would do well to consider the price Jesus paid for it. You are at peace with God because Jesus satisfied His demands for justice. Live in such a manner that shows your gratitude.

Father, You knew humanity would never follow You as we ought,
so You put Your wrath on Jesus in our place. Empower me to live
the Spirit-filled life in such a way as to bring honor to Your name.

THE COMFORTER

As for Me, this is My covenant or league with them, says the Lord:
My Spirit, Who is upon you [and Who writes the law of God inwardly
on the heart], and My words which I have put in your mouth shall
not depart out of your mouth, or out of the mouths of your [true,
spiritual] children, or out of the mouths of your children's children,
says the Lord, from henceforth and forever.
ISAIAH 59:21 AMPC

Does the message of today's verse sound familiar?

In John 14:16 (AMPC), Jesus said something similar: "And I will ask the Father, and He will give you another Comforter (Counselor, Helper, Intercessor, Advocate, Strengthener, and Standby), that He may remain with you forever."

Long before Jesus was born in the flesh, God planned to send His Spirit into His people to advocate for, strengthen, and comfort them. And not just for the current generation but for many to come after them.

That's where you come in. After receiving the Holy Spirit, what are you doing to make sure God's words do not depart from your mouth, nor from the mouths of your children? Are you making the scriptures a priority in your home? Are you setting aside enough time to spend in them? Are you able to recite verses as situations present themselves?

Father, I love Your Word, but I confess to not spending
as much time in it as I should. That changes today.

REBUILD THE ANCIENT RUINS

*They shall build up the ancient ruins; they shall raise
up the former devastations; they shall repair the
ruined cities, the devastations of many generations.*

ISAIAH 61:4 ESV

Believers in the old covenant were all about rebuilding, raising up, repairing, and redeeming. But believers in the new covenant have a better, clearer picture of what that looks like when they transform something that was sinful into something that is used for the Lord's purposes.

A West Palm Beach church took over a former strip club in 2019 with plans to open in 2020. The reverend of NewSound Church said the former facility was being transformed into a church building that would hold six hundred to seven hundred people.

"I don't mind being in a building that was a strip club any more than I mind somebody walking in our doors that had at one time in their life been a stripper," the pastor said in a CNN story. "I believe that God is opening up some doors that a 20-month-old church can't open by themselves."

What are you currently doing to rebuild ancient ruins or to transform something for God's glory? It doesn't have to be a major overhaul. You can restart a church library, offer to fix the cars of single mothers, become a mentor, or many other things.

Lord, use me as a means of transformation.

SHARE YOUR TESTIMONY

You welcome those who gladly do good, who follow godly ways.
But you have been very angry with us, for we are not godly.
We are constant sinners; how can people like us be saved?
ISAIAH 64:5 NLT

A man named Dustin knew how it felt to be a constant sinner. He grew up in a household that liked to party, and he says it was easy to find substances to abuse. That led to time alone with girls, which led to a pregnancy when he was just fifteen years old, and an abortion. Both he and his girlfriend were heartbroken afterward.

"We couldn't bear to talk about it," he told Christian Broadcasting Network (CBN). "And it plunged us into this spiral of drug addiction that was just awful and that ultimately took my girlfriend's life."

Dustin ended up in jail on the suicide floor. That's when he remembered something his grandmother used to tell him: God is present. Jesus is the Savior, and He is who Dustin needed. Dustin cried out to Jesus and his heart was changed. As of the taping of the CBN interview, he was working for a pro-life medical sharing ministry.

Your story might not be as dramatic as Dustin's. But you still know how it feels to battle with constant sin. Share your testimony. One day, someone might remember what you said and call on the Savior.

Lord, embolden me to tell others
about how You changed my life.

NO MORE EXCUSES

"Do not say, 'I am too young.' You must go to everyone I send you to and say whatever I command you. Do not be afraid of them, for I am with you and will rescue you," declares the LORD.
JEREMIAH 1:7–8 NIV

God's people have been using excuses to not do what He's called them to for thousands of years. Moses said he couldn't speak well, Abraham and Sarah thought they were too old, and in today's verses, Jeremiah claims he is too young. But the Lord stops that right away, just as He did with Moses, Abraham, and Sarah.

Just go, the Lord told Jeremiah, and do not fear because He would go with him.

Take note of what Matthew Henry said in his concise commentary about these verses: "It becomes us to have low thoughts of ourselves. Those who are young, should consider that they are so, and not venture beyond their powers. But though a sense of our own weakness and insufficiency should make us go humbly about our work, it should not make us draw back when God calls us."

What's your excuse? Isn't it time to go humbly about the work God has called you to? Cast down your excuse and trust God to go with you.

Lord, I've held on to my excuse for so long, but I believe that as I let it go today, You will walk with me.

KEEP BLUSHING

*"Were they ashamed when they committed abomination?
No, they were not at all ashamed; they did not know how to
blush. Therefore they shall fall among those who fall; at the time
that I punish them, they shall be overthrown," says the LORD.*
JEREMIAH 6:15 ESV

Today's verse is a sobering one—a warning for those who not only have committed abomination (a vile act) but who were so far gone that they no longer even knew how to blush. As a result, they were to be counted as unbelievers. This was probably a reference to false prophets and wicked priests who were leading people astray.

First Timothy 4:1–2 says that people who devote themselves to deceitful spirits and teachings of demons end up with a "seared" conscience. They have a false sense of comfort. It'd be like not having any feeling in your arm, so when you set it against a hot grill, you wouldn't feel a thing; therefore, you wouldn't feel the need to remove it. The subsequent effects would be devastating to your skin. The same can be said for sin.

When you stop fighting against your sinful nature, you'll slowly lose the ability to blush or feel guilty. When that happens, you are in danger. Never allow yourself to get to that point.

*Lord, never allow me to take my sin lightly. May I always
be sensitive to the Spirit's conviction and quick to repent.*

MOVE ON

"Do people fall down and not get up? Or take the wrong
road and then just keep going? So why does this people
go backward, and just keep on going—backward!"
JEREMIAH 8:4–5 MSG

If you've ever been in an unfamiliar city or on an unfamiliar highway and been totally dependent on your GPS device, you know that it doesn't always steer you in the right direction. New roads may not show up on your GPS. And it may insist that you take roads that no longer even exist. But once you finally figure out that you're going in the wrong direction, you override the GPS and point your car in the right direction.

The people Jeremiah was writing to were indeed God's people (see verse 8), but oddly, they routinely took the wrong road—spiritually speaking—then just kept going. The context suggests that their leaders were the GPS, leading them down the wrong road without any understanding that they needed to turn around.

Just because a religious leader says something, it doesn't mean it's right. Verse 9 (MSG) says, "Look at them [the religious leaders]! They know everything but GOD's Word." If you've been sitting under teaching in a church for a long time that is moving away from the scriptures, it's time to find a new fellowship right away.

Lord, make me a Berean—someone who studies everything
religious leaders say to make sure it lines up with Your Word.

CORRECT ME, O LORD

Correct me, O LORD, but in justice; not in
your anger, lest you bring me to nothing.
JEREMIAH 10:24 ESV

Adam and Eve hid from God after they sinned. Jonah ran from God. When Jesus opens the sixth seal, people will hide in rocks and caves, trying to avoid the face of God. Hiding and running from God is the norm for the sinner, especially one who doesn't have a strong relationship with Him.

In today's verse, however, a remnant of God's people not only didn't run from Him, they *asked* for His correction—not in His anger, lest He crush them, but in His justice. It's similar to a teenage son who makes a poor decision, but rather than hiding from his dad, he picks up the phone and confesses, asking for mercy. Dad would still correct him, but he would be satisfied, knowing he's done a good job in helping his child to develop his conscience.

When David was faced with a choice of punishment for his sin, he chose to "fall into the hand of the LORD, for his mercy is great" (2 Samuel 24:14 ESV).

How can you do anything less after you've sinned? You'll not only restore your broken fellowship with God; you'll be made white as snow.

Lord, may I never run from You after I've sinned.
Instead, make it my default setting to run to You.

ONE MORE CHANCE

"If you repent, I will restore you that you may serve me; if you utter worthy, not worthless, words, you will be my spokesman."
JEREMIAH 15:19 NIV

God had reached His limit with His people. He told Jeremiah to not even pray for their well-being because He would not listen (Jeremiah 14:11–12). Even if Moses and Samuel were to stand before Him, His heart would not go out to this people (Jeremiah 15:1). And yet, Jeremiah pled God's people's case anyway (Jeremiah 14:19–22), and God heard his prayer. You can read His response in today's verse.

Do you have a prayer ministry that is anything like Jeremiah's—one in which you pray for people who seem so far from God? Maybe even for people who have ticked you off or done something horrible to you or someone you love? God is slow to anger, but there does come a time when His anger demands justice, leaving the sinner in a dangerous place.

Make it a standard practice to pray for your enemies, for those everyone else has forgotten, for those who seem beyond the reach of hope. God may hear and relent, offering them one more chance to repent and turn toward Him.

Lord, give me a heart for my enemies, the forgotten, and for those who have given up hope. I long for them to taste Your mercy.

STAYING FAITHFUL

But my people are not so reliable, for they have deserted me;
they burn incense to worthless idols. They have stumbled
off the ancient highways and walk in muddy paths.
JEREMIAH 18:15 NLT

I s it possible for God's people to desert Him for other gods? Today's verse would indicate that it certainly is possible, and it happens when believers stumble off the "ancient highways." In many ways, America is both the easiest country to be a Christian in and the most difficult. Easy because of the freedom. Difficult because of the ease and comfort.

In a 2007 radio broadcast, John Piper talked about the difficulty aspect: "You go to church, the music is nice, the AC is nice, the lighting is nice, the friends are there, the children have something fun to do, the sermon is more-or-less interesting, and we can go home saying that we've been Christians."

This would change if the church were under heavy persecution and pushed underground. But it doesn't need to come to that. What are you doing to make sure your family isn't deserting God in favor of the idols of comfort and ease? How are you conveying that the American way isn't necessarily the Christian way, as Piper said in that same broadcast?

Lord, decrease my desire for ease and comfort, and increase
my faith and ability to lead my family to worship well.

A SPIRIT OF GRATITUDE

I spoke to you in your [times of] prosperity, but you said,
I will not listen! This has been your attitude from
your youth; you have not obeyed My voice.
JEREMIAH 22:21 AMPC

The prosperous often believe they don't need God. They can meet all their own needs and many of their wants, so obedience to God isn't high on their priority list. While this isn't always the case, it certainly was in today's passage regarding God's people. God spoke, but they disobeyed, and they'd been doing so since their youth.

Have you noticed this pattern in your own life regarding prosperity? When all the bills are paid and you've got extra money in your pocket, is your heart less sensitive to the Spirit's leading, and do you tend to be less obedient to clear biblical principles?

What's a believer supposed to do during times of prosperity? Pray for lack? Not at all! But maintaining a spirit of gratitude to God, given that He is the source of every good and perfect gift (as James 1:17 says), will go a long way toward keeping you humble and, therefore, willing to obey God whether you are in seasons of plenty or want.

Lord, may I always maintain a spirit of gratitude toward You.
Indeed, You are the source of every good and perfect gift.
Everything belongs to You. May I never lose sight of that.

IS THE GOSPEL STILL CHANGING YOU?

"Behold, the days are coming, declares the LORD, when I will raise up for David a righteous Branch, and he shall reign as king and deal wisely, and shall execute justice and righteousness in the land."
JEREMIAH 23:5 ESV

Throughout Israel's history, the country was hot then cold toward God. One generation would be faithful and the next two would not. He brought judgments, plagues, and even death to express His displeasure, but even when they understood the message, they often fell away shortly thereafter.

In today's verse, the Lord is talking about a different plan. A better one. One that doesn't depend on humanity. He would raise up a righteous Branch who will reign as a king and deal wisely, executing justice and righteousness in the land. God was faithful to do so in the form of Jesus. And in His death, burial, and resurrection, He conquered sin and death, removing the sting of death to give the believer victory.

Does the simple yet profound Gospel message still move you to action? Is it still changing you? Would you put your life on the line for it? Are you passing it along to the next generation? Are you still praying for opportunities to share it with others?

Lord, the Gospel is the greatest story ever told.
May it always be a sweet sound in my ear
and the motivating force in my heart.

SPEAK UP

"GOD sent me to preach against both this Temple and city everything that's been reported to you. So do something about it! Change the way you're living, change your behavior. Listen obediently to the Message of your GOD. Maybe GOD will reconsider the disaster he has threatened."
JEREMIAH 26:12–13 MSG

The prophets and priests were at their wit's end with Jeremiah. He'd been warning them about impending judgment from God, and they weren't interested in what he had to say. In Jeremiah 26:11, they called for him to be put to death.

People who speak the truth in a situation in which others are going astray are rarely appreciated. Nobody wants to hear that he is wrong. But this was Jeremiah's calling and he had to be faithful. As a Christian, this is your calling as well. Matthew 5:14 (MSG) says, "You're here to be light, bringing out the God-colors in the world. God is not a secret to be kept. We're going public with this, as public as a city on a hill."

In what ways is your faith in Christ public? Do your neighbors know you are a Christian? How about your coworkers? Do you say the hard but truthful thing when the situation warrants it? How can you improve?

*Lord, I'm not as vocal as I should be. Prompt me
to speak up to testify to Your truth more often.
May I never shirk from my responsibility.*

STAY THE COURSE

This is what the LORD says: "When seventy years are completed for Babylon, I will come to you and fulfill my good promise to bring you back to this place. For I know the plans I have for you," declares the LORD, "plans to prosper you and not to harm you, plans to give you hope and a future."
JEREMIAH 29:10–11 NIV

You've probably seen Jeremiah 29:11 on plaques and memes. It's a wonderful promise, but it cannot be fully understood apart from verse 10. God's plan to prosper His people—who were in Babylonian captivity—would not occur for seventy years. That meant that most of the people who heard the Lord's promise from Jeremiah's lips would not be alive when it came to fruition.

In the meantime, they were supposed to build houses, plant gardens, get married, have children, and work for the well-being of the city. God doesn't always rescue His people from their circumstances right away. Sometimes He even chooses not to. Either way, He expects His people to remain faithful.

Are you in a season of waiting for God? Maybe you are waiting for a promotion or waiting for God to heal a loved one. Or maybe you are waiting for Him to solve your financial crisis. It's perfectly acceptable to ask God for whatever you need. But while you're waiting for an answer, stay the course.

Lord, give me patience to endure my hardship.

WORSHIP EXUBERANTLY

"They shall come and sing aloud on the height of Zion, and they shall be radiant over the goodness of the LORD, over the grain, the wine, and the oil, and over the young of the flock and the herd; their life shall be like a watered garden, and they shall languish no more."
JEREMIAH 31:12 ESV

Zion is one of the seven hills on which Jerusalem is built. At one point in Israel's history, David took it from the Jebusites (2 Samuel 5:6–7) and it became known as the city of David. In today's verse, Jeremiah is prophesizing about a time when God's people would come to the height of Zion and sing while exhibiting radiance over the goodness of the Lord.

You've probably seen the articles about the trend toward men not singing in worship services anymore. Many reasons are cited, including a simple lack of fervor in Christian men, a modern tradition of songs that are more feminine in nature, and the songs' keys being too high. Don't succumb to these excuses. Worship with all your heart and all your lungs.

The New Testament equates Zion to the church (1 Peter 2:1–6) and even to heaven (Revelation 14:1). How can the Christian man do anything but sing and exhibit radiance over what Jesus has done for him?

*Lord, may I always worship You
exuberantly, for You are worthy!*

FREEING CAPTIVES

*"Therefore, thus says the LORD: You have not obeyed me
by proclaiming liberty, every one to his brother and to his
neighbor; behold, I proclaim to you liberty to the sword,
to pestilence, and to famine, declares the LORD."*

JEREMIAH 34:17 ESV

God always hears the cries of the oppressed. In today's verse, He's upset with His people for oppressing their own. One commentary points out that as soon as Nebuchadnezzar withdrew his army, the Jews took back their own slaves. But they weren't allowed to hold anybody in servitude for more than seven years.

This all seems like a foreign concept to Christians today. Even so, today's passage is still applicable for you. People all around you are trapped in sin with no hope of redemption other than Jesus.

One Sabbath, Jesus went into a synagogue in Nazareth and read from Isaiah, saying this prophecy was indeed about Himself: "The Spirit of the Lord is upon me, because he has anointed me to proclaim good news to the poor. He has sent me to proclaim liberty to the captives" (Luke 4:18 ESV).

This is your mission as well. You have been anointed and commissioned. Proclaim freedom from sin in the name of Jesus to anybody who will listen.

---

*Lord, You've given me a clear mission: to set the captives
free by proclaiming the Gospel. Embolden me to do so.*

HANDWRITING SCRIPTURE

*Take a scroll [of parchment] for a book and write on it all the words I
have spoken to you against Israel and Judah and all the nations from
the day I spoke to you in the days of [King] Josiah until this day.*
JEREMIAH 36:2 AMPC

A scroll was a significant amount of parchment that was cut and
stitched together. Then it was rolled together in a "book." Today,
Jewish synagogues still use such scrolls. Writing everything the Lord told
Jeremiah on the scroll would have been done to preserve the message
for future generations.

Deuteronomy 17:18–20 records another time in Israel's history
when Moses instructed future kings to write a copy of the law by hand
in a book. And each king was to read from it all the days of his life so he'd
learn to fear the Lord.

Have you ever handwritten significant portions of the scriptures for the
same purpose? Or maybe to help you memorize it? Several recent studies
have indicated that copying information by hand makes the material
easier to remember. If you've never done so, consider picking a portion
of scripture—maybe one that will speak to an area you are struggling
in—then write it out by hand. You may experience a breakthrough.

*Lord, show me which portion of scripture to write
out by hand that I might learn to fear You better.*

SERVE THE KING

And Gedaliah son of Ahikam, the son of Shaphan, swore to them and
their men, saying, Do not be afraid to serve the Chaldeans; dwell in
[this] land and serve the king of Babylon, and it shall be well with you.
JEREMIAH 40:9 AMPC

Gedaliah, the newly appointed governor over the poorest of Judah who hadn't been taken into exile, made a promise of safety to them then said something similar to what God had promised those who were in exile: dwell in the land, serve the king, and all will be well with them.

Political leaders will come and go. You'll agree with some and disagree with others. However you feel about a political leader, you have work to do while that person is in office—and it's not all that different from what the people of Judah were to do. Continue to work, gather food, build houses, give away your children in marriage, work for the good of your city, and pass along the faith.

During the next election, vote your conscience. But don't allow the results to discourage you to the point that you cannot function or work for the good of your city and family. Politics and elections matter, no doubt. But the Christian is called to a life of faithfulness, regardless of political ebbs and flows.

Lord, temper me when I'm overzealous politically,
and remind me to stay faithful to what You've called me to do.

DARING SINNERS

"We will not listen to what you have said to us in the name of the Lord!
But we will do everything that we have said we would do. We will burn
special perfume to the queen of heaven and pour out drink gifts to her."
JEREMIAH 44:16–17 NLV

The men of Judah who spoke the above words were in a dangerous place spiritually—unwilling to listen to what God was telling them through Jeremiah.

"These daring sinners do not attempt excuses, but declare they will do that which is forbidden," Matthew Henry writes in his concise commentary. "Those who disobey God, commonly grow worse and worse, and the heart is more hardened by the deceitfulness of sin."

These men were so hardened that they were burning special perfume to the queen of heaven (the moon). These are people who knew better, but their consciences were becoming hardened.

Are you aware of a clear biblical mandate that you aren't obeying? Listen to Jeremiah's response (Jeremiah 44:23 NLV): "Because you have burned special perfume and have sinned against the Lord and have not obeyed the voice of the Lord or walked in His Laws or done what He said to do, this trouble [their land was laid to waste] has come upon you, as it has this day."

Repent before God's judgment arrives.

Lord, I confess my sin before You. I repent of doing
things my way. I will walk with You and obey You.

FORGET YOUR BIG PLANS

"So forget about making any big plans for yourself.
Things are going to get worse before they get better.
But don't worry. I'll keep you alive through the whole business."
JEREMIAH 45:5 MSG

Baruch, one of Jeremiah's scribes, apparently had plans that weren't in line with the way things were unfolding. Commentators suggest that maybe he had his sights set on advancing to a higher post or office, where he might accumulate wealth and the applause that comes with it. Since he wasn't getting his way, he complained to Jeremiah, so Jeremiah set him straight in today's verse.

What do you have your sights set on? Climbing the corporate ladder? Buying a bigger, nicer home? Moving to a nicer part of the city? Something else? What happens if God has other plans? Are you willing to ask Him? Are you willing to submit to His plans once He reveals them?

God promised to keep Baruch alive during the exile, but He also promised that things would get worse before they got better. God has a plan to take you through your times of lack. But you have to stay the course. Forget your big plans and seek Him instead. He'll be your guiding light when darkness seems to surround you.

Lord, I lay my big plans on the altar and offer
them as a sacrifice. I desire Your presence and
Your guidance more than I desire getting my way.

RESTORATION PLANS

"Yet I will restore the fortunes of Moab in
days to come," declares the LORD.
JEREMIAH 48:47 NIV

The Moabites were known for being gross idolaters. Numbers 25:1–3 (NIV) records a shameful time in Israel's history when her men engaged in sexual immorality with Moabite women who invited them to make sacrifices to their gods. They bowed down before these gods, making God furious.

In Jeremiah 48, we read all about how Moab faced destruction. And yet, at the end of that chapter, the Lord says He will restore the fortunes of Moab in days to come. It's a head-scratcher, for sure. They hadn't done anything to warrant such favor. And yet, God planned to restore them in some fashion.

Do you have an enemy who got what he had coming to him? Maybe he was caught with his hand in the cookie jar or maybe he's an atheist who continues to mock you for your faith in Christ. In Matthew 5:44–45 (NIV), Jesus said, "I tell you, love your enemies and pray for those who persecute you, that you may be children of your Father in heaven." Offer mercy and grace when none is warranted. As you do, you'll show the world that Jesus really can restore and transform anybody.

Lord, I want to be a shining example of Your
mercy and grace. I didn't deserve it. Nobody else
does either. But as I show it, may they see You.

ONE IN CHRIST JESUS

*"In those days and in that time, declares the LORD, the people
of Israel and the people of Judah shall come together, weeping
as they come, and they shall seek the LORD their God."*
JEREMIAH 50:4 ESV

I n today's reading, Jeremiah prophesies about the glorious homecoming of the Jews at the overthrow of Babylon. As the people of Judah return home, they will weep and seek the Lord their God. It's a beautiful picture of the various tribes coming together as one people.

In John 17:11 (ESV), Jesus prayed, "I am no longer in the world, but they [those whom the Father had given Him] are in the world, and I am coming to you. Holy Father, keep them in your name, which you have given me, that they may be one, even as we are one."

God's plan has always been for His people to come together and be one. Few Christians would dispute this. But it's much more difficult in practice. Do you know the name of the pastor of the church across the street from yours? When is the last time you served with believers who don't share your theology?

Don't wait for something catastrophic to occur before bonding with fellow believers. They are your brothers and sisters in Christ. Love them now.

*Father, may Your Body be one, even as You
are one with Jesus and the Holy Spirit.*

HE'LL NEVER FORSAKE YOU

*"For Israel and Judah have not been forsaken by their God,
the LORD of hosts, but the land of the Chaldeans is
full of guilt against the Holy One of Israel."*
JEREMIAH 51:5 ESV

As far as Israel and Judah had strayed from the Lord—and it was about as far as humanly possible—the Lord hadn't forsaken His people. He allowed them to face the consequences for their sin, no doubt, and it came at a great cost, including their freedom and many of their lives. But at just the right time, the Lord promised to "stir up the spirit of a destroyer against Babylon" (Jeremiah 51:1 ESV), Judah's oppressor.

Have you ever experienced severe consequences for your sin? Did it make you feel distant from God? Did you maybe even doubt His existence? Sadly, distance and doubt are the fruit of rebellion against Him. But He never intended for you to live this way perpetually, no matter what you've done. Hebrews 13:5 says He will never leave you nor forsake you.

No matter how distant you might feel from God right now, He stands at the ready to embrace you. Run toward Him and eat from the fattened calf He has prepared for you. Then resolve to never leave His table again.

*Lord, I've felt the distance between us, and I know it's all my fault.
Forgive me, Father. Welcome me back. Let me dine with You.*

WOULD YOU BE A GO-TO CHRISTIAN?

My eyes are blind with tears, my stomach in a knot.
My insides have turned to jelly over my people's fate.
LAMENTATIONS 2:11 MSG

Jeremiah is known as the "weeping prophet." Lamentations 1–2 will give you an idea why. Jerusalem lies in ruins. It was once teeming with people, now it is desolate. Her roads are said to be weepy, empty of pilgrims headed to feasts. Her city gates are deserted. And, Jeremiah says, "GOD abandoned his altar, walked away from his holy Temple and turned the fortifications over to the enemy" (Lamentations 2:7 MSG).

Imagine how you would react if the church in America were in shambles. Imagine if worship services were silent, pews were empty, and the doors were locked. And finally, imagine it was the church's fault. How could you not weep over such a scenario?

Even if all of this came to fruition, the church isn't a place, it's a people. And even in countries that outlaw Christianity, it flourishes because believers can still recite scripture and sing hymns from memory. They can still pray. And they still have the Holy Spirit.

Are you someone fellow Christians could count on if the faith were outlawed? How much scripture and how many hymns do you know by heart?

Lord, I want to know more scripture and hymns
by heart than I do anything else. Help me to
set a plan in place to make this a reality.

PEACE IN TIMES OF CRISIS

Because of the LORD's great love we are not consumed,
for his compassions never fail. They are new every
morning; great is your faithfulness.
LAMENTATIONS 3:22–23 NIV

As the prophet Jeremiah looked around the smoldering rubble of the once-great city of Jerusalem after the Babylonians had destroyed it, his heart was filled with crushing sorrow. He knew it didn't have to be this way, but he also knew that his own people's rebellion had brought the city to ruin.

Jeremiah had plenty to be grieved over. Yet in the midst of the horrors he sees around him, he's still able to thank God for His love, compassion, and faithfulness. Though his heart was shattered, the prophet still saw God for who He really is.

How would you respond if you were faced with a personal catastrophe—the loss of a loved one, a financial crisis, a divorce, or a bad medical diagnosis? It's not easy to keep praising and trusting God during very difficult times. But this is the key to persevering, to finding peace and comfort when it feels like your world is falling apart around you.

You can do it. Just start by opening your mouth and praising God for who He is and how good He is to you.

God of compassion, thank You that in the midst of the
craziness of this world, I can always count on Your
amazing, never-ending love and mercy.

WILLING TO SPEAK UP

"Nevertheless if you warn the righteous man that the righteous should not sin, and he does not sin, he shall surely live because he took warning; also you will have delivered your soul."
EZEKIEL 3:21 NKJV

We live in a time when many Christians are reluctant to speak up when they see a professing brother or sister in Christ drifting away from their faith and toward sin. The reason? They, like most people in our world today, don't want to be seen as "judgmental."

Today's verse, however, suggests that we who follow Jesus Christ are responsible for confronting fellow believers we see straying. This isn't just a nice suggestion either; it's a God-given responsibility.

God has designed the Christian faith so that we believers need one another, and not just so we can spend quality time with like-minded people. We are to hold one another accountable, even when doing so makes us feel uncomfortable. It often not easy to do that, but God calls us to love our brothers enough to tell them difficult truth.

The life direction of someone you care about could be changed. . .if you are willing to speak the truth to them. Are you willing to speak up?

Father in heaven, it's not easy to confront my brothers in You when I know they are headed in a wrong direction. Help me to always speak the truth in love, knowing that You want my brothers and me to hold one another accountable.

HURTING GOD?

"Then when they are exiled among the nations, they will remember me. They will recognize how hurt I am by their unfaithful hearts and lustful eyes that long for their idols."
Ezekiel 6:9 nlt

You probably already know that the Bible teaches that God can be angered at the sinful, rebellious actions of His people. That was true in Old Testament days, and it's true today. God does not change!

But did you ever consider that the God who created us and saved us can also feel emotional hurt when we stop following Him as He has called us to do? Today's verse tells us that God's heart was broken—that He was hurt—when His beloved people turned their backs on Him and chose other things to love.

Genesis 1:27 tells us that God created humans in His own image. That means several things, but it points to one single motivation on God's part: He wanted a created being that He could love and that could choose to love Him in return. And when that object of God's love chooses another, God feels heartbreak in much the same way a husband does when his wife chooses to leave him for another man.

God has given each of us a choice, and the right one is to choose to love Him with everything within us.

Loving heavenly Father, keep me mindful that You have created me and saved me so that I could enjoy a mutually loving relationship with You.

AN UNDIVIDED HEART

"I will give them an undivided heart and put a new
spirit in them; I will remove from them their
heart of stone and give them a heart of flesh."
EZEKIEL 11:19 NIV

If you've ever listened closely to the good minister's words during a wedding ceremony, you'd have to conclude that he's reminding both the bride and groom that they should be entering into their marriage with undivided hearts and undivided minds (the phrase "forsaking all others" comes to mind, doesn't it?).

Sadly, many a marriage has failed—or at least been badly damaged—because one or both of the spouses allowed their hearts and minds to become divided. That leads to no place good! Good marriages, on the other hand, happen when both parties love one another with undivided hearts.

Just as you would want your beloved to love you with an undivided heart, God wants you to love Him with an undivided heart, soul, and mind. That, Jesus taught, is God's greatest commandment.

This commandment isn't an easy one to follow on our own. In fact, it's impossible! But when you turned to Jesus for salvation, He put the Holy Spirit inside you, giving you the ability to love God and follow Him with a completely undivided heart.

Dear Father in heaven, I confess that I don't always
love You with a completely undivided heart and mind.
May Your Holy Spirit fill me more and more every day,
so that I may forsake all others and serve You completely.

TURNING FROM IDOLS

*"Therefore say to the people of Israel, 'This is what
the Sovereign LORD says: Repent! Turn from your
idols and renounce all your detestable practices!' "*

EZEKIEL 14:6 NIV

Christians today don't think or speak much about idols or idolatry. To most of us, that's Old Testament stuff. Besides, we don't worship actual, literal idols—like people in ancient times did.

Sounds like we have this idolatry thing licked, doesn't it?

In reality, though, idolatry is as much of a danger for the man of God today as it was in Old Testament times. We may not worship statues or other inanimate objects, but the world offers all kinds of temptations toward idolatry. That is why the apostle John warned, "Dear children, keep yourselves from idols" (1 John 5:21 NIV).

What kinds of things do you find yourself tempted to "worship"? Money? Position? Social standing? There's a long list of things that, in themselves, aren't sinful. But when we become fixated on them, when we start believing that they can bring us the satisfaction and security we should find in God alone, then they can become idols.

So be careful. Make sure you keep God alone as your object of loving worship.

*Father God, there are so many things in this world that could
become idols to me if I'm not careful. Help me to guard my
heart from any form of idolatry and to cleanse my life of
those things I've held in a higher place than I should.*

HUMBLE GIFTEDNESS

*"So you were adorned with gold and silver; your clothes were
of fine linen and costly fabric and embroidered cloth. Your food
was honey, olive oil and the finest flour. You became very beautiful
and rose to be a queen. And your fame spread among the nations
on account of your beauty, because the splendor I had given you
made your beauty perfect, declares the Sovereign LORD."*

EZEKIEL 16:13–14 NIV

T he words above were addressed to a very gifted, very blessed people: the people of God's chosen nation, Israel. It's a long list of blessings God had poured out on His people. But in the following twenty verses, God chided them because they had somehow forgotten that everything they had was a gift from Him.

This part of Israel's story should stand as a reminder for us today to heed these words of the apostle Paul: "What do you have that you did not receive? And if you did receive it, why do you boast as though you did not?" (1 Corinthians 4:7 NIV).

Confidence isn't a bad thing, and an awareness of our strengths and abilities can help us in our work and in our ministries. But those things must be tempered with an awareness that everything we have and everything we are comes from the hand of our generous heavenly Father.

*Generous Father, it's easy sometimes for me to forget that
everything good about me is because of who You are and not
because of anything about me. Please keep me humble.*

GOD'S HEART FOR SINNERS

*"Do I take any pleasure in the death of the wicked?
declares the Sovereign LORD. Rather, am I not pleased
when they turn from their ways and live?"*
EZEKIEL 18:23 NIV

Have you ever found yourself, if only a little bit, secretly condemning certain people—or groups of people—as irredeemable, as beyond God's reach?

Humanly speaking, it's hard to understand how God could save what we consider the vilest of sinners. But truthfully speaking, God has been doing just that from the very beginning. More times than we can possibly count, God has joyfully saved those many of us would consider beyond reach.

Right now, God is giving humans—even those we might think of as "unreachable"—time to turn to Him so that they can live eternally. This is how the apostle Peter put it: "The Lord is not slow in keeping his promise, as some understand slowness. Instead he is patient with you, not wanting anyone to perish, but everyone to come to repentance" (2 Peter 3:9 NIV).

So let's let God be God and pray that He does the same kind of miracles in others as He did in us when He saved us.

*Lord, I confess that I sometimes think of some people as beyond
Your reach. But You are a God who does miracles—one of the biggest
of which was when You saved me. May I never think of someone as
beyond redemption. Instead, remind me to pray for those who,
humanly speaking, seem hopelessly lost.*

BEING AN INTERCESSOR

"I looked for someone who might rebuild the wall of righteousness that guards the land. I searched for someone to stand in the gap in the wall so I wouldn't have to destroy the land, but I found no one."
EZEKIEL 22:30 NLT

A s we moved into the 2020s, more and more people stopped watching or reading the news, simply because they find it so discouraging and depressing. Maybe you're one of them!

For the Christian man though, the bad or discouraging news he sees about his community, his state, his nation, and the rest of the world give him the opportunity to engage in what is call *intercessory prayer*. That's the kind of prayer in which someone "stands in the gap" before God and pleads for His mercy and intervention on behalf of another—including friends, family members, government leadership. . .that list goes on and on.

God has given each of us an amazing responsibility—and privilege: to be men of prayer, men who come to Him and plead fervently with Him on behalf of others. Who can you begin praying for today?

Lord God, I believe that You are looking for men to stand in the gap and pray for their friends, their family members, for their communities, and their nation. Help me to be the man of prayer who can make a difference in this world and in the lives of people around me.

REMAINING FOCUSED

The word of the LORD came to me: "Son of man, with one blow I am about to take away from you the delight of your eyes. Yet do not lament or weep or shed any tears. Groan quietly; do not mourn for the dead."
EZEKIEL 24:15–17 NIV

Today's scripture presents a directive from God that, at first glance, looks insensitive, even harsh. Ezekiel was about to suffer the wrenching loss of his wife, and one would expect that he'd need to spend a period of time mourning her death.

But God instructed Ezekiel to skip all the traditional outward signs of grief and instead mourn the loss of his wife quietly and privately. God knew that Ezekiel would be grief-stricken, and He almost certainly comforted His prophet during his private time of praying and seeking His will.

It may be difficult to understand why God commanded Ezekiel to forgo the traditions of mourning. But we can take one important lesson from this passage: when we serve God, there may be times when tragedy can discourage us or steal our joy. When you suffer loss, you can and should mourn. But your heavenly Father will be right there with you through your season of mourning, strengthening you and encouraging you in what He's called you to do.

God of compassion, strengthen me and help me to remain focused on serving You, even when my heart is breaking.

A LAMENT FOR SINNERS

The word of the LORD came to me:
"Son of man, take up a lament concerning Tyre."
EZEKIEL 27:1–2 NIV

———————

In the prophet Ezekiel's day, Tyre was an amazing Mediterranean coastal city known throughout the region as a leader in shipping and commerce. But, as so often happens to the powerful and influential, Tyre became filled with pride and self-sufficiency (see Ezekiel 28), and God was about to judge the city.

Ezekiel was not happy about the eventual fate of Tyre, and neither was God. Our heavenly Father always prefers that people turn to Him so they can live (see Ezekiel 18), but eventually there comes a time when He must judge unrepentant sinners.

Have you ever looked down on sinners—especially people whose sin hurts others badly—hoping God would just drop the hammer? It's not a bad thing to want God to act on behalf of those who are mistreated, but at the same time, we should keep our hearts soft toward sinners.

We should feel grief over injustice in our world, but we should join Ezekiel—and God—in feeling a sense of sorrow over those who are lost and without direction from the God who loved us enough to save us.

Sovereign God, keep my heart soft toward those who need to hear the message You have for a fallen, sinful world. Give me the courage to say what You want me to say, when You want me to say it.

WHEN OTHERS SPEAK WELL OF YOU

Son of man, say to the ruler of Tyre, "This is what the Sovereign LORD
says: 'In the pride of your heart you say, "I am a god; I sit on the
throne of a god in the heart of the seas." But you are a mere mortal
and not a god, though you think you are as wise as a god.' "
EZEKIEL 28:2–3 NIV

The king of Tyre was a talented and wise leader who built the city into one of the most beautiful, richest cities in the world. Sadly, though, the king allowed what others had said about him to cause him to be filled with extreme pride. He actually began to see himself as a god and not a mere man.

One of the biggest potential dangers in accomplishing great things—as a leader, as a businessman, as a minister—is the praise people heap on you. If you're not careful, the things others say can go to your head and cause you to think more highly of yourself than you should.

That happened to the king of Tyre, and it can happen to us today too.

When people say good things about you, respond graciously. But it's always good to also remind them—and yourself—that God deserves all the credit for who you are and what you do.

Lord, please keep me humble by reminding me
often that everything I am and everything
I do is on account of Your generous love.

THE COST OF PRIDE

*"Therefore thus says the Lord GOD: 'Because you have increased
in height, and it set its top among the thick boughs, and its
heart was lifted up in its height, therefore I will deliver it into
the hand of the mighty one of the nations, and he shall surely
deal with it; I have driven it out for its wickedness.' "*
EZEKIEL 31:10–11 NKJV

Today's scripture verse is part of God's pronouncement of judgment on Egypt for its pride and arrogance. God was about to judge and humble Pharaoh using "the hand of the mighty one of the nations," meaning Nebuchadnezzar of Babylon.

The lesson of Ezekiel 31 for us today is this: when we live in humility before God, we put ourselves in a place where He can give us refuge and protection from our spiritual enemies. But when we live in pride, believing we can take care of ourselves without God's help, the enemy has free rein.

This is why wise King Solomon wrote, "Pride goes before destruction, a haughty spirit before a fall" (Proverbs 16:18 NIV). Strong words indeed!

If you want to live under God's mighty hand of protection, remember that you can't defeat your spiritual enemies on your own. Make sure to keep yourself humble and dependent on your mighty heavenly Father.

---

*God of Wisdom, forgive me when I think more of myself than
I should. Keep me humble by reminding me often that You
are my source of protection against my spiritual enemy.*

RIGHTLY MOTIVATED

*"So they come to you as people do, they sit before you as My people,
and they hear your words, but they do not do them; for with their
mouth they show much love, but their hearts pursue their own gain."*
EZEKIEL 33:31 NKJV

As a professing Christian man, you probably attend church services regularly. That's a good thing. You might also go to a weekly men's Bible study. That's also a positive. And you might even give till it hurts to your church or other ministry. God approves!

There are a lot of things we Christians do and say because we know God wants us to do them. But how often do we take the time to examine our real motives for the things we do? How often do we look into our hearts to make sure that the things we do and say are truly motivated out of true love for God and not out of what we consider proper religious duty?

God sees our hearts first, not our outward religious acts. That's why it's important to engage in some regular self-examination to ensure that we're not just doing the right things, but doing them for the right reasons.

*Lord, it's so easy to play the part of a Christian man in today's world.
But I know that You look at the heart first. Help me to examine my heart
often so that all I say and all I do is motivated by my true love for You.*

A NEW HEART

*"I will give you a new heart and put a new spirit in you;
I will remove from you your heart of stone and give you
a heart of flesh. And I will put my Spirit in you and move
you to follow my decrees and be careful to keep my laws."*
EZEKIEL 36:26–27 NIV

On December 3, 1967, a large team led by surgeon Christiaan Barnard performed the world's first human-to-human heart transplant. This groundbreaking medical accomplishment took place at Groote Schuur Hospital in Cape Town, South Africa.

As incredible as this medical event was, God did something even more amazing when He saved you. At the moment you humbled yourself before Him, He replaced your old, stony heart with a new, soft heart. When He performed that spiritual heart transplant, He changed you in every way; He actually made you a completely new person. That's what the apostle Paul referred to when he wrote, "If anyone is in Christ, the new creation has come: The old has gone, the new is here!" (2 Corinthians 5:17 NIV).

That's right! Through the work of His Holy Spirit, God gave you a new, undivided heart that can hear Him and respond to what He says to you. Not only that, your new heart will never fail and never need to be replaced again.

*Lord Jesus, I could never thank You enough for putting a new
heart in me and giving me new life. Thank You for giving me
Yourself in the form of a sacrifice for my sins and for sending
Your Holy Spirit so that I can be the man You've saved me to be.*

A GOD OF THE IMPOSSIBLE

He led me back and forth among them, and I saw a great many bones on the floor of the valley, bones that were very dry. He asked me, "Son of man, can these bones live?" I said, "Sovereign LORD, you alone know."

EZEKIEL 37:2–3 NIV

When God showed the prophet Ezekiel a vision of a valley filled with dry bones, He asked him a question that is of eternal importance to all of us today: "Can these bones live?"

Ezekiel knew that God was the God of the impossible, and his vision ended with a miracle: dry bones being covered with flesh and coming to life.

Ezekiel's vision speaks to us today. The apostle Paul wrote, "But because of his great love for us, God, who is rich in mercy, made us alive with Christ even when we were dead in transgressions" (Ephesians 2:4–5 NIV).

Today, God is showing each of us our own valleys filled with dry bones—the people in our lives who don't know Jesus—and asking us, "Can these bones live?"

The answer, of course, is *Yes, they can!* Our part in making that miracle happen is to speak the words of life we know as the Gospel of Jesus Christ.

Lord, I know that it's Your will for me to speak life to men and women who are spiritually dead. Please give me the faith and courage to speak the message of eternal life through Jesus Christ.

BE PREPARED

The man said to me, "Son of man, look carefully and listen closely and pay attention to everything I am going to show you, for that is why you have been brought here. Tell the people of Israel everything you see."
EZEKIEL 40:4 NIV

Have you ever been in a situation where you knew you needed to open your mouth and speak the Gospel message, only to freeze up at the moment of truth because you weren't sure what to say?

Moments like that are exactly why the apostle Peter wrote, "Always be prepared to give an answer to everyone who asks you to give the reason for the hope that you have" (1 Peter 3:15 NIV).

So how can you be prepared? Ezekiel gives us a good clue. Before an angel of the Lord showed the prophet a vision of the rebuilt temple in Jerusalem, he told Ezekiel to pay close attention to what he was about to hear and see—and then tell the people of Israel everything he had heard and seen.

Obviously, Ezekiel wouldn't have been able to tell the people about something he hadn't paid proper attention to when it happened. That's why we Christian men need to pay attention to what God teaches us in our times of prayer and Bible reading. When we do that, we'll be prepared when it's time to tell others about Jesus.

Lord Jesus, thank You for teaching me and preparing me to share my faith with those who need You.

ATTENTION TO DETAIL

And the LORD said to me, "Son of man, take careful notice.
Use your eyes and ears, and listen to everything I tell you about
the regulations concerning the LORD's Temple. Take careful note
of the procedures for using the Temple's entrances and exits."
EZEKIEL 44:5 NLT

If you've read some of the listings on one of those online job sites, you may have noticed that one of the qualifications listed is "attention to detail." That usually means it's a job that requires the worker to pay close attention to "the little things."

God gave Ezekiel some detailed instructions for the Jewish priesthood when the Jews returned to Jerusalem after the Babylonian Exile. That's why He told the prophet, "take careful notice."

There may be times in your walk with the Lord when He seems to be telling you, "Pay close attention. This is very important!" And if God says it's important, you'd do well to listen closely!

When you follow your Bible reading with a time of prayer, it's a good idea to make sure you don't just talk to God. Make sure you pay close attention to what He may be saying about what you've just read.

Lord God, You have so much to show me and teach me. Help me to pay
close attention to all You show me and tell me so that I can grow
in my knowledge of You and so I can live as You want me to live.

HONESTY

"Use only honest weights and scales and honest measures, both dry and liquid. The homer will be your standard unit for measuring volume. The ephah and the bath will each measure one-tenth of a homer. The standard unit for weight will be the silver shekel. One shekel will consist of twenty gerahs, and sixty shekels will be equal to one mina."
EZEKIEL 45:10–12 NLT

The Bible makes a big deal about honesty in every part of our lives, including in our work and business practices. Even most non-Christian businessmen understand that honesty is the best policy. After all, having a reputation for shady dealings, especially in the internet age, can quickly lead to business failure.

Of course, honesty is all the more important for the man who follows Christ, simply because God calls us to be honest in every way.

How important is honesty to you? Do you always do your best to speak truthfully? Do you always make sure that you don't waste your company's time when you're on the clock at work? Do you always treat business clients honestly and truthfully?

You demonstrate your love for God—and for your neighbor—when you practice integrity and honesty in every area of your life.

Righteous Father, I know You want me to be honest with people in all areas of life, including business, work, and finances. Help me always to treat people fairly and justly, and please show me where I need to do better in this area.

LIVING WATERS

He asked me, "Have you been watching, son of man?" Then he
led me back along the riverbank. When I returned, I was surprised
by the sight of many trees growing on both sides of the river.
Then he said to me, "This river flows east through the desert into
the valley of the Dead Sea. The waters of this stream will
make the salty waters of the Dead Sea fresh and pure."
Ezekiel 47:6–8 nlt

A spring creek is a stream that originates from an underground spring that produces enough water to keep the stream flowing at a consistent level. One well-known spring creek in the United States is the Metolius River in central Oregon, which originates at its headwaters at Metolius Springs.

A spring creek is a good illustration of what God wants us to be to the world around us. It brings to mind these words from Jesus: "Whoever believes in me, as Scripture has said, rivers of living water will flow from within them" (John 7:38 niv).

God calls us to be a source of life-giving water to a world around us, a source of blessing to those who need it. So don't keep it inside you. Let it flow into you from above and then out to a thirsty, needy world.

Lord Jesus, You are my source of living water. I want that
water to flow from me into the world around me. Show me
how I can bless others with what You've given me.

OUR SOURCE OF UNDERSTANDING

Daniel replied, "No wise man, enchanter, magician or
diviner can explain to the king the mystery he has asked
about, but there is a God in heaven who reveals mysteries."
DANIEL 2:27–28 NIV

Today's scripture contains the words of the Old Testament prophet Daniel to Babylonian King Nebuchadnezzar, who had asked him to interpret a troubling dream he'd had. The king had already turned to his astrologers and magicians, but they couldn't help him. So, he turned to the man of God, Daniel.

With God's help, Daniel solved the mystery of the king's dream. But first he stated some wisdom that is still important to us today. God had given Nebuchadnezzar his dream, and only God could explain what it meant—not wise men, not enchanters, not magicians, and not diviners.

Daniel interpreted the king's dream. But he could only do it because he was in constant communication with his Father in heaven. So when he spoke the interpretation, he was speaking God's own message to the king.

It's sometimes tempting to turn to sources of worldly wisdom when we're desperate for answers. But we should always trust God and His written Word when we need wisdom and understanding.

Lord God, You are the ultimate source of wisdom and understanding.
Through Your Holy Spirit, You help me to understand what
otherwise would only be a mystery. Thank You for giving me
the wisdom and understanding I need to live for You.

EVEN IF HE DOESN'T. . .

Shadrach, Meshach, and Abednego replied, "O Nebuchadnezzar, we do not need to defend ourselves before you. If we are thrown into the blazing furnace, the God whom we serve is able to save us. He will rescue us from your power, Your Majesty. But even if he doesn't, we want to make it clear to you, Your Majesty, that we will never serve your gods or worship the gold statue you have set up."
DANIEL 3:16–18 NLT

Have you ever prayed for God to get you out of what seemed like an unsolvable pickle, only to hear nothing from Him but silence? Sometimes, we think that if we just pray about a certain pressing situation, He'll come through for us, and promptly. But God doesn't always work that way. In fact, sometimes He leaves us in a tough situation. . .and for reasons only He understands.

How do you respond when you don't immediately receive the deliverance you've prayed for? You won't go wrong when you take the same approach Shadrach, Meshach, and Abednego took—remain steadfast in your relationship with God and refuse to compromise as you wait for answers.

Glorious Father, I've learned that there will be times in life when You don't deliver me from my problems. Though my flesh may want to cry "It's not fair!" I want You to strengthen me and give me courage to worship You and You alone, especially when You allow me to suffer.

RESPONDING TO A CRISIS

*Now when Daniel knew that the writing was signed, he went home.
And in his upper room, with his windows open toward Jerusalem,
he knelt down on his knees three times that day, and prayed and
gave thanks before his God, as was his custom since early days.*

DANIEL 6:10 NKJV

D aniel knew his life was on the line. King Darius of Persia had issued a decree stating that anyone who prayed to anyone but the king would be put to death by being fed to lions. Daniel was in deep trouble, so he did the only thing he could: he prayed.

Daniel was a man of prayer. He prayed three times a day, every day. And as he prayed that particular day, he *gave thanks to God*. That's right! With his life hanging in the balance, he thanked God!

When we're in the midst of difficult times, it's easy to forget to speak words of thanks to God. But that should be our exact response when life gets tough. No matter how difficult your situation may be, you can always speak words of gratitude to your Father in heaven.

God hears those prayers. . .and He responds to them too.

---

*Loving Father, sometimes I forget that You are my source
of encouragement and strength when it seems like my
world is coming apart. Help me to come to You regularly and
faithfully in prayer, in good times and tough times alike.*

WHEN YOU RECEIVE A PROMISE

I, Daniel, learned from reading the word of the LORD, as revealed to Jeremiah the prophet, that Jerusalem must lie desolate for seventy years. So I turned to the Lord God and pleaded with him in prayer and fasting.

DANIEL 9:2–3 NLT

In yesterday's scripture verse, you saw that the prophet Daniel was a devoted man of prayer. In today's passage, you'll see that he was also devoted to the Word of God.

Daniel, who lived in Babylon during the Babylonian Exile, had read the inspired writings of the prophet Jeremiah, and he learned that the Jewish people's seventy years of captivity would end and that they would return to their home in Jerusalem.

That had to be great news to the prophet, and you might think he would plan some kind of celebration. But instead, Daniel took the time to go to God with prayers of confession and pleas for His mercy and blessing on His people.

When you receive a promise straight from God's written Word, how do you respond? Daniel's example should encourage you to seek God all the more in prayer, knowing that He has something good for you. When you do that, you prepare your heart to receive His very best.

Father in heaven, thank You for encouraging me and strengthening me in my prayer life through Your written Word. May I never neglect reading my Bible and applying it to my prayers.

GREATLY BELOVED

*Then again, the one having the likeness of a man touched me
and strengthened me. And he said, "O man greatly beloved,
fear not! Peace be to you; be strong, yes, be strong!"*
DANIEL 10:18–19 NKJV

We earthly fathers who want to raise confident, courageous children can take a huge step toward making that a reality when we make sure we let our children know one thing: they are genuinely loved.

That's true for children, and it was true of a certain Old Testament prophet.

God encouraged Daniel toward courage by starting with the words, "O man greatly beloved." And because he embraced his value in the eyes of God, Daniel went on to accomplish some amazing things.

The apostle Paul gave New Testament voice to the truth of God's love for us when he wrote, "But because of his great love for us, God, who is rich in mercy, made us alive with Christ even when we were dead in transgressions—it is by grace you have been saved" (Ephesians 2:4–5 NIV).

As a Christian, you can think of yourself as many things in God's eyes: saved, redeemed, blessed, set aside. . .it's a long list you can find in the pages of scripture. Don't forget, though, that you are all those things and more because you are, above all, *greatly beloved*.

---

*Loving God, today's verse tells me that I can take courage
and strength just in knowing that You love me so deeply.*

PUTTING YOUR PAST BEHIND YOU

"When that day comes," says the LORD, "you will call me 'my husband' instead of 'my master.' O Israel, I will wipe the many names of Baal from your lips, and you will never mention them again."
HOSEA 2:16–17 NLT

The main theme of the book of Hosea is God's faithfulness to an unfaithful people of Israel, who had chosen the idol Baal over the God who had loved them and fulfilled His every promise to them. Though God would judge these people, He would also bring them back to Himself.

Indeed, God lovingly worked to bring reconciliation, to steer the people back to fellowship with Himself.

And He does the very same thing with us today.

You may have gone through a time in your walk with the Lord when you strayed from Him. Or maybe you lived a life of high sin before you knew Him. The good news is that He worked to bring about restoration and forgiveness. But here's some more good news: He will never bring up your past to shame you or cause you to feel insecure in His love.

You really can put your past life of rebellion and idolatry behind you for good. After all, that is exactly what God has done for you.

Thank You, Lord, for loving me and for saving me from my past sinful thoughts and actions. Help me to remember that You've cleansed me and that You've chosen to forget that part of my life.

THE GOD WHO RESTORES

"Come, let us return to the LORD. He has torn us to pieces; now he will heal us. He has injured us; now he will bandage our wounds. In just a short time he will restore us, so that we may live in his presence."

HOSEA 6:1–2 NLT

Good parents know that as important as discipline is to bringing up their children, restoration is also essential. *Without* restoration, the parent/child relationship can remain strained, even to the point of fracturing over time. *With* restoration, the child can know that the parent meted out the discipline out of real love and not just anger.

Our Father in heaven isn't just a good Father—He's the *perfect* Father. When He disciplines us, it's out of His perfect love for us. And when that time of discipline has passed, He invites us back into His presence—where we can know we are fully restored, forgiven, and loved.

Are you going through a time of discipline right now? You can endure it, knowing that God will restore you into full loving fellowship with Himself. He loves you too much to do anything different.

Lord, like any loving father, You've disciplined me in the past when I've strayed from Your ways. But when You've done that, You've also reached down to me and restored me so that I could again know the joy of Your presence. Thank You!

HIS WAYS ARE RIGHT

Who is wise? Let him understand these things. Who is prudent?
Let him know them. For the ways of the LORD are right;
the righteous walk in them, but transgressors stumble in them.
HOSEA 14:9 NKJV

It has been said that "common sense isn't so common today." The same thing can be said of wisdom, can't it? In the age of Twitter and other social media, people are more often drawn to the witty aphorism than they are to true words of wisdom.

Today's verse points us to true wisdom, and it's in the ways and words of our Father in heaven. It's an amplification of these words from Solomon: "The fear of the LORD is the beginning of wisdom, and knowledge of the Holy One is understanding" (Proverbs 9:10 NIV).

In today's world, we can turn to many sources for wisdom. But it's worldly wisdom, and it's almost always either incomplete or completely wrong. That's why God's words to Hosea are as important to us today as they were when they were written. God is our source of complete wisdom, and His ways are the best ways for us to follow, no matter what the world says.

God of wisdom, I live in a time when it seems as though everyone
lives by their own standards and values. The sad results speak
for themselves. Thank You for showing me Your ways
and for empowering me to walk in them daily.

RENDING YOUR HEART

Rend your heart and not your garments. Return to the LORD
your God, for he is gracious and compassionate, slow to anger
and abounding in love, and he relents from sending calamity.
JOEL 2:13 NIV

Back in biblical times, God's people sometimes tore their garments as a demonstration of grief or mourning—sometimes over their own sin. But in today's verse, God tells His people that they showed true brokenness and remorse—and their need for God's grace and mercy—when they rent their own hearts and not just their clothes.

If we're not careful, we Christian men can get too caught up in outward expressions of our need for God. There's nothing necessarily wrong with those expressions, but we must always remember that God looks at what's going on in our hearts first.

What do you do when you know you need God's mercy, forgiveness, and compassion? A good place to start is talking with Him about it. That means confessing your sins, repenting, and asking for the grace you need to change your behavior. After that, regularly praying and studying God's Word will strengthen you in heart and mind so that you can live as He calls the man of God to live.

Gracious Father, You have shown me many times over that You
are a compassionate, merciful God who loves me. May that part
of You help me to change my heart first then change whatever
behavior, speech, or thinking You want to change in me.

HELD TO A HIGHER STANDARD

Hear this word, people of Israel, the word the LORD has spoken against you—against the whole family I brought up out of Egypt: "You only have I chosen of all the families of the earth; therefore I will punish you for all your sins."

AMOS 3:1–2 NIV

A certain high school football coach was known for being a strict disciplinarian who held his players to high standards of behavior on and off the field. But when his own son was old enough to play for him, it seemed like he was stricter on the boy than on the other players.

The father/coach told his son/player early, "Son, it might seem like I'm harder on you than I am on the other players. But it has to be that way. You're not just one of my players—you're my son, and I want the very best for you."

Our heavenly Father is like that with us, isn't He? The Bible teaches that God disciplines His own people as an earthly father disciplines his children (see Hebrews 12:4–11). But this isn't God being hard on us just because He can. It's because He loves us and holds us to the standards He's set for His own family.

Father in heaven, I don't enjoy it when You discipline me for my sins. But I thank You for doing just that, for it shows me that You have chosen to love me as one of Your very own.

PRAYER CHANGES SITUATIONS

*This is what the Sovereign LORD showed me: The Sovereign LORD
was calling for judgment by fire; it dried up the great deep and
devoured the land. Then I cried out, "Sovereign LORD, I beg you, stop!
How can Jacob survive? He is so small!" So the LORD relented.*

AMOS 7:4–6 NIV

———◆———

Just imagine what was going through Amos's mind when God revealed to
him that He was about to judge the nation of Israel for its rebellion—in
fact, this judgment had already begun. Amos loved his nation and its people,
and his heart must have been breaking. So, in addition to everything else
God had given him to do, Amos got on his knees and pleaded on behalf of
Israel. In response to Amos's prayers, "the LORD relented."

This is a remarkable example of prayer changing situations. When
Amos pleaded with God, He showed mercy to the land of Israel.

Do you know of a situation that needs to be changed? You never know
how God will respond if you spend some time praying over that matter.
So go to God and offer Him specific prayers about your situation. Then
just wait for Him to respond!

*Righteous God, thank You that You hear my prayers and that You love
showing mercy to me and those I love in answer to those prayers. Make
me a man of prayer so that I may make a difference in the world.*

ENDURANCE IN THE DEPTHS

"Those who cling to worthless idols
turn away from God's love for them."
JONAH 2:8 NIV

On his way down to the depths of the Mediterranean, Jonah's prayer reveals an important personal discovery: when people love anything more than God, they miss God's love in everything.

Jonah nearly missed the life-changing impact of God's love in his everyday moments because he marginalized what God had asked him to do. He knew God's love would transform a group of people he couldn't tolerate (the citizens of Nineveh), so when God asked him to talk to them, he went the opposite direction.

But as he endured the depths of the sea, Jonah learned the suffocating truth that idolatry always intensifies isolation—isolation from the love of a God whose everyday interventions make life meaningful. Jonah's self-love and respect for his own ideas led him into a boatload of panic. Clinging to worthless idols always does.

Enduring in the depths of your overpowering experiences can teach you too. It can help you refocus your thoughts and energies on loving the people God sends into your life, so that you don't "turn away from God's love."

Father, help me cling to Your words and to love people,
so that I can turn toward, not away from, Your love.

ENDURING HUMILITY

He has shown you, O mortal, what is good.
And what does the LORD require of you? To act justly
and to love mercy and to walk humbly with your God.
MICAH 6:8 NIV

Charles Shulz's first *Peanuts* cartoon strip was published on this day in 1950. Although Shulz never liked the name of the strip, his humorous depictions of the humble (and often humbled) Charlie Brown continue to resonate with readers.

When the prophet Micah summarizes what God desires from those who follow Him, he mentions three specific behaviors: doing the right thing in every business and personal transaction, extending mercy to those who need it, and demonstrating humility. Perhaps Micah's deep compassion for the broken and disenfranchised (Micah 4:6) made it easy for him to mention the importance of humility.

In a media-saturated culture where screenagers reverence their rights, humility is often replaced with a worldview philosophers call "meism." Like the *Peanuts* cartoons that often opposed ego-centrism, Micah reminds us that God's directives are dishonored in a worldview in which humility itself has been humbled to the point of insignificance.

There will likely be at least one moment today when you will have to choose between your rights and humility, between what benefits you and what blesses another person. When that moment appears, remember Micah's counsel that our self-promoting sacrifices (6:6–7) mean little to God—and practice enduring humility.

Father, help me to walk humbly with You and to
pursue another's benefit more than my own.

ENDURING OBSERVATIONS

*"Look at the nations and watch—and be utterly amazed.
For I am going to do something in your days that
you would not believe, even if you were told."*
HABAKKUK 1:5 NIV

Marshall McLuhan's maxim, "the medium is the message," asserts that the mediums we expose ourselves to influence how we experience life. The internet medium's instant access to any information anywhere, for instance, has changed how societies process patience and contentment.

Habakkuk's counsel to "look at" and "watch" what God is doing so that believers can enjoy the wonder in being "utterly amazed" deepens McLuhan's insight.

Habakkuk's prophecy explains how God will use an unlikely nation to accomplish His purposes. This certainly "amazed" anyone who took the time to observe what God was doing. This is often God's way: to use the unlikely and the unexpected so that His followers can find Him, as John Fischer put it, even where they least expect Him.

What are you hoping to spend your free time looking at and observing today? Spend time looking at what God is doing in the world through this devotional book, ministry blogs, and in your life, and you'll find yourself "utterly amazed." Perhaps you'll experience God, as Nahum wrote, surrounding you like castle walls in the day of distress (1:7), or maybe you'll find yourself so overwhelmed by Him that you can't help but celebrate with Habakkuk "on the heights" (3:19).

Father, amaze me!

ENDURING HUNGERS

"Give careful thought. . . .
From this day on I will bless you."
HAGGAI 2:18–19 NIV

A lovesick student once told his teacher, "At breakfast, I can't eat because I'm thinking about her. At lunch I can't eat because I'm thinking about her. At dinner I can't eat because I'm thinking about her. Then I can't sleep at night. . ."

The teacher interrupted, "Let me guess, because you're thinking about her." The student looked puzzled.

"No," he said. "I can't sleep because I'm *so* hungry."

Twice the prophet Haggai wrote, "Give careful thought" (2:15, 18). Although he wasn't writing about appetite or lovesickness, he repeated his admonition because careful thought helps us examine our hidden hungers.

Haggai's first admonition prompted God's people to consider how unprofitable life was when their first thoughts were about improving their houses, while God's didn't even have permits (2:15). In the second admonition, God reminded them that when they began putting Him first, He honored them—He increased their earnings and pleasures (2:19).

In distracted cultures, it's difficult to "give careful thought." The time required doesn't seem as immediately satisfying as gratifying other hungers like hobbies and amusements. But when believers think carefully about the good God does for those who work on His kingdom first, they do more than avoid the unprofitable hours Haggai describes; they honor God—and He so often returns the favor.

Father, help me examine my hidden hungers
so that I can work first on Your place in my heart.

ENDURING LOVE

*Therefore tell the people: This is what the LORD Almighty
says: "Return to me," declares the LORD Almighty,
"and I will return to you," says the LORD Almighty.*
ZECHARIAH 1:3 NIV

Before Benny Hester's song "When God Ran" became the number six best-selling song in Christian music history, people struggled with the title. After all, God doesn't run from anyone or anything. But as listeners heard the first few lines, they recognized the title's profound truth—God *does* run.

Zechariah writes about God's desire to "return" to those who have chosen to return to Him. Like the forgiving father who "runs" to greet a prodigal son returning home after a period of rebellion (Luke 15:11–32), God celebrates those who return to Him. When studied alongside today's reading in Zechariah, it's obvious that the parable and the prophecy show that Hester's song title got it right—God doesn't wait until you crawl back to Him, He runs to meet you along the way.

Maybe the song "When God Ran" is one of the longest-running songs in Christian music history because it reminds listeners of one of scripture's most compelling and comforting truths—no matter where you've been or what you've done, God not only wants to welcome those who return to Him. . .He's running!

*Father, no matter how distracted I
get today, help me return to You.*

ENDURING MOTIVES

"Ask all the people of the land and the priests, 'When you fasted and mourned in the fifth and seventh months for the past seventy years, was it really for me that you fasted?' "

ZECHARIAH 7:5 NIV

On this day in 1926, Babe Ruth hit a World Series record three home runs in a single game.

Ruth was famous for saying, "The way a team plays as a whole determines its success. You may have the greatest bunch of individual stars in the world, but if they don't play together, the club won't be worth a dime." Ruth reminded everyone that the reasons teammates show up to play are important—that motives matter.

Before the game, the Sultan of Swat sent two baseballs and a note to a young John Sylvester, who was confined to a hospital bed. The note read, "I'll knock a homer for you." Ruth's critics said he sent the note as a publicity stunt, but John Sylvester never believed that. He recovered, served his country, and became a company president. The story demonstrates that although it's difficult to evaluate another man's motives, it's fairly easy to examine your own.

Zechariah's prophecy asked God's people, "was it really for me. . . ?" His question reminds readers that following Him involves a moment-by-moment assessment of motives. How would you answer the question God asked in Zechariah's prophecy?

Father, use Zechariah's prophecy to remind me that motives matter.

ENDURING COMPASSION

"I will strengthen Judah and save Israel: I will restore them because of my compassion. It will be as though I had never rejected them, for I am the LORD their God, who will hear their cries."

ZECHARIAH 10:6 NLT

Jim Elliot once wrote, "Most laws condemn the soul and pronounce sentence. The result of the law of my God is perfect. It condemns but forgives. It restores—*more than abundantly*—what it takes away."

Elliot's words were influenced by readings like today's. Zechariah reminded God's people that after receiving His forgiveness, they would live as though He had never rejected them. God knew His people needed this reminder. They still do. Believers live, too often, like their repentance only produces forgiveness, rather than restoration.

In today's reading, Zechariah also performs a linguistic miracle. Five hundred years before Jesus dies, Zechariah prophesies about the one who was "pierced" (12:10), a prophecy fulfilled when Jesus was "pierced" on the cross (John 19:31–37). But even this prophetic miracle dims in comparison to the kind of forgiveness Jesus' sacrifice offers. His death not only frees people from the death they deserve, His sacrifice restores them "more than abundantly." That is the enduring character in God's generous compassion. As Zechariah put it earlier, "Return. . .I will restore twice as much to you" (9:12 NIV).

Father, help me to live like a son who has been not just forgiven but also restored!

ENDURING EFFORT

"You say, 'It's too hard to serve the LORD,' and you turn up
your noses at my commands. . . . Think of it! Animals that
are stolen and crippled and sick are being presented as
offerings! Should I accept from you such offerings as these?"
MALACHI 1:13 NLT

It's just for church!" Have you ever heard a musician, small group leader, or Sunday school teacher say this?

Since God doesn't directly challenge your offerings or good works, it's easy to let your efforts slide. It's easy to accept the idea that God wouldn't want to make serving Him more difficult than it needs to be. But that's not how God made humanity. He made people to enjoy giving their best.

Athletes know their best games are the ones where they "left it all on the field." Musicians know their best performances are the ones in which they were fully engaged. Whenever believers give less effort, they disengage from the way they were designed and dishonor the One who made them.

Whenever you say, "It's just for church," and give God less than your best, He offers a challenge similar to the one He proposed in Malachi: " 'Test me in this,' says the LORD Almighty, 'and see if I will not throw open the floodgates of heaven and pour out so much blessing that there will not be room enough to store it' " (3:10 NIV).

Father, help me leave it all on the field for You today!

ENDURING PRODUCTIVITY

"Produce fruit in keeping with repentance. And do not think you can say to yourselves, 'We have Abraham as our father.' I tell you that out of these stones God can raise up children for Abraham."

MATTHEW 3:8–9 NIV

John the Baptist called out the religious leaders of his day. Dressed in camel's hair and a leather belt, he reminded them that God doesn't need leaders who take pride in their position as God's children. After all, God can "raise up children" from rocks if He wants to.

Do you ever descend into this way of thinking? You start believing you're special because you had something to do with becoming a believer? John reminds his readers that their work is to "produce fruit in keeping with repentance," rather than to luxuriate in the fruits of repentance.

What fruit is John describing? Paul summarizes it this way: "But the fruit of the Spirit is love, joy, peace, forbearance, kindness, goodness, faithfulness, gentleness and self-control" (Galatians 5:22–23 NIV). It's helpful to ask at lunch every day, "What fruit is God producing in and through my life?" If you spend time looking for evidence of love, joy, etc., you'll find it, and the Spirit will also use your thoughtfulness to show you other fruit to work on. Maybe self-control? Maybe gentleness?

Father, help me join the work of Your Spirit
in producing fruit in keeping with repentance.

ENDURING RICHES

"Blessed are the poor in spirit,
for theirs is the kingdom of heaven."
MATTHEW 5:3 NIV

I'm not one who's got it all in place/ Tellin' you what you should do, no/ I'm just one old hungry beggar/ Showin' you where I found food" (John Fischer, "Beggar").

When cultures celebrate personal achievement more than personal piety, Jesus gets reduced to a human celebrity. But when even unbelieving cultures value humility, Jesus becomes one of their heroes.

For the early disciples, Jesus' words were often startling. How could the "poor" be blessed? Many of them were following Him hoping this miracle-working "king" would make them rich. "Blessed are the poor" certainly wasn't the preferred branding of most Jerusalem PR firms in His day.

Today's reading showcases Jesus' humility: "If anyone slaps you on the right cheek, turn to them the other cheek also. And if anyone wants to sue you and take your shirt, hand over your coat as well" (5:39–40 NIV); "Be careful not to practice your righteousness in front of others to be seen by them. If you do, you will have no reward from your Father in heaven" (6:1 NIV); "Do not judge, or you too will be judged" (7:1). The "poor in spirit" choose to champion these truths.

Despite popular wisdom, there is a sense in which "beggars" can be "choosers."

Father, help me resist believing I've got it all together so that, rather than preaching at people, I can show them where to find food.

REFEREEING RIGHTEOUSNESS

Jesus said, "It is not the healthy who need a doctor, but the sick.
But go and learn what this means: 'I desire mercy, not sacrifice.'
For I have not come to call the righteous, but sinners."

MATTHEW 9:12–13 NIV

J esus ate with people who used the tax system of the time to steal money, often condemning families to poverty and ruining lives.

When asked why He would do this, Jesus reminded His questioners that He didn't come to referee the righteous. He came to redirect sinners and heal the hurting.

Jesus constantly confronted pious people, pointing out the lack of compassion in their arduous rules:

- requiring the *priests* to deal with the rule-breaking healing of the leper (8:1–4),
- telling the faithless in *Israel* that a centurion had more faith than they did (8:13), and
- confronting the *teachers of the law* with their lack of mercy when He healed a paralyzed man (9:3).
- Jesus' friendship with the despised and rejected irritated and infuriated the *pharisees* (9:11–13). Why sip lattes with losers?

Like these religious evangelists, God's people often spend more time refereeing righteousness than referring the lost to Jesus. They think it's wiser to focus on people who further their comforts, so they invite the socially righteous to dinner. Jesus didn't think this way.

Jesus ate with the marginalized because He knew His sacrifice could move the margins.

Your sacrifice of comfort and time can do the same.

Father, help me spend more time referring than refereeing.

ENDURING QUESTIONS

"Are you the Messiah we've been expecting,
or should we keep looking for someone else?"
MATTHEW 11:2–3 NLT

A common question in small groups or after church services is "Why doesn't God share more information with us?"

John the Baptist certainly felt this confusion. Jesus said that no human being was "greater than John the Baptist" (Matthew 11:11 NLT), but John still wasn't given the inside information he wanted. Sitting in prison, he sent his disciples to ask Jesus if He was the Messiah.

When Jesus walked in human flesh, He sometimes knew the inside information and other times He didn't. He knew the past life of the woman at the well (John 4:16–19) but didn't know when the "the son of man" would come (Matthew 24:36). Why? Jesus was fully God but chose to be "born as a human being" and submit Himself to the Father's will, which included not having all the information (Philippians 2:7 NLT).

Like John, on earth you serve the Father's purposes. He is using your life to teach the angels who "are eagerly watching these things happen" (1 Peter 1:12 NLT), and He is showing you that your deepest meaning comes from a faith that embraces "the evidence of things we cannot see" (Hebrews 11:1 NLT), a faith that finds its greatest joy somewhere between the questions and the answers.

Father, help me to trust that You both
have and are the answer I need.

ENDURING MERCY

"If you had known what these words mean, 'I desire mercy, not sacrifice,' you would not have condemned the innocent."
MATTHEW 12:7 NIV

On this day in 2006, Muhammad Yunus of Bangladesh earned a Nobel Peace Prize for providing loans to encourage economic development among the world's poor.

Like him, Jesus labored to help the underprivileged. He explained that hungry individuals, like His disciples (Matthew 12:1–2), and the disenfranchised, like the man with the withered hand (12:9–13), should experience mercy rather than condemnation. Jesus pointed out that precedent had already been established when David fed his soldiers (12:3–6) and the priests ate the food at the temple (12:5).

Jesus also documents how the religious leaders often misunderstood the scriptures and sacred traditions, which led to their judgmental attitudes and behaviors. He confronted their critical spirit, making it clear that God desires "mercy, not sacrifice."

Like the religious leaders Matthew writes about, you are profoundly influenced by the cultures and traditions you grew up in. They deeply impact the amount of mercy you extend. It's wise to examine where your values come from and how they align with scripture. Otherwise, you can end up following your church's traditions instead of Jesus.

Even though you may never receive a peace prize for helping the poor, remember that God is more impressed when you prize the peace that mercy brings.

Father, show me where my values truly come from so that I might live out the mercy You desire.

ENDURING NEEDS

He withdrew by boat privately to a solitary place. Hearing of this,
the crowds followed him on foot from the towns.
MATTHEW 14:13 NIV

The moments that most test your compassion for others are the moments you most need the compassion of others.

After John the Baptist's death, Jesus "withdrew." He felt sorrow both as a human and as John's creator. But Jesus didn't stay in hiding. Matthew's description reveals not only Jesus' compassion for John; it reveals a method for dealing with grief.

Although Jesus intended to spend time in a "solitary place," His empathy interrupted His intent. When He stepped out of the boat, hurting and alone, a crowd came to Him. Instead of following His culture's grieving process and meeting His own needs, Jesus had "compassion on them and healed their sick" (Matthew 14:14).

This rare form of empathy takes profound inner strength—strength energized not by a desire to meet the expectations of others, but by a desire to meet their needs. Jesus' compassion caused Him to step out of His boat into a crowd of requests. He turned grief into grace.

The next time you face sorrow, consider mowing a neighbor's lawn, detailing a car, or making tea for someone who is ill. Charles H. Spurgeon said, "Carve your name on hearts, not on marble." Stepping out of your isolation to meet another's needs can soften the pain and etch your emotions and efforts into eternity.

Father, show me healthy ways to
turn my grief into Your grace.

ENDURING EXPERIENCE

Jesus' appearance was transformed so that his face shone like
the sun, and his clothes became as white as light. Suddenly,
Moses and Elijah appeared and began talking with Jesus.
MATTHEW 17:2–3 NLT

In his essay "Why I am Not a Christian," Bertrand Russell claimed that Jesus' words "some standing here right now will not die before they see the Son of Man coming in his Kingdom" (Matthew 16:28 NLT) demonstrate how wrong He was when He said His second coming would occur "before the death of all the people who were living at that time." Russell could have benefitted from today's reading.

Had Russell read the next paragraph, he would have noticed that when "some" of the disciples who had been "standing" with Jesus watched as He met with Moses and Elijah, they saw the Son of Man "coming in his Kingdom."

Like the disciples, our experience of the "coming of the kingdom" is not any less real because it is still coming. We enjoy experiences from the kingdom's influence every day through the indwelling of the Spirit: kindness, selfless love, peace, wisdom, and more.

As sad as it is that Russell saw today's reading as a "defect" in Christ, it is sadder that he missed the human experience of all that the "coming of the kingdom" offers. Will you?

Father, remind me to pray and live the way
Jesus taught: "Your kingdom come, Your will be done."

ENDURING GENEROSITY

*"Don't I have the right to do what I want with my own money?
Or are you envious because I am generous?"*
MATTHEW 20:15 NIV

Organizational research recommends addressing envy regularly to promote productivity. When companies coach employees about envy, they create more positive climates, improve relationships, and further the organization's mission. The same is true of the church.

Jesus used a parable about envy to coach His followers. Instead of focusing on the strategies used in many businesses, He reminded them of the mission—to love God and our neighbors. Focusing on a mission statement can help any organization, and it is a preferred method for reducing envy in the church.

Jesus' point is that life isn't about fairness; it's about God being "generous" with all of us (Matthew 20:16). Jesus wants His followers to remember that the things they possess and the successes they achieve aren't significant compared with remembering God's generosity.

Later, Jesus adds, "You know that the rulers of the Gentiles lord it over them, and their high officials exercise authority over them. Not so with you. Instead, whoever wants to become great among you must be your servant" (20:25–26).

Celebrating the success and the blessing of others reduces envy and helps us spend our energies on enjoying God together, forever—regardless of who came to Him first.

*Father, help me avoid envy at work, at church,
and in my family by celebrating, rather than envying,
the generosity You have extended to others.*

ENDURING VALUE

Then he said to them, "So give back to Caesar what
is Caesar's, and to God what is God's." When they heard
this, they were amazed. So they left him and went away.
MATTHEW 22:21–22 NIV

When the religious leaders were trying to "trap him in his words" (Matthew 22:15), Jesus provided an answer that reached beyond the question. He often does.

When the leaders asked if it was right to pay a highly controversial tax, Jesus asked them whose image was on their coins. When they replied, "Caesar's," He explained that they should "give back to Caesar what is Caesar's, and to God what is God's" (22:20–21). Jesus' answer didn't end with giving to Caesar what belonged to him; it ended with giving what belonged to God.

John Hockman maintains, "while ancient kings carved stone statues in their images to remind their subjects of their greatness, magnificence and authority, God created living beings in his image, breathing into them an infinite sense of value."

Jesus' answer reached beyond the question, beyond paying taxes. It reminded His accusers that being stamped in God's "own image" (Genesis 1:27) answered one of the deepest human needs—to feel valued.

As Matthew records the rest of the chapter, Jesus' answers left His accusers speechless: "No one could say a word in reply" (22:46). His answer should leave you speechless for other reasons!

Father, thank You for creating me in Your image so
I might experience its intrinsic, infinite value!

ENDURING MOTIVATIONS

"His master replied, 'Well done, good and faithful servant!
You have been faithful with a few things; I will put you in charge
of many things. Come and share your master's happiness!' "
MATTHEW 25:23 NIV

As Jesus continued to employ parables to reeducate the religious leaders and instruct His followers, He often used motivational appeals seldom mentioned in locker rooms or advertising agencies.

Few coaches or creatives in marketing firms would consider motivating people through appealing to their desire to please "the Maker of all things" (Isaiah 44:24). Have you ever wondered why this motivation, though relatively unused by some of the world's major motivational forces, works so powerfully within God's people?

Working for the One who made you, who left the luxuries of heaven to live with humanity and who later suffered the agonies of the cross for you promotes a cosmic happiness. It rises above all other motivations and shines its warm light into the cold darkness of self-promotion and greed.

The parable illustrates this principle, and just when you might ask, "What efforts are the best to invest my talents in?" Jesus answers by explaining the work that pleases Him most: "The King will reply, 'Truly I tell you, whatever you did for one of the least of these brothers and sisters of mine, you did for me' " (Matthew 25:40 NIV).

Will you "come and share your Master's happiness"?

Father, help me give my best to others
by dedicating every effort to You.

ENDURING SINCERITY

*When the disciples saw this, they were indignant.
"Why this waste?" they asked. "This perfume could have
been sold at a high price and the money given to the poor."*
MATTHEW 26:8–9 NIV

George Herbert, the younger friend of the poet John Donne, captured the irony in today's reading in his poem, "The Sacrifice":

For thirty pence he did my death devise/ Who at three hundred did the ointment prize,

Not half so sweet as my sweet sacrifice:/ Was ever grief like mine?

Herbert's insight follows today's reading. According to John's Gospel, Judas Iscariot was indignant about the expensive ointment poured on Jesus. He said it should have been sold for three hundred pence (a year's wage) and given to the poor (John 12:5). Ironically, this was ten times the amount he sold Jesus for (Matthew 26:15). Maybe this irony in the devaluation of Jesus' life became part of the anguish that caused Judas to take his own.

As sad as the irony in Judas' treatment of Jesus appears, it's even more ironic that Jesus sacrificed His life for people like Judas—people who cared more about their lives than His love.

Like Judas, your living can trade a friendship with Jesus for nothing of value. God takes His relationship with you personally. He still watches sadly as His people make ironic choices. Maybe that's why Herbert ends his stanza with Jesus' question, "Was ever grief like mine?"

Father, help me to avoid an ironic life.

ENDURING EMOTIONS

So they departed quickly from the tomb with
fear and great joy, and ran to tell his disciples.
MATTHEW 28:8 ESV

Trying to imagine the despair the disciples felt after Jesus died is difficult; how could they feel any hope when the person who created that hope had died? But as difficult as it is to imagine the utter sense of loss, it's also hard to imagine the sudden emotional rebirth they experienced at the empty tomb.

Matthew describes their emotions as "fear and great joy." Encountering the more-than-natural always produces some kind of fear. Although the fear produced by a scary movie or story is much more common in our culture, there is a delightful kind of fear as well—a fear that creates anticipation. Talking with an angel filled both Marys with this kind of fear.

Alongside that fear ran a "great joy." The adjective means "too much." It's as if Matthew wanted to communicate that it was more than too much joy to write about—it was too much to feel.

Encountering the more-than-natural produced fear and great joy in the disciples; it can do the same in you. As you read this week, look for God in His Word and in how He uses it in you and through you. Maybe finding His more-than-natural presence will cause you to feel the same emotions these disciples did as they "took hold of his feet and worshiped him" (Matthew 28:9 ESV).

Father, help me experience enduring fear and joy!

TIME MANAGEMENT

Very early in the morning, while it was still dark, Jesus got up,
left the house and went off to a solitary place, where he prayed.
MARK 1:35 NIV

In 1967, Charles E. Hummel published "The Tyranny of the Urgent," a pamphlet that became a time-management classic. He wrote, "Your greatest danger is letting the urgent things crowd out the important."

Hummel's essay promoted new commitments in managers, pastors, and other leaders who were well aware they had become consumed by the "urgent." In today's reading, Mark chronicles Jesus visiting a "solitary place, where he prayed," pointing out the method He used to avoid the energy-sapping tyranny that inconveniences most believers.

As God in human flesh, Jesus experienced the urgencies you do. He knew, more than you ever could, what it felt like to have crowds of people need Him. Helping was easy in His divinity, but not in His humanity (Philippians 2:5–8). Jesus needed times of prayer. These times reminded Him that His purpose on earth required leaving one crowd full of "urgent" needs to minister to another (Mark 1:38). Christians need the reminder too.

Does the tyranny of the urgent keep you from helping your family, wife, church friends, or neighbors? If so, schedule regular time in a solitary place to talk things over with God. He will help you avoid allowing the urgent to crowd out the important.

Father, free me from every tyranny that keeps me
from helping the people You want me to help.

ENDURING INSIGHTS

"Pay close attention to what you hear. The closer you listen, the more understanding you will be given—and you will receive even more. To those who listen to my teaching, more understanding will be given."
MARK 4:24–25 NLT

Has someone you looked up to ever said things like, "Now, pay close attention here" or "Listen carefully"?

Maybe you were learning to work with power tools or fishing tackle. Maybe you were experimenting with brushstrokes on a canvas or clay on a potter's wheel. Maybe you were learning to make lattes or flip pancakes. No matter the situation, the words "pay close attention" promised a higher quality picnic table, a larger catch, an engaging painting, a durable bowl, or a tasty mocha.

Most people have been told at some point that good things happen when they listen more closely, when they pay attention to the details. When you trusted these people, you usually found their advice confirmed—the pleasures of life were more deeply satisfying.

Jesus told His followers "the closer you listen, the more understanding you will be given." He understood the temptation in partial, preoccupied hearing. If you want the deeply satisfying pleasures the listening-life offers, ask God to help you hear the delight in every detail.

Father, help me to walk the miles between hearing from a distance and listening more closely, so I will understand more deeply the satisfactions in knowing You.

ENDURING RULES

So the Pharisees and teachers of the law asked Jesus,
"Why don't your disciples live according to the tradition
of the elders instead of eating their food with defiled hands?"
MARK 7:5 NIV

In His answer to the religious leaders, Jesus quotes the Old Testament: "Isaiah was right when he prophesied about you hypocrites; as it is written: 'These people honor me with their lips, but their hearts are far from me. They worship me in vain; their teachings are merely human rules' " (Mark 7:6–7 NIV).

Jesus' point about rules is the same as Isaiah's. They end up moving your heart away from the things that matter and from the One who matters most.

David F. Miller said, "The Christian life is not a list of rules; it's a life of righteousness."

Every time you put pressure on yourself or others to follow man-made rules, you move further away from the heart of God. Instead of valuing Him, you value your ability to adhere to human systems of righteousness. You esteem and respect your ability to perform instead of His ability to transform.

The Bible's rules about envy, lust, sex outside of marriage, eating more than our bodies need, and other clear instructions are not human. They promote your relationship with God and fit remarkably well into Jesus' summary: Love God with your entire being and love your neighbor as yourself (Mark 12:30–31).

Father, help me to replace my list of
rules with a life of righteousness.

ENDURING SECURITIES

"Truly I tell you, anyone who will not receive the kingdom of God like a little child will never enter it."
MARK 10:15 NIV

On this day in 1929, Wall Street suffered its infamous Black Thursday. Markets collapsed and the security of United States citizens collapsed along with them.

As banks closed and families lost jobs, the new poor began to look for more secure investments, not only financially but spiritually. Church attendance grew, evangelists attracted huge crowds, and Christian nonprofits increased in number and influence. Their trust and dependence on wealth evaporated, and believers began to redirect their security toward God.

It feels good to provide for yourself and your family, to put food on the table and fuel in the car, and pay off a home. But being able to provide security only through personal industry can yield a hundred dark Thursdays. Jesus reminded His followers only those who "receive the kingdom of God like a little child" find a home there. The trust and sense of wonder that characterize childhood should characterize your life.

If the bank closed and you lost your job today, would you be able to roll with it? Would you relax "like a little child" in the arms of a loving Father? This month, when you evaluate your securities, maybe you can extend that evaluation to childlike matters of the heart.

Father, help me evaluate my spiritual portfolio and reinvest in the security that matters most.

ENDURING WEALTH

*Jesus called his disciples to him and said, "I tell you the truth,
this poor widow has given more than all the others."*
MARK 12:43 NLT

———————

Jesus sees what others overlook.

The media notices the generosity of the wealthy. When millions are donated in the name of philanthropy, the reports fill the papers, news programs, and blogs. It's easy to celebrate large financial gifts that benefit large companies and ministries, and even easier to overlook the little guys.

But God sees more. When a poor widow offers two small copper coins, Jesus calls His disciples over and points out what others missed—the offering of "everything" (Mark 12:44).

In a similar encounter, Jesus praises a woman who, at a small gathering, breaks an expensive alabaster vase and pours a year's wages worth of perfume on Him to prepare Him for His burial (Mark 14:3).

Both of these women, though largely overlooked by their cultures, offered "everything."

When the unrecognized do something extravagant from the heart, Jesus points it out. He sees the significant in culturally insignificant people.

The same religious leaders who shamelessly cheated "widows out of their property," should have noticed the extravagant gift this widow made, but they did not (Mark 12:40). As you walk through today, will you see the significant in the insignificant?

———————

*Father, thank You for noticing the little people who do
the truly great things. Help me see what You see.*

ENDURING APPRECIATION

"For the spirit is willing, but the body is weak."
MARK 14:38 NLT

Have you read some of the literature on how to deal with people who disappoint you?

If you have, Jesus' example in today's reading will startle you. He rejects contemporary wisdom and replaces it with the ancient wisdom of Solomon.

When Solomon's wife disappoints him by hiding from him emotionally and physically, he asks her to let him see her "face" and hear her "voice," since both are beautiful to him. He ends his confrontation by reminding her that despite hiding her heart, their relationship is still "in bloom" (Song of Songs 2:15). Solomon doesn't crush her spirit or her efforts to improve. He comforts her with a reminder of how much their relationship means to him.

Jesus follows the same pattern when His disciples disappoint Him. After He asks them to pray through His hours of agony, they let Him down by falling asleep. Instead of responding to the disappointment in the two most typical ways—avoidance or condemnation—Jesus ministers, like Solomon, to their needs. He reminds them not only that their "body is weak" but that their "spirit is willing." The appreciative part, "your spirit is willing," promotes hope and encourages the desired improvement.

If someone disappoints you today, do more than point out how that person has let you down—let that person know you appreciate the willing spirit.

Father, when someone lets me down, help me build them up
the way Jesus built up His disciples when they failed Him.

ENDURING THANKS

*"Blessed is she who has believed that the
Lord would fulfill his promises to her!"*
LUKE 1:45 NIV

When a job doesn't work out, the truck breaks down, or a relationship deteriorates, do you find it difficult to believe, as Mary did, that God will fulfill His promises?

During these times, it helps to read passages like today's because they illuminate the unseen forces at work on earth. Forces like God's angels and His miracles, or even forces like faith itself—the ability to believe in impossible outcomes.

Mary, Zechariah, and Elizabeth's faiths were encouraged by Gabriel's reminder, "For no word from God will ever fail" (Luke 1:37 NIV). Do you feel the deep, personal happiness that comes with believing like they did? Regardless of your immediate circumstances, God means it when He says His words will never fail you.

In response to God's promises, Mary wrote the song in today's reading (Luke 1:46–55). She committed hours to expressing her thanks, because she experienced it so deeply. Maybe this is part of the reason God chose her to mother the Messiah—He appreciates those He knows will spend time showing their thankfulness.

Will you celebrate God's faithfulness in significant ways, like Mary did? You could express your thankfulness by writing a song, fixing someone's car, raking a neighbor's leaves, or financing a church mission trip—anything that serves Him.

---

*Father, help me believe and respond to Your
faithfulness, like Mary, in significant ways.*

ENDURING WORSHIP

She had lived with her husband seven years after her marriage,
and then was a widow until she was eighty-four. She never left
the temple but worshiped night and day, fasting and praying.
LUKE 2:36–37 NIV

A widow most of her life, Anna walked the lonely corridors, met the temple visitors, and prayed and fasted.

Luke doesn't explain what kept Anna working as a prophetess. All he reveals is that rather than growing bitter toward God for the loss of her husband and the resulting loneliness, Anna worshipped.

Most believers would not choose Anna's life. There is so much to experience—so much laughter in families, so much meaning in friendships. As a result, most Christians find it difficult to look beyond their screens, to stare out through their living room blinds at the import in a cloistered life. But Anna did.

Anna got up each morning to the same food, clothing, and conversations she had known the day and decade before. Though overlooked by most who entered the temple, Anna continued serving, never receiving the accolades she deserved or tasting the happiness of those she waited on.

But then, Anna saw Jesus. And for her, earth's loneliness and longings finally made sense. They always do when heaven enters a room.

Is it hard to worship when your life doesn't feel as vibrant as other lives? Let Anna's story encourage your patience. Then one day, you too can celebrate the moment Jesus walks in.

Father, help me to worship like Anna.

ENDURING TEMPTATION

The devil said to him, "If you are the Son of God, command
this stone to become bread." And Jesus answered him,
"It is written, 'Man shall not live by bread alone.' "

LUKE 4:3–4 ESV

Pastor Don Mogford once said, "When you're being tempted, and you will be, quote scripture."

Mogford's youth group had just completed a ten-week program that included memorizing sections of the Bible. The verses/passages the high schoolers committed to memory covered the "seven deadly" sins: envy, gluttony, greed, lust, pride, laziness, and anger. He also added passages from the Bible about bitterness, sadness, and anxiety. He wanted these teens to practice the process Jesus used to face direct temptation.

Every time He faced the devil's enticements in the wilderness, Jesus cited the Bible. Instead of pointing out fallacies or trying to outsmart the devil, which He certainly could have done, He simply quoted the scriptures. You should too.

Paul told Timothy "All Scripture is inspired by God and is useful to teach us what is true and to make us realize what is wrong in our lives. It corrects us when we are wrong and teaches us to do what is right" (2 Timothy 3:16 NLT).

This weekend, use an online Bible app or concordance to help you look up and begin memorizing scripture verses you can use to confront your strongest temptations. You'll be glad you did.

Father, help me help myself, so that I can confront the
temptations that come my way the way Jesus did.

ENDURING SUCCESS

"Then your reward will be great, and you will be children of the Most High, because he is kind to the ungrateful and wicked. Be merciful, just as your Father is merciful."
LUKE 6:35–36 NIV

I n *Being Happy in an Unhappy World*, John C. Hagee wrote, "Mercy requires that we learn to love others, to value their welfare more than our own!"

It is unproductive to head to work without mercy on our minds. Organizations can't thrive without it. Employers need it. Parents need it. Because of the human propensity to sin, mercy becomes mandatory.

Mercy keeps communication climates warm, relationships strong, and productivity high. Mercy melts bitterness and reignites the passions that make employees and organizations successful. But even though mercy makes working with people manageable, it rarely appears in books about management. Why?

Mercy violates your human right to fair treatment. After all, you expect diligence, kindness, and respect—and the conduct that should come with them. They're in your relational DNA. But mercy requires that you show these to the very individuals who least extend them. It means learning "to love others, to value their welfare more than our own."

God constantly shows you His mercy. Jesus said God is even "kind to the ungrateful and wicked." His point was not that you can be too. It was that your success and happiness depend on it.

Father, help me rejoice in the mercy
You extend me and offer it to everyone.

ENDURING HARVEST

*"The seed on good soil stands for those with
a noble and good heart, who hear the word,
retain it, and by persevering produce a crop."*
LUKE 8:14–15 NIV

In the northern hemisphere, October has become an internationally recognized time for celebrating the end of harvest—Octoberfest sausages, pumpkin-spice donuts, and apple cider fill the ads, store marquees, and our shopping carts.

In today's passage, Jesus discusses a spiritual harvest cultivated in those "who hear the word and retain it." A harvest of more than temporal "riches and pleasures." A harvest whose crops produce eternal joys, but whose success is determined by diligence.

In *Loving Your Neighbor: Surprise! It's Not What You Think*, David Sanford wrote, "We have overlaid the American dream on top of our Christian faith. As a result, we're expecting too much from this brief life, and are too little focused on eternity with God and His people." Diligence in the right direction makes all the difference.

A good harvest requires the determination to focus on eternity, to see beyond the festivities and shopping carts—the "riches and pleasures." It requires a tenacious diligence that begins with spending time in the Word.

As you allow the devotionals in this book—as well as the daily scripture readings they accompany—to condition the soil of your heart, God will produce an enduring harvest in you and through you.

Father, help me produce soil that promotes Your efforts.

THE HARVEST IS GOD'S RESPONSIBILITY

*These were his instructions to them: "The harvest is great,
but the workers are few. So pray to the Lord who is in charge
of the harvest; ask him to send more workers into his fields."*

LUKE 10:2 NLT

Jesus assured His followers that the desire and need for God is great in the world, but He also said that those willing to carry that message are few in number. In fact, Jesus told them to specifically pray for God's intervention in the harvest so that more people would respond to His message.

Have you stepped out into ministry or gone about your day with the assurance that the harvest is abundant? Or have you been tempted to believe that there is no interest in God or in the message of Jesus? If the harvest doesn't appear abundant to you, it may be worthwhile to consider where that perception is coming from—since Jesus states that the one need is for more workers.

As you look to God's Spirit for guidance and empowerment, never lose sight of the reality that the harvest is God's and that the power is His as well. Look to Him for your results and trust that He will direct you where you need to go and to say what needs to be said.

*Jesus, send more workers to gather the
abundant harvest. Help me to do my part.*

WHAT ARE YOU STORING AWAY?

"God said to him, 'You fool! This very night your life will be demanded from you. Then who will get what you have prepared for yourself?' This is how it will be with whoever stores up things for themselves but is not rich toward God."
LUKE 12:20–21 NIV

At what point did the rich man's material abundance become a trap keeping him from the abundance of God? Perhaps that line is different for every person, but at a certain point, the man made himself a servant to his wealth and personal security and not to God. As he prepared larger and larger barns for his own personal enjoyment and comfort, he failed to see the ways he had lost sight of God and became bankrupt.

How can you avoid the kinds of traps that ensnared the rich man consumed with building bigger barns? Perhaps one place to start is to consider your abundance and security as resources to share with others. Your abundant "harvest" can be put to better use blessing others—like when John the Baptist commanded those with two jackets to share with those who had none (Luke 3:11).

You can also watch for ways wealth distracts you from God. Like the man who spent so much time building new barns, the use of money can lead to more diversions and expenses that draw your attention away from the wealth of God's present love and mercy.

Jesus, help me to become rich toward God today.

REJOICE WHEN SINNERS REPENT

"He said to him, 'Son, you are always with me, and all that
is mine is yours. It was fitting to celebrate and be glad, for this
your brother was dead, and is alive; he was lost, and is found.' "
LUKE 15:31–32 ESV

The older brother in the parable of the Prodigal Son didn't betray his family or squander the family wealth, but he did know how to hold a grudge. Faced with his brother's return, he could only see what his brother had done wrong in contrast to all he had done right. Lost in his accounting was his brother's restoration, which prompted his father's celebration.

Comparing yourself with others is a fast track to killing your compassion for them. . .and to turning yourself into a hero. When you need to preserve a certain narrative about yourself, mercy for others can evaporate pretty quickly. What's more, focusing on the failures of others makes it easy to overlook your own mistakes and vices. The son who stayed home didn't consider his own bitterness a flaw, so it was hard for him to have compassion for his brother. Instead, he used the prodigal's actions as a smokescreen to hide his own flaws.

Failing to show mercy can result in missing out on God's joy. . .and quite a few parties, sometimes literal ones. God always prefers mercy, and that means celebrating a sinner's homecoming.

Jesus, help me to see others with compassion
and mercy so that I can rejoice with You.

FREEDOM FROM MONEY'S MASTERY

*"No one can serve two masters. For you will hate one
and love the other; you will be devoted to one and despise
the other. You cannot serve God and be enslaved to money."*
LUKE 16:13 NLT

It may seem counterintuitive to think that God and money are in competition for the position of master in your life. But in today's verse, Jesus strongly suggests that money can indeed function much like a master.

Money demands time, planning, and hard work. Money can promise security, solve problems, and lead to comfort and even peace—that is, until you run out of it. It's hard to control some of the forces that determine how much money you can earn or keep, and that's what makes it a fickle, if not demanding, master.

Has money become a master in your own life? Do you find yourself craving a little more security or a little more comfort? While money may deliver on some of its promises, you can trust that God is *always* present and *always* offers a different kind of comfort and security.

While praying that God will provide your daily bread, you can trust that He will care for your needs. . .as long as you put love for Him and your neighbors first. When you release your cares to God, you are free to love your neighbors without the burden of depending on your own wealth or of providing your own security.

Lord, I trust that You can provide for all of my needs.

WHAT REPENTANCE LOOKS LIKE

Zacchaeus stood up and said to the Lord, "Look, Lord!
Here and now I give half of my possessions to the poor,
and if I have cheated anybody out of anything, I will pay back
four times the amount." Jesus said to him, "Today salvation has
come to this house, because this man, too, is a son of Abraham."
LUKE 19:8–9 NIV

Zacchaeus, an unscrupulous tax collector, didn't just admit his wrongdoing or change his ways. He also vowed to pay back everyone he had cheated, making things right with people who had suffered most from his dishonesty. His faith in Jesus so greatly prompted this turnaround that Jesus immediately recognized how deeply Zacchaeus had adopted the Gospel message.

What do you need to make right today? There may be a relationship you've neglected, a friend you've failed to help, or a bad habit you need to be leave behind. Whatever it is, God's mercy and grace are present for you. . .if you make a move toward them. Mercy doesn't just change your life on its own. Faith must be joined with action.

Salvation belongs to your house today when you follow up your faith with the choices you make. There is no other way to demonstrate your faith. One simple choice at a time to follow God's commands will make your faith come alive.

Jesus, help me to see the ways I can make my failures right.

THE GREATEST LEADERS SERVE

"But not so with you. Rather, let the greatest among you become as the youngest, and the leader as one who serves. For who is the greater, one who reclines at table or one who serves? Is it not the one who reclines at table? But I am among you as the one who serves."
LUKE 22:26–27 ESV

Jesus described leadership as a position from which we can serve others, not as one from which we demand respect and prestige. As you consider ways to steward the influence and power God has given you, think of the ways you can overturn the assumptions of today about greatness and power. If Jesus overturned the standards of His time for power, then His example may lead you to consider ways you can find to go last, to put others ahead of yourself, and to accept less than you think you deserve.

This is a tough exercise in humility that will cause you to rethink some assumptions about yourself and what your goals may be. It may feel like settling for less, but it's really an opportunity to place others ahead of yourself. As challenging as this may be, it will free you from the pressure to fight for what you think you deserve and give you an increased awareness of the challenges your neighbors face. You may even become the kind of person others want to follow.

Jesus, help me to let go of my illusions about myself so that I can serve others in freedom and humility.

TOO GOOD TO BE TRUE

*Then Jesus said to them, "You foolish people! You find it so
hard to believe all that the prophets wrote in the Scriptures.
Wasn't it clearly predicted that the Messiah would have to
suffer all these things before entering his glory?"*
LUKE 24:25–26 NLT

As His disciples struggled to believe the reality of the coming resurrection, Jesus expressed dismay that they had failed to believe something spelled out clearly in the scriptures and in His own teachings. Is it possible that such promises were too good to be true? Why was it so hard to believe the *really* good news of Jesus?

Perhaps you haven't quite imagined how wonderful the promises of the resurrection or your home with God really are. Perhaps you haven't fully grasped that God's Spirit is dwelling in you or that Jesus could never forsake you. It's understandable that you may not want to be disappointed if it's not true. . .or perhaps you just find it a little too "out there."

Yet, the many eyewitness accounts, generations of Christians, and the power of God on display today all serve as reminders that these stories are true and offer real comfort to the suffering and needy today. After the resurrection, a risen Savior walked among His people and more or less said, "What did you *expect* would happen?"

*Jesus, help me to believe the wonderful
promises You give Your people.*

A SIMPLE TEST OF OBEDIENCE

Everyone who does evil hates the light, and will not come into the light for fear that their deeds will be exposed. But whoever lives by the truth comes into the light, so that it may be seen plainly that what they have done has been done in the sight of God.

JOHN 3:20–21 NIV

You can know if you are living in confidence or shame before God by doing a little self-examination. If you are willing to stand before God without hiding anything or making some kind of excuse for yourself, you are living by God's truth and obeying His commands with a clear conscience. However, if your first inclination is to hide from God, to add a lengthy excuse, or to delay such an encounter at all, then you are most likely not living in obedience to Him. If that's the case, you'll need to confess your sins to God, lest you miss out on the intimacy and peace He offers His people when they come to Him in the confidence of His light.

Jesus assures you that He will never leave or forsake you. God is working in your favor in many ways, even if you are afraid of His light. The goal in the end is your complete renewal so that you can see God, yourself, and others clearly and live free from shame and fear.

Jesus, help me to boldly confess my sins so I can live in the freedom of Your light.

DOING GOD'S WILL SUSTAINS YOU

But he said to them, "I have food to eat that you do not know about." So the disciples said to one another, "Has anyone brought him something to eat?" Jesus said to them, "My food is to do the will of him who sent me and to accomplish his work."

JOHN 4:32–34 ESV

You may have sung that the joy of the Lord is your strength, but Jesus told His disciples that obedience to God the Father's will sustained Him like a full meal. While Jesus surely followed up that declaration with a substantial meal eventually, how could such an encounter leave Him feeling strong and steady, filled up, and satisfied?

By doing God's will and blessing others, you will find yourself moving in step with Him. . .with nothing to hide, nothing to explain away, and a peace that your decisions are leading you in the right direction as you bless others. Just as Jesus found His place in the world, obedience to God can also place you in a position to feel settled over your own place here. As you watch God moving through others, leading them to freedom, you'll find a sense of satisfaction greater than anything food can offer.

Everyone has a hunger to find a purpose in life, and Jesus offers the recipe no one else can beat.

Jesus, help me to find satisfaction and fulfillment in doing the Father's will.

WHAT ARE YOU HUNGRY FOR?

Jesus replied, "I am the bread of life. Whoever
comes to me will never be hungry again.
Whoever believes in me will never be thirsty."
JOHN 6:35 NLT

Since Jesus described Himself as the "bread of life" and as a well of water that would satisfy any thirst, then perhaps you should consider today what you're hungry for and what could satisfy your thirst. Are you trying to satisfy your hunger with food that could never leave you feeling whole and satisfied? Are you even aware of what you're hungry for in the first place?

If you can work backward, consider the areas of your life where you struggle with desires or anxieties. What are you most concerned about or ashamed of before God? Those are the places where you are experiencing hunger and thirst. But those are also the areas where you are most likely to seek inadequate food and drink to bring satisfaction.

The challenge today is to ask how Jesus can become the food and drink that satisfies those longings and struggles in your life. Your hunger is an important clue. Face that emptiness in your life, and ask God to help you find what can truly fill it.

Jesus, help me to rely on You as bread for my life today.

BEWARE OF THE TRAP OF TOO MUCH CONFIDENCE

Jesus said, "If you were blind, you would not be guilty of sin; but now that you claim you can see, your guilt remains."
JOHN 9:41 NIV

I f you have children—or remember your own childhood—you may be familiar with a child protesting, "I didn't know that was wrong! It's not fair to punish me!" after doing something wrong. Children expect mercy when they act out of ignorance—or if they can at least claim they didn't know the rules. Such mercy is right in line with Jesus, who reserved His judgment of sin for those who claimed to be free from it.

It turns out that hypocrisy over sin is far worse in God's eyes than the sinful acts themselves. By committing sin and then denying their need for repentance or forgiveness, people cut themselves off from God's mercy and forgiveness.

Are there areas in your life where you may be a little too confident in yourself? Are you certain that you are doing what's right? While confidence rightly placed is a wonderful thing, beware of the trap of considering yourself more righteous and holy than you really are.

Jesus, I look to Your mercy and kindness to forgive and restore me for my failures.

A VERY SIMPLE COMPROMISE

But one of them, Caiaphas, who was high priest that
year, said to them, "You know nothing at all. Nor do you
understand that it is better for you that one man should die
for the people, not that the whole nation should perish."
JOHN 11:49–50 ESV

Insulting the intelligence of the high council, Caiaphas made a simple argument based on math. By killing one man, Jesus, the religious leaders could prevent Him from arousing suspicion from the Roman authorities. It was the simplest compromise to make, especially when he framed any alternatives as foolishness. The fear of appearing foolish and of risking the fate of their nation weighed heavily on these religious leaders, who reasoned that framing Jesus was in fact a way to preserve the greater good.

One little compromise can lead men to terrible places, as one deception builds on the other. Such retreats from truth and honesty rarely make things better or yield results even close to the original aims of those who make such calculations.

It is better to come clean today with your areas of compromise or deception than to allow them to fester and grow. Even if the math seems simple and the end result is a net good, beware of the ways that living in a falsehood can undermine even your best intentions.

Jesus, You experienced the painful results of compromise.
Guide me in the path of integrity in my decisions today.

LET GO OF YOUR ATTACHMENTS

"Those who love their life in this world will lose it. Those who care nothing for their life in this world will keep it for eternity. Anyone who wants to serve me must follow me, because my servants must be where I am. And the Father will honor anyone who serves me."
JOHN 12:25–26 NLT

There is nothing in this life you can keep or take with you into eternity other than what springs from your love for God. Your obedience and selfless service to others demonstrates your faith in God and confidence in the life that's to come.

Clinging to what you can gain for yourself today at the expense of your soul is a bad trade. The more you concentrate on accumulating in this world, and the more you worry about what you can possess or protect in this life, the less capacity you'll have to hold on to what God cares about most.

Think of the things that can weigh you down or slow your steps toward God. Think of your attachments to this world—whether emotional, relational, or physical—that hold you back. They are burdens that keep you from the only prize that matters.

The more you surrender to God, the less you have to worry about defending. The more you've emptied from your life, the better prepared you are to receive what God wants to give you.

Jesus, open my eyes to what holds me back from You.

LOVE LEADS TO OBEDIENCE

Jesus replied, "Anyone who loves me will obey my teaching. My Father will love them, and we will come to them and make our home with them. Anyone who does not love me will not obey my teaching. These words you hear are not my own; they belong to the Father who sent me."

JOHN 14:23–24 NIV

Jesus makes the stakes of obedience very clear in today's verse. He's not interested in enforcing rules for their own sake. He views God's way of living not just as an intellectual checklist but as a path to life and relationship and as a sign of one's devotion and love. Jesus is looking for followers who are committed to Him and listen to Him out of a desire for Him, not out of fear or duty.

Perhaps this teaching today is an opportunity to examine your motivation and desires. Are you motivated to follow Jesus out of a sense of love and commitment, or out of duty and obligation? The Father sent Jesus to bring you back to fellowship with Himself. He left the Holy Spirit with you because He would never abandon you. The abundant life of God is yours, provided you do the kinds of things that lead to that life.

Fellowship with God is yours to claim because of the Father's great love for you, but you must be careful to keep any distractions from obscuring the wonder of His heavenly presence.

Jesus, help me to see how great the Father's love is for me.

GOD'S LOVE REMAINS IN YOU

*"O righteous Father, even though the world does not know you,
I know you, and these know that you have sent me. I made known
to them your name, and I will continue to make it known, that the
love with which you have loved me may be in them, and I in them."*
JOHN 17:25–26 ESV

The love of God the Father that resided in Jesus the Son is also within you. This love originates in the Trinity's perfect love. Peace is present in your life today, affirming and restoring you. . .if you will receive it. And as if God the Father's love weren't enough in your life, Jesus Himself promises to remain in you.

God affirmed Jesus as His own Son who is deeply loved, and He also sees Jesus in you and sees you as His beloved child. This is the shocking good news of Jesus—God is present as King and has come to rest and reside among His people.

When you fail or stumble into sin, God still sees you as a beloved child who is sheltered by the presence of His Son. There is forgiveness and restoration for you when you repent because you can never lose your place. You have been adopted and indwelt by God's love and His Son. Your hope is in the spiritual reality of God dwelling in you.

Father, may Your love guide and restore me today.

DO YOU LOVE WHAT JESUS LOVES?

A third time he asked him, "Simon son of John, do you love me?" Peter was hurt that Jesus asked the question a third time. He said, "Lord, you know everything. You know that I love you." Jesus said, "Then feed my sheep."

JOHN 21:17 NLT

As Jesus restored Peter, He gave him the specific commission to care for His followers who had come to depend on Him. The mark of Peter's love and commitment to Jesus in the years to come would be his ability to love and care for Jesus' followers.

This truth is an opportunity for self-examination and an invitation for you to evaluate your priorities. Each day there are different opportunities to "feed" or care for your own desires. . .or for the aspirations of others. You can feed your desire for comfort or security. Or you can feed the needs of others around you, seeking out those who are overlooked or forgotten and sharing God's love and blessings with them.

Perhaps the first step is to remember that you are Jesus' "sheep," that He loves and cares for you. He will never leave you or forsake you. He wants you to have the fullness of God's life in you. Now He asks that you respond by sharing His teachings, kindness, and mercy with others.

Jesus, remind me that I am Your beloved sheep today so that I can love others like You do.

IS GOD ASKING YOU TO WAIT?

On one occasion, while he was eating with them, he gave them this command: "Do not leave Jerusalem, but wait for the gift my Father promised, which you have heard me speak about. For John baptized with water, but in a few days you will be baptized with the Holy Spirit."
ACTS 1:4–5 NIV

Has there ever been a time when you felt God compelling you to wait? How about a time when a trusted spiritual leader suggested waiting? Waiting is a big task for those inclined toward action. There aren't awards or respected positions for people who wait the best. But what if the most important part of your ministry to others is your ability to wait?

The big caveat is whether you are waiting for the right reason—such as waiting for God's Spirit. Rather than rushing forward with your own plans and relying on your own abilities, you wait for God's Spirit to empower and direct you, just as the apostles did. Can you imagine how different the book of Acts would be if the apostles had moved forward on their own without waiting for God's Spirit?

Waiting takes the pressure off you to bear the burdens of others with your own strength, or to serve others with your own wisdom. By waiting for the Spirit, you can acknowledge your dependence on God and ensure that you serve others out of God's abundance.

Spirit, teach me to wait for You as I serve others.

FREEDOM TO SERVE OTHERS

Thus Joseph, who was also called by the apostles Barnabas (which means son of encouragement), a Levite, a native of Cyprus, sold a field that belonged to him and brought the money and laid it at the apostles' feet.

ACTS 4:36–37 ESV

B arnabas emerged as one of the most important missionaries mentioned in the book of Acts—he joined Paul's missionary journeys, stood by John Mark in his time of failure, and worked tirelessly to share the Gospel. The first mention of Barnabas in Acts reveals something significant about him: he sold his field to generously provide for the needs of the poor. Before setting out on his missionary work, he unburdened himself of his field to become a worker in God's harvest.

While we can't say for sure how much of a burden or responsibility that field had been for Barnabas, there's no doubt that selling it freed him to serve others and to minister once he had passed the proceeds of the sale to the apostles.

Is it possible that something you own is keeping you from seeing God's calling with clarity or preventing you from taking a step of faith? While there is nothing wrong with owning a field, or other possessions, the burden of more wealth can obscure what God wants to accomplish in your life and through your actions.

Today, ask God if He wants you to unburden yourself of something you own so you can serve Him, and others, better.

Jesus, show me the ways that my possessions keep me from serving You, and others, better.

LISTEN FIRST

But as the believers rapidly multiplied, there were rumblings of discontent. The Greek-speaking believers complained about the Hebrew-speaking believers, saying that their widows were being discriminated against in the daily distribution of food.

ACTS 6:1 NLT

The Greek-speaking widows were among the most powerless members of the early church. They depended on charity in a foreign land and culture and were unsure about what would become of them after their husbands passed. How would the church respond to them in their time of crisis?

You may think you know why people are poor, destitute, or struggling. You may think you have the perfect solution to make everything better for them. But do you really listen to what they have to say about their situations, about what they really need?

Just as the apostles listened to these overlooked women and found a solution that honored their God-given dignity and met their needs in concrete ways, your ability to help others is largely based on how well you listen. You can only help as much as you understand and engage with those who are in need or suffering. Only then can you offer a solution.

Jesus, help me to see You in the faces of those who are suffering, and give me ears to listen.

NEW LIFE THROUGH ENCOURAGEMENT

Barnabas took him and brought him to the apostles.
He told them how Saul on his journey had seen the
Lord and that the Lord had spoken to him, and how in
Damascus he had preached fearlessly in the name of Jesus.
ACTS 9:27 NIV

Things appeared hopeless for Paul after his long history of persecuting Christians. How could God bring new life to someone who appeared so set in his ways and so determined to destroy the work of God among many? Miraculous visions aside, Paul never would have stepped into his larger role in the church without the faith and encouragement of Barnabas.

Perhaps you feel like you have a long way to go before you are able to serve others effectively, or maybe you're simply wondering whether you'll ever have God's life to share with others. It's possible that the missing piece is someone in your community who can lift you up at a time of confusion and uncertainty. You may need to lean on the wisdom of a mentor or friend who can help you see the potential that God has stored in you.

As you take stock of your outlook and hope for the future, consider how someone else could make a difference the way Barnabas did. Perhaps you can also play that same role for someone who also needs that encouragement in the near future.

Jesus, I trust that You can bring new life
and restoration where I have no hope.

WHAT IF GOD SURPRISES YOU?

Peter said, "By no means, Lord; for I have never eaten anything that is common or unclean." And the voice came to him again a second time, "What God has made clean, do not call common."
ACTS 10:14–15 ESV

The only thing that may have surprised Peter more than his unusual dream was its highly unexpected message that Jews and Gentiles were equally important to God. Peter had to quickly rethink his understanding of scripture.

The apostle Paul spent a good deal of time writing letters to Jewish Christians who were slow to catch on to this paradigm-shifting message. Despite not fully accepting the message of the dream, despite struggling to make sense of God making all people "clean," Peter still followed God's command.

Faith doesn't assure us that everything will make sense right away. God may lead you in ways that seem confusing, or even appear to be contradictory. You may not know what is waiting on the other side. Perhaps God will surprise you. Are you willing to accept God's judgment of others, believing Him when He calls them "clean"?

When you step into uncertainty, your faith will grow and your trust in God will develop. At a time when your steps only make sense to God, you are learning to submit your own wisdom and knowledge to His ways.

Lord, I trust You to direct my steps today.

HOW TO PREPARE FOR A CHALLENGE

Paul and Barnabas also appointed elders in every church.
With prayer and fasting, they turned the elders over to
the care of the Lord, in whom they had put their trust.
ACTS 14:23 NLT

The recently planted churches in the apostle Paul's time faced adversity and even physical harm. As their newly appointed leaders prepared to guide their churches through difficult, if not dangerous, times, Paul and Barnabas were preparing to leave town. What could Paul and Barnabas pass on to them to help them endure the trials before them?

What if the odds you're facing are so steep that you can only rest in God's guidance and provision? When facing a challenge, it's tempting to work overtime on plans and on accumulating wisdom. But prayer and fasting take the situation out of your hands and place the future in God's hands.

In your weakness and emptiness, you can acknowledge that God is the source of your strength and hope. There's no way you can overcome everything set against you based on your own resources. It's far better to start off completely relying on God than to fail and seek Him as a last resort!

Jesus, I trust that You can lead me through adversity
and the seemingly hopeless challenges of today.

HOW TO ENDURE BEING STUCK

*About midnight Paul and Silas were praying and singing hymns
to God, and the prisoners were listening to them, and suddenly
there was a great earthquake, so that the foundations of the
prison were shaken. And immediately all the doors were
opened, and everyone's bonds were unfastened.*
ACTS 16:25–26 ESV

Paul and Silas were chained and locked down in a gloomy prison,
awaiting their fate. Did God truly call them to this dead end of beatings,
chains, and locked doors among criminals? How could they respond when
so many things stood against them?

Rather than despairing that God's favor or blessing had departed their
ministry, they turned to Him in faith, singing hymns and praying. They
trusted in God's direction and power when they could have despaired.

As you encounter your own trials, roadblocks, and suffering, prayer
and praise can break the chains of despair that could otherwise hold you
back. Physical circumstances don't reveal much about God's proximity
in times of suffering or trial. Focusing on God's presence and love can
become your first step toward freedom. Even if you remain stuck, locked
down, or struggling for a season, God has not abandoned you.

Perhaps God won't shake you loose from your chains right away, but
regardless of how He sends help in the end, a faith that endures continues
to sing even in the darkness.

*Jesus, I trust that You are with me
when I feel trapped or hopeless.*

REPENTANCE BRINGS "MAGICAL" CHANGE

Many who became believers confessed their sinful practices.
A number of them who had been practicing sorcery brought
their incantation books and burned them at a public bonfire.
The value of the books was several million dollars.

ACTS 19:18–19 NLT

What did the people of Ephesus hope to gain from their magic books? This wasn't the fantasy section of today's libraries. These were real spells used to gain power, control, wealth, and even favor with false deities. Turning to God in repentance meant a clean break from the magic books they had relied on, even making a dramatic break by burning them in a public bonfire.

Today may be a good time to consider what you rely on. Perhaps a smartphone, bank account, position, or a possession has become a source of security or status for you. Just as you can't serve both God and money, you also can't serve God and your own security. Anything you rely on rather than God may be an obstacle that needs to be confessed before Him.

Much like the people of Ephesus, who made a public display of their change, it may be most helpful to make a confession along with others. You're surely not alone in your struggles! A public confession with others is far more likely to endure.

Jesus, I confess that I have not always relied on You.
Grant me the wisdom to turn to You today.

AVOIDING THE TRAPS OF POWER AND MONEY

"In all things I have shown you that by working hard in this way we must help the weak and remember the words of the Lord Jesus, how he himself said, 'It is more blessed to give than to receive.' "
ACTS 20:35 ESV

Paul recognized that power and money could become the two greatest temptations among the Ephesian church. He shared his example, and the example of Jesus, noting that he worked hard to provide for his own financial needs, and he did not hold his position over anyone.

Most importantly, Paul placed himself under the same teachings as everyone else. There were no exceptions: hard work and generosity could save the Ephesian church and its leaders from the traps of power and money.

What do you value? Are you driven to protect your money? Are you jealous of the position or influence of others? Today's passage is an opportunity to examine your own life in order to identify these root causes of so many conflicts and division.

Power and money drive people to make bad choices and then rationalize them in retrospect. By committing to hard work, rather than demanding status, and by sharing your money generously with others, you'll enjoy the fruitful blessings of humility and generosity. There is freedom when you let go of the very things that may be holding you back.

Jesus, I give You thanks for the many blessings I enjoy and celebrate today. Help me to avoid the desires for power and money, which can never be satisfied.

REPENTANCE ISN'T CONVENIENT

As he reasoned with them about righteousness and self-control and the coming day of judgment, Felix became frightened. "Go away for now," he replied. "When it is more convenient, I'll call for you again."

ACTS 24:25 NLT

Have you ever resolved to get your act together before God. . .*in the future*? Perhaps you've believed that in time you would get around to prayer, confession, or repentance—putting off something that is necessary but remains challenging and costly.

Waiting to make a spiritual change until a convenient time is really just another way of saying no. As Felix, the Roman governor of Judea, listened to Paul, he wrestled with the appeal of his message while also realizing how inconvenient it could become for himself and his career.

There will never be a convenient time to follow Jesus. He will always disrupt your plans, change your goals, and cause you to change your values. There will always be something you need to release into His care. It won't get any easier to make that first step. Yet, as long as you can make the choice, there is time to turn to God.

By God's grace, you have the choice today to turn away from the sins that hold you back and to stop living with regret or shame. You have God's inconvenient mercy offering you restoration today.

Jesus, I receive Your disruptive mercy and restoration today.

HOW FAST CAN GOD CHANGE A LIFE?

Then Agrippa said to Paul, "Do you think that in such a short time you can persuade me to be a Christian?" Paul replied, "Short time or long—I pray to God that not only you but all who are listening to me today may become what I am, except for these chains."
ACTS 26:28–29 NIV

As Agrippa listened to Paul's compelling message about God's salvation, he found himself in a moment of decision. Could he become a Christian so quickly? Everything would have to change, including his powerful position most likely.

If you feel like you're too far from God, or that a change could be too costly, perhaps Paul's words are for you today. Whether a short time or long, God's saving love is here for you today. God is able to reach you no matter your situation. Your doubts, your career, or your failures aren't enough to keep God away, and your life can change in an instant if you'll simply surrender to Him.

That moment of surrender is a leap of faith into the unknown. There could be some steep costs at first, but the end result will be God's loving presence in your life. You may be able to count the costs accurately today, but there are unknown joys waiting for you tomorrow.

Jesus, I trust that You can free me even today.

GOD'S PATIENCE IS NOT INDIFFERENCE

*Do you suppose, O man—you who judge those who practice
such things and yet do them yourself—that you will escape
the judgment of God? Or do you presume on the riches of his
kindness and forbearance and patience, not knowing that
God's kindness is meant to lead you to repentance?*

ROMANS 2:3–4 ESV

Does God care if you obey His commands? Are there consequences for following your own wisdom or resisting God's wisdom in your decisions?

The Psalms remind us that it can seem as if the evil and disobedient succeed while the righteous struggle. There is despair that obedience will never pay off in the long run while those committed to their own way enjoy success and prosperity.

Paul suggests that we can look at this in a different way. God's patience delays judgment, but it is not indifference to sin or disobedience. These are signs of God's mercy for all people. There is hope that those living in rebellion will reconsider their ways, repent of their sins, and escape God's certain judgment.

God will judge each person justly according to their deeds, even those who talk a good game but lead a secret life of indulgence and rebellion. There may still be some time to delay, but not forever.

*Father, thank You for Your mercy and patience. May I
build my life on the solid rock of obedience to Your will.*

ADVERSITY BUILDS ENDURANCE

We can rejoice, too, when we run into problems and
trials, for we know that they help us develop endurance.
And endurance develops strength of character, and
character strengthens our confident hope of salvation.

ROMANS 5:3–4 NLT

At a time when Paul and the early church faced discrimination, financial loss, and violent attacks, he suggested a counterintuitive response to problems and trials: *rejoice*. Why would he ever encourage anyone to rejoice in a time of suffering and struggle?

Simply put, adversity leads to endurance that strengthens your hope in salvation. Adversity offers a blunt but useful test for what you value and whom you trust in. Will you endure and continue to trust in God, or will you turn elsewhere for your hope? If everything was smooth sailing all the time, you may begin to trust more in yourself or in others rather than in God. Each trial is an opportunity to examine the state of your faith.

While God surely remains with you in your times of suffering and mourns with you in your darkest hours, your faith can take a step forward when it seems that everything is moving backward or spinning out of control. You will renew your strength when you rely on God in troubling times.

Jesus, I trust that You are near in my trials, and I ask that You
would increase my faith so that I can endure difficult times.

GOD'S RIGHTEOUSNESS IS GIVEN, NOT MADE

For I can testify about them that they are zealous for God, but their zeal is not based on knowledge. Since they did not know the righteousness of God and sought to establish their own, they did not submit to God's righteousness.

ROMANS 10:2–3 NIV

Can you make yourself more worthy of God? Is there a level of holiness you must reach before God grants you His favor?

The people of Israel were eager to please God. They committed themselves to the hard work of obedience and added an abundance of additional guidelines to make sure they were on the straightest, most narrow path. Tragically, Paul characterized them as zealous but ignorant, unaware of what God had given to them for free.

It's possible to be so committed to your own plans and desire for God that you rebel against His path toward holiness. It can feel discouraging to realize that, even with the best intentions, you've gone on the wrong path. Even if you've meant well, God's measure for your life will be whether you've submitted to Him.

Committing to the wrong direction with all of your heart will not bring your heart any closer to God. Stopping to check your direction may be what sets you on the right path.

Father, grant me the clarity to see the direction and commitments of my life so that I can live wholly submitted to You.

ENDURANCE THROUGH TRANSFORMATION

*Do not be conformed to this world, but be transformed by the
renewal of your mind, that by testing you may discern what is
the will of God, what is good and acceptable and perfect.*
ROMANS 12:2 ESV

When a potter makes a jar, two important things happen to the clay.
First, it is shaped. Second, it is hardened. Only after clay is hardened
does it become waterproof and useful as a vessel.

Isaiah 64:8 (ESV) says "But now, O LORD, you are our Father; we are
the clay, and you are our potter; we are all the work of your hand."

In his letter to the Romans, the apostle Paul warns his readers that
the world will try to change the clay of our identities to fit its mold. If we
want to be useful vessels for God, we need to be more than conformed—we
need to be fundamentally changed by the fire of God's influence. Though
the process of transformation will be painful to our selfish desires, it will
make us useful for God's plans.

If you feel like you are in the fire today, thank God for transforming
you into someone who will be more useful for His purposes.

*Lord, I am clay in Your hands. Shape me into a useful vessel.
Keep me from conforming to the world's mold. Help me endure
through the fire to be good and acceptable and perfect for You.*

HARMONIOUS LIVING

May the God of endurance and encouragement grant
you to live in such harmony with one another, in accord
with Christ Jesus, that together you may with one voice
glorify the God and Father of our Lord Jesus Christ.
ROMANS 15:5–6 ESV

Think back to the last sporting event you attended where the crowd sang a song. Maybe it was the national anthem or a song meant to pump up the team. There's a good chance that the song's power was in its volume rather than its harmony, because there are always people in the crowd who are completely tone deaf.

Now think of a professional orchestra, where the musicians are trained and have been practicing the same song for a while. There is beauty in the orchestra where there wasn't in the sports crowd.

Our lives are like music being played for God. He desires us to live in harmony with the musicians around us, to be like the professional orchestra more than the tone-deaf crowd. But living in harmony takes practice. It means that we aren't playing alone. It means that we need to follow the sheet music and the Conductor.

Take a listen to your life's music. Is it in harmony with the musicians around you?

Lord, I want my life's music to glorify You. May I live in
harmony with the people around me. Help me stop trying
to be a solo act when I'm called to be in an orchestra.

STRONG TO THE END

*Now you have every spiritual gift you need as you eagerly
wait for the return of our Lord Jesus Christ. He will keep
you strong to the end so that you will be free from all
blame on the day when our Lord Jesus Christ returns.*

1 CORINTHIANS 1:7–8 NLT

Milo of Croton lived in the sixth century BC and dominated strength competitions across the ancient Greek world. According to legend, Milo once carried a four-year-old bull around the arena then butchered and ate it all in the same day.

Physical strength is often part of a man's identity, but it isn't the most important form of strength in the Christian life.

In his first letter to the Corinthians, Paul says that God will keep believers strong to the end so they'll be blameless when Christ returns. This isn't a strength we can supply on our own. It comes by the grace of God. In essence, God's grace is strong enough to overcome our sin.

By ourselves, we are as powerless as the bull Milo of Croton carried. Our diets and workout routines, physical and spiritual, mean nothing before the Almighty's righteousness. Thank God that Jesus has worked out our salvation for us.

Live today in God's strength. Exercise your spiritual gifts for Him. Feast on His words. Rest in His goodness.

*Almighty God, I am strong in Your love.
Help me exercise it for others today.*

KEEP RUNNING

Do you not know that in a race all the runners run, but only one gets the prize? Run in such a way as to get the prize.
1 CORINTHIANS 9:24 NIV

———————◆———————

Eric Liddell, the son of Scottish missionaries to China, discovered a love of running while enrolled in boarding school in south London. In time, Liddell was called "The Flying Scotsman" and was the fastest man in Scotland.

Then, at the 1924 Olympics Liddell refused to run in his favored event, the 100-meter race, because one of the heats was held on Sunday. Instead, Liddell chose to compete in the 400-meter race, which was held during the week. His performance in the race set a European record that stood for twelve years.

After the Olympics, Liddell became a missionary to China. When asked whether he missed his glory days of racing, he responded "It's natural for a chap to think over all that sometimes, but I'm glad I'm at the work I'm engaged in now. A fellow's life counts for far more at this than the other."

Eric Liddell knew what it meant to run for the greater prize. He died as a missionary in a Japanese internment camp in China during World War II, just months before the camp was liberated. But his legacy of commitment to God lives on and on.

Lord, strengthen my legs to run the race before me.
Be my prize worth running for. May others see me
running and run alongside me toward You.

CARRY ON

Love bears all things, believes all things,
hopes all things, endures all things.
1 CORINTHIANS 13:7 ESV

Kevan Chandler has good friends and a love of adventure. So when he was offered the opportunity to backpack across Europe, he was all in. But Kevan Chandler didn't carry a backpack. . .he rode in it.

Chandler has spinal muscular atrophy and would normally be confined to a wheelchair. Since Kevan's wheelchair would only get in the way during the trek, his friends carried him in a specially designed backpack.

Their adventure, documented in the book *We Carry Kevan*, has redefined what accessible travel looks like and shined a spotlight on the strength of friendship in the face of adversity.

The love that moved Kevan's friends to carry him across the world is the kind of love that literally bears all things. The love we Christians have for one another should be no less.

True love believes the best about people and hopes that the Lord will work in their lives.

God calls His people to work toward greater unity, regardless of our differences, even when that means that we must carry one another along.

Lord, give me love for others that believes the best about them
and works to help them toward it. You have done no less
for me. Help me carry others even as You carry me.

ACT LIKE MEN

Be watchful, stand firm in the faith, act like men,
be strong. Let all that you do be done in love.
1 Corinthians 16:13–14 esv

The Greek word *andrizomai* is used only once in the New Testament. In 1 Corinthians 16:13, it is translated as the imperative statement, "Act like men."

There are a lot of stereotypes associated with men, but the apostle Paul wasn't encouraging the believers of Corinth to act macho, cheer on their favorite sports team, or belch loudly. The word *andrizomai* is something a commanding officer might say to his soldiers. Be courageous!

The interesting thing about Paul's command is that he follows it up with a reminder to act in love. This is a profound juxtaposition. Prepare for war, but arm yourself with love.

Paul knows that a believer's life is a battleground. We must watch out for invisible enemies. We must stand firm in our Savior's grace. We must be strong against temptations. We must act like men, courageously loving others when it feels more natural to fight.

In the battles you face today, arm yourself with the Savior's love, and you will show the world what it really means to act like men.

Father God, You are the commander of heaven's armies, and You
know about the battles I face every day. Give me the strength to
do more than fight my enemies. Give me the strength to love them.

LIFELINE

We are hard pressed on every side, but not crushed;
perplexed, but not in despair; persecuted, but not
abandoned; struck down, but not destroyed.
2 CORINTHIANS 4:8–9 NIV

On December 7, 1941, the Japanese attack on Pearl Harbor took the lives of 2,341 American service members. Almost half died on the battleship USS *Arizona*.

USS *Arizona* crew member Lauren Bruner recalled, "I and five others were located on the antiaircraft gun directors platform above the bridge when the forward powder magazine blew. All of us were badly burned. I was burned over 80% of my body. At that point, the only possibility to evacuate the ship was to dive in the water, which was 80 feet below and was fully engulfed in flame. That was not an option for survival."

Moored next to the USS *Arizona* was the USS *Vestal*, a smaller repair ship. On board, crew member Joe George saw the trapped men and threw them a rope. In spite of their horrific burns, the men were able to shimmy across to safety.

Believer, this world is under attack just like the USS *Arizona*, but Jesus has seen you and thrown you a lifeline. Though in this world you will get burned, by God's grace you shall not fall into the fiery depths below. Praise God for giving you the only option for survival!

Lord, You are my lifeline in a world on fire. Keep me from
despair, and use me to bring others to Your safety.

UNEXPECTED RICHES

You know the generous grace of our Lord Jesus Christ.
Though he was rich, yet for your sakes he became poor,
so that by his poverty he could make you rich.
2 CORINTHIANS 8:9 NLT

For about ninety minutes, Manhattan native Dan Levene was a multimillionaire.

"I just started laughing. I mean I really laughed. Clearly this account did not have this much money in it to start the day," Levene said.

Levene noticed that his stock trading account had $89.9 million more in it than it should have and that it was available for immediate withdrawal. Instead of rushing out to spend his new funds or trying to reinvest the money, Levene called the bank that made the error to his account.

When unexpected money shows up in your bank account, it is probably a banking error. As Christians, even the unexpected wealth we are promised after death didn't come without a cost. Jesus paid our penalty, becoming poor for our sake. His sacrifice has given us a windfall that we get to keep for eternity.

Thank God for His rich mercy and grace!

Lord, I am rich because of Your poverty. Thank You for taking
the punishment on my behalf. Thank You for giving me a
share in Your kingdom. Help me generously share the
wealth of Your grace with others around me.

STRENGTH IN WEAKNESS

For the sake of Christ, then, I am content with weaknesses,
insults, hardships, persecutions, and calamities.
For when I am weak, then I am strong.
2 CORINTHIANS 12:10 ESV

I t isn't natural to be content with weakness, especially for men. And when others see our weaknesses, we are likely to feel shame, maybe even anger. These feelings may cause us to question our usefulness to Christ. After all, how can God use someone who keeps falling into sin?

In his second letter to the Corinthians, the apostle Paul mentions a weakness of his own. No one knows exactly what Paul meant when he said that he was given a "thorn in the flesh," but it is clear that Satan used this weakness to attack Paul and cause him to sin.

Three times Paul asked God to remove this weakness, but God responded, "My grace is sufficient for you, for my power is made perfect in weakness" (2 Corinthians 12:9 ESV).

No matter what weaknesses you have, what insults you endure, what hardships you live through, remember that God's grace is sufficient for you. Stop trying to overcome your weakness with your own strength, and allow God to work in you. And if others see your example of weakness transformed, they'll have reason to praise God instead of you.

Lord, forgive me for the times when I hide my weakness from
others and from You. Give me Your strength to be content.

INDEPENDENCE VS. FREEDOM

So I say, walk by the Spirit, and you will
not gratify the desires of the flesh.
GALATIANS 5:16 NIV

Take a minute and think of all the advertising campaigns and slogans that appeal to your selfishness. *Have it your way. Just do it. Obey your thirst.* You can probably think of others.

Why do these advertisements work? Because they appeal to our independence. They give us the illusion of freedom by saying that we should do whatever we want. And while these companies don't openly encourage us to sin, they do encourage us to act selfishly.

Oswald Chambers once wrote, "Whenever God touches sin it is independence that is touched, and that awakens resentment in the human heart. Independence must be blasted clean out, there must be no such thing left, only freedom, which is very different. Freedom is the ability not to insist on my rights, but to see that God gets his."

When you became a believer, God gave you the Holy Spirit, but He did not remove your natural, fleshly self. When you listen to your natural desires, you trade your freedom for something less than God's goodness. Stop listening to the ads that appeal to your selfishness, and start listening to the God who knows what is best for you.

Lord, let me live by the Spirit. Keep me from acting on my selfish desires.
May your Word be louder than the advertisements I see today.

GOOD WORKS

*For we are God's handiwork, created in Christ Jesus to do
good works, which God prepared in advance for us to do.*
EPHESIANS 2:10 NIV

Born in Poland in 1894, Maximilian Kolbe knew early that he wanted to serve the Lord. Ordained as a Franciscan friar, Kolbe traveled the globe, building monasteries in Japan and India before returning to Poland for health reasons in 1936.

When his religious work contrasted with the Nazi invasion of his country, Kolbe was taken to the German death camp in Auschwitz. While there, Kolbe continued his priestly duties in spite of the extra beatings that came with them.

After ten individuals escaped Auschwitz, the camp's commander ordered that ten of the prisoners were to starve to death as retribution. Though he wasn't one of the ten chosen, Kolbe volunteered to take the place of one of them. Maximilian Kolbe used his last days to lead the other condemned men in prayer, and he was the last of them to die.

Since we have been created in Christ Jesus and adopted by God, we should seek opportunities to be like Him. Throughout his life, Maximilian Kolbe did good works for others, even dying in someone else's place.

Whether or not they are as extreme as Maximilian Kolbe's example, God has good works planned for you today. How can you show others that you are His child?

*Lord, help me see and do the good works
You've prepared for me today.*

THE LAMP SHADE OF NEGATIVITY

Do all things without grumbling or disputing, that you
may be blameless and innocent, children of God without
blemish in the midst of a crooked and twisted generation,
among whom you shine as lights in the world.
PHILIPPIANS 2:14–15 ESV

B elievers in Christ are called to be lights shining in the world, but nothing puts a lamp shade on your light like negativity.

Robert Sapolsky, professor of neurology and neuroendocrinology at Stanford University's School of Medicine, has studied the effects on the brain of exposure to negativity. He found that exposure to stressors for more than thirty minutes can lead to increased levels of cortisol, which can harm brain function and increase cell death. So, negative people literally hurt your brain.

When believers engage in the kind of grumbling and fighting that is common in the world, people naturally distance themselves, tuning out whatever positive message the negative people are trying to convey.

In order to be an effective light in the darkness, you need to take off the lamp shade of negativity. Don't let God's people become known for fighting among ourselves. Instead, let God be known to others through love.

Lord, You are the Light of the World and You call me to shine too.
May Your light shine in me so others can see You. Keep me from doing
anything that would cast shade on Your name or Your people.

GET DRESSED

Since God chose you to be the holy people he loves, you must clothe yourselves with tenderhearted mercy, kindness, humility, gentleness, and patience. Make allowance for each other's faults, and forgive anyone who offends you. Remember, the Lord forgave you, so you must forgive others. Above all, clothe yourselves with love, which binds us all together in perfect harmony.
Colossians 3:12–14 NLT

You've probably heard that "clothing makes the man." It is an old phrase. In fact, Shakespeare used a variant of it in *Hamlet*, when Polonius tells his son Laertes that "apparel oft proclaims the man."

While people do tend to make snap judgments about others based on the clothes they wear, the truth is especially poignant when considering our spiritual clothing. When people look at your life, do they see someone dressed in mercy, kindness, humility, gentleness, and patience? Or do they see selfishness, immorality, anger, slander, and obscene talk?

It's time to take off the old clothes the world gave you and put on Christ's love for others. Get dressed so that people know that you are God's because they see you wearing His clothes.

Lord, dress me in Your clothes today. Stop me from putting back on the worldly clothes I used to wear.

GOD'S WILL FOR YOUR LIFE

*Be thankful in all circumstances, for this is
God's will for you who belong to Christ Jesus.*
1 Thessalonians 5:18 nlt

"What are you going to be when you grow up?"

It's a common question for small children. But when those children grow up and get ready to leave home, the question takes on new significance. High school graduates might be tempted to look for heavenly signs to point them in the right directions. The question may even become, "What is God's will for my life?"

Unfortunately, the Bible doesn't specifically say which job you should have, or what your spouse's name is, or any of those other big life decisions. But it may be comforting to know that God does have a perfect plan that your indecisiveness cannot thwart. And though it may leave out the specifics of your circumstances, the Bible does tell you what God's will is.

Be thankful.

If you belong to Christ, then no matter what you become when you grow up, you need to give thanks to God for what you are: His child. Whether you are rich or poor, married or single, a plumber or a rocket scientist, or a writer or a computer programmer, you are called to be thankful.

---

*Thank You, Lord, for allowing me to be Your child.
When I worry about the specific details of my life,
remind me to be thankful in every circumstance.*

ALL SORTS OF PRAYERS

First of all, then, I urge that supplications, prayers,
intercessions, and thanksgivings be made for all people.
1 TIMOTHY 2:1 ESV

If you had a neighbor who only talked to you when he needed to borrow something, how would you feel toward him? There probably wouldn't be much of a relationship there. But if he were the type of neighbor who talked with you about the weather, complimented your lawn, and asked for some advice on behalf of his sister-in-law, you'd probably be a bit closer to him.

You see where this is going, right?

Our prayer life is not only an indicator of our relationship with God; it is one of the primary means by which we form a strong and growing relationship with Him.

If your prayer life consists of just asking God for things, you may be treating Him like a cosmic vending machine. But even if you are praying in a variety of ways to God, but only for how His love affects your life, your prayer life is still too small.

God wants to hear from you about everything, and He wants you to pray for everyone. Next time you pray, shift your focus off yourself and widen it to the world around you. See what God will do when you recognize His prominence over everything!

Lord, You are awesome in so many ways! Thank You for Your love.
Expand my love for others as You expand my ability to see them.

VITAL CONFLICT

For the time will come when people will not put up with sound doctrine.
Instead, to suit their own desires, they will gather around them a great
number of teachers to say what their itching ears want to hear.

2 Timothy 4:3 niv

N o one likes being wrong. It's unpleasant when someone disagrees with you, but in business, in life, and in your walk with Christ, such conflict is vital to success.

Walter Wrigley, founder of Wrigley Chewing Gum, once said, "When two people always agree, one of them is unnecessary." Businesses thrive when managers empower their employees to speak the truth. Conversely, businesses fail when their leaders listen to bad counsel.

One of the factors that led to the bankruptcy of Lehman Brothers bank was its habit of firing employees who voiced dissent. Though it was the fourth-largest investment bank in the United States, its size couldn't overcome bad counsel.

The Christian life is no different. If you surround yourself with people who tell you just what you want to hear, your relationship with Christ will suffer. You need people who will give you sound doctrine, even when (*especially* when) it hurts.

If you haven't been offended at church recently, ask yourself if you're listening to sound doctrine. If not, it's time to get your itchy ears checked and find some teachers who will give you the truth.

Lord, keep my ears from itching for comfort when I need
to hear uncomfortable truths. Surround me with
good teachers, and help me follow their advice.

SHAME

Let us therefore come boldly to the throne of grace, that we may obtain mercy and find grace to help in time of need.
HEBREWS 4:16 NKJV

The internet has created some strange trends over the years. One trend that emerged in 2012 was the practice of "dog shaming," which features photos or videos of dogs acting guilty when faced with the evidence of their misdeeds.

Perhaps the videos became popular because they are relatable. When faced with shame, we often hide our wrongdoings, but this temporary solution leads to greater shame later.

"The less we talk about shame, the more power it has over our lives," says Dr. Brené Brown, PhD, LMSW in her book *Daring Greatly*. "If we cultivate enough awareness about shame to name it and speak to it, we've basically cut it off at the knees."

Christians can go one step further than naming our shame. We are invited to receive forgiveness. Don't let guilt and shame stop you from being forgiven.

God doesn't get laughs by creating "human shaming" videos for heaven's YouTube channel. He wants a close relationship with you. The next time you feel tempted or guilty, boldly approach God's throne and restore your relationship with Him. He is ready to give you mercy and grace, even when you think you least deserve it.

Lord, thank You for Your mercy and grace. Thank You for not giving up on me when I am tempted to hide from You.

DESERTION

We are not of those who shrink back and are destroyed,
but of those who have faith and preserve their souls.
Hebrews 10:39 esv

During World War II, the US military tried 2,864 army personnel for desertion. Of those, forty-nine were convicted and sentenced to death, but only one sentence was actually carried out. On January 31, 1945, twenty-four-year-old Pvt. Eddie Slovik was executed by a firing squad.

Before the war, Slovik was in and out of prison for petty theft, breaking and entering, and stealing cars. His record would have made him ineligible for military service, but Slovik settled down, got married, and cleaned up his act. A year after his wedding, he was drafted and sent to France, where the fight against the Nazis was hottest.

After seeing war up close, Slovik decided that a court-martial was preferable to dying on the battlefield, so he decided to desert. Though he was encouraged repeatedly to retake his post and avoid punishment, Slovik was committed. He never believed that he would be sentenced to death.

In the Christian fight against sin, you are on the front lines. You may not believe that the consequences of your faithlessness are serious, but a man has already been executed for them. Jesus took the punishment for your desertion. Would you desert Him now?

Lord, give me strength for the fight against sin. Keep my faith
strong and preserve my soul, so I don't desert You.

RUNNING FOCUS

Therefore, since we are surrounded by such a huge crowd of witnesses to the life of faith, let us strip off every weight that slows us down, especially the sin that so easily trips us up. And let us run with endurance the race God has set before us. We do this by keeping our eyes on Jesus, the champion who initiates and perfects our faith.
HEBREWS 12:1–2 NLT

In 1977, a group of sports psychologists published a paper that changed how long-distance runners ran. The researchers interviewed elite runners and midpack runners, asking what they thought about while they ran. The elite runners said they focused on things like breathing and form. Suddenly, that's what every runner started to do.

Then in 2013, another group of researchers decided to rerun the study, only instead of interviews, they tested the oxygen levels of runners in a lab. The new research found that when runners focused on their breathing and form, they used more oxygen than those who didn't.

By focusing on their in-the-moment performance, runners actually ran worse than others who thought about things outside of themselves.

In order to run with endurance as Christians, we too need to focus less on ourselves. When sin trips you, don't focus on it. Give it to God. Be forgiven. Refocus on the Savior. Run strong!

Lord, be my focus. Keep me from tripping. Help me start running toward You again when I do.

MIRRORS

Anyone who listens to the word but does not do what it says is like
someone who looks at his face in a mirror and, after looking at
himself, goes away and immediately forgets what he looks like.
JAMES 1:23–24 NIV

P icture this: You are about to make an important presentation at work. The owner of the company is sitting in the front row. The meeting will start soon, but you have enough time for a bathroom break. While washing your hands, you glance in the mirror and notice that your fly is down, your shirt is buttoned incorrectly, and a glob of toothpaste has dried on your chin. You smile at your reflection and walk straight into the meeting.

You wouldn't do that, would you? If your fly was down, you'd zip it up. If your shirt was buttoned wrong, you'd redo it. If you had dried toothpaste on your chin, you'd clean it off.

The Word of God is a mirror for our spiritual lives. By reading the Bible, we should see the areas of our lives that need attention. So when we read the Bible and don't change the way we live, something's wrong.

Don't stop at looking in the mirror of God's Word. Start doing something about it.

Lord, thank You for the Bible. Help me see myself in the mirror
of Your Word. Give me the will to change what needs changed.

WINTER

For you have been born again, not of perishable seed, but of imperishable, through the living and enduring word of God.
1 PETER 1:23 NIV

Today marks the winter solstice in the northern hemisphere. We'll experience the shortest day and the longest night of the year. Because of its place in the yearly cycle, many cultures have celebrated the solstice as a time of death and rebirth.

Winter may be a time when the world looks dead, but since the days will get longer and the nights shorter, hope isn't lost. The natural world with its seasons and agricultural cycles might inspire some to believe that even the afterlife works cyclically, but Christians know better.

For you, rebirth isn't part of a cycle. It's a onetime event. By being exposed to the truth of God's Word, by experiencing His love, you have been pulled out of the earthly cycle. Death doesn't work the same once you've been born anew.

Being born again for a Christian doesn't mean that the days will get longer and nights shorter from here on out. It means that day never turns to night. The plants don't die at the end of the season, because winter is a thing of the past.

Creator God, You made this world with beauty and order, and gave us seasons that hint at the possibility of rebirth. Thank You for Your sacrifice, which pulls me out of the cycle of death and into eternal life with You.

BUILDING FAITH THAT ENDURES

*For this very reason, make every effort to supplement your faith with
virtue, and virtue with knowledge, and knowledge with self-control,
and self-control with steadfastness, and steadfastness with godliness,
and godliness with brotherly affection, and brotherly affection with love.*
2 PETER 1:5–7 ESV

Houses are built from the foundation up. Once the foundation is solid,
then the walls can be framed with studs. After the wall's studs are
in, plywood gets added to the outside, then house wrap, then siding.
Inside the house, insulation is put in, then drywall, which gets sealed
and then painted.

It starts with a strong foundation, but for people inside the house to
be protected from storms, they need to keep building onto that foundation.

Christ has laid the perfect foundation for the Christian life. Building your faith on any other foundation won't work. But if you stop building after the foundation, the storms of this life will be more dangerous
and uncomfortable. For your faith to protect you well, keep building.

Live a virtuous life. Grow in knowledge. Control your desires. Be
steadfast, godly, and kind. Above all else, paint your life with love so
others will see it and want to visit.

*Lord, You are the Master Builder. Help me use the tools You have
given me to build a secure faith that is inviting to others. Don't let
me settle for a strong foundation when You want more for me.*

CONFESSION

*If we confess our sins, he is faithful and just and will forgive
us our sins and purify us from all unrighteousness.*
1 JOHN 1:9 NIV

I n *Scientific American* magazine, psychologist James W. Pennebaker
writes that the act of confession, whether religious or through expressive writing, is linked to less stress, better sleep, and improved cardiovascular function. Science agrees that confession isn't just good for the soul. . .it is good for the body too.

But while the health benefits are great, they aren't the best part of confession; forgiveness is, because it sets us on the path to restoring our broken relationship with God.

Confessing our sins to God doesn't give Him any new information. He already knows what we've done. The act of confession allows us to take responsibility for our actions. God won't necessarily take away the consequences of our sins, but He will take away the barrier that stops us from having a right relationship with Him.

Do you have sins you need to confess? Is something holding you back from being in a right relationship with God? Confess, be forgiven, and start living the life God intended for you. Even science agrees that you'll sleep easier once you have!

*Lord, I need Your forgiveness. You know the ways I have hurt
our relationship, but You've promised to forgive me anyway.
Help me avoid the need for forgiveness in the future, but keep
me coming back to You when I do need it.*

LEGACY OF JOY

*I have no greater joy than to hear that my
children are walking in the truth.*

3 JOHN 4 ESV

Christmas is a time of family gatherings. It is a time of sharing stories of recent events and reminiscing about family times long past. It is a time of traditions like decorating Christmas trees and baking cookies. As you gather together with loved ones during the holidays or reminisce about past gatherings while on your own, this is a perfect time to think about the legacy of faith your family is building.

There's no better place to begin a legacy than with the arrival of Jesus Christ. Make it a point to read Luke 2 aloud with someone this year. Rejoice together that God's love provided a Savior for a world that didn't deserve saving.

Do your utmost to live peaceably with your friends and families during the stressful times that holidays bring. Speak truth in love and share the Gospel with the lost people you know.

Walk in the truth of God's love this Christmas and you will do more than spread joy to the world. You will give God joy as well.

Lord, may I walk in the truth and bring joy to Your face. Thank You for sending Your Son to earth. As I go to family gatherings or holiday parties, don't let me forget to show others the love You have shown me.

THE ETERNAL GOD'S BIRTHDAY

*"I am the Alpha and the Omega," says the Lord God,
"who is and who was and who is to come, the Almighty."*
REVELATION 1:8 ESV

When you think about it, celebrating the birthday of the eternal God is a little silly. God exists outside of time. He has always been. He always is. He always will be. He is the beginning and end of all creation, the sustainer of existence, and the One to whom all creation will bow down for eternity. Does it make sense to celebrate the birthday of One who has always been?

Actually, it is because of His eternal nature that the birth of Jesus Christ is doubly worth celebrating. Because of the love God has for us, He entered into the world as a frail human baby. The all-powerful God humbled Himself and submitted to the rules He made for us, becoming the only sacrifice His holy nature could accept.

We celebrate the birth of Christ because it shows us the lengths God's love is willing to go for the world He created. We celebrate because He has extended His holiness to us, making it possible for us to be with Him eternally. Today, give thanks that the eternal God was willing to be born so you could be born again into His eternal love.

*Jesus, Happy Birthday! Thank You for sharing Your
holiness with me so I can be with You forever.*

ANGELS' SONG

In a loud voice they were saying: "Worthy is the Lamb,
who was slain, to receive power and wealth and wisdom
and strength and honor and glory and praise!"
REVELATION 5:12 NIV

Picture yourself as a shepherd outside Bethlehem at the time of Christ's birth. First, one angel arrives with good news, then thousands more pop into view singing, "Glory to God in the highest heaven, and on earth peace to those on whom his favor rests" (Luke 2:14 NIV).

At that time, the people of Israel were waiting for an earthly Messiah who would save them from earthly rulers. They expected Him to come in power and seize control of the government. They were expecting the Lion of Judah. Instead, they got the Lamb of God.

Jesus came in a humble way, and though He demonstrated His power through miracles and teaching, His revolution was different from what the people of Israel were expecting. When they decided that their hope in Jesus was misplaced, they had Him crucified. But that was God's plan all along!

Peace on earth wasn't possible before Jesus took the punishment for our sins on the cross. Only once He was slain could He become both the Lion *and* the Lamb, worthy to receive power and wealth and wisdom and strength and honor and glory and praise. Today, sing praises with the angels because Jesus made a way for peace!

Lord, You are worthy of all praises.
Bring Your peace into my life.

SUPERMAN AND FAITH

When the seven thunders spoke, I was about to write.
But I heard a voice from heaven saying, "Keep secret
what the seven thunders said, and do not write it down."

REVELATION 10:4 NLT

Christopher Reeve, the actor famous for playing Superman from 1978 through the 1980s, once said, "A hero is someone who, in spite of weakness, doubt or not always knowing the answers, goes ahead and overcomes anyway."

Reeve knew weakness. In 1995, he was in an accident while horseback riding that resulted in paralysis from the neck down. Though he went through dark times and even considered suicide, he pressed on toward recovery, relearning how to do everything as he went. In time, Reeve returned to filmmaking, both behind the scenes as a director and in front as an actor.

From the time of his accident until the time of his death in 2004, Christopher Reeve did not know what to expect from life. No one does. What matters is what you do when you don't have answers.

God leaves room for mysteries in life, partly so you will have chances to show your trust in Him and His goodness. Even when times are dark, you can overcome by placing your faith in the One who overcame death itself.

Lord, help me trust in You when I don't have all the answers.
Keep my faith strong through my many weaknesses.

SATAN'S END

So the great dragon was cast out, that serpent of old,
called the Devil and Satan, who deceives the whole world;
he was cast to the earth, and his angels were cast out with him.
Revelation 12:9 nkjv

From his first appearance to humanity in the Garden of Eden to the very end of days, Satan has fought against God's supremacy. Unfortunately, he's good at inspiring people to do the same.

In his book *The Screwtape Letters*, a fantastical correspondence between two demons, C. S. Lewis writes, "You see, it is so hard for these creatures to persevere. The routine of adversity, the gradual decay of youthful loves and youthful hopes, the quiet despair (hardly felt as pain) of ever overcoming the chronic temptations with which we have again and again defeated them, the drabness which we create in their lives and the inarticulate resentment with which we teach them to respond to it—all this provides admirable opportunities of wearing out a soul by attrition."

It *is* tiresome living in a fallen world. It's true. But it's also true that the end has already been written. Satan loses. He is simply trying to bring as many people down with him as he can. Christians sometimes forget that they needn't go along with sin, because Christ has already overcome it. Remember the end of the story and persevere!

Lord, my future is secure in You. Give me the
power to overcome sin's temptation today.

WORK AND REST

Here is a call for the endurance of the saints, those who keep the commandments of God and their faith in Jesus. And I heard a voice from heaven saying, "Write this: Blessed are the dead who die in the Lord from now on." "Blessed indeed," says the Spirit, "that they may rest from their labors, for their deeds follow them!"
REVELATION 14:12–13 ESV

Hard work is important. There is a lot of talk in the proverbs about the value of working hard and the dangers of laziness. Check out Proverbs 12:11, Proverbs 13:4, and Proverbs 14:23 to see just a few.

Rest is important too. On the seventh day of creation, God rested. When leading the Israelites through the wilderness, God provided twice the normal amount of manna on the sixth day so they could rest on the seventh.

Rest is one of the rewards for hard work. If you know you won't be able to stop doing a job until it is finished, it behooves you to finish the job quickly so you can rest.

Living in a fallen world is hard work. That's probably why there are so many verses that encourage it. But the reward is coming. Keep working hard because you'll be able to rest soon. And it is going to be the best rest you've ever had.

Lord, give me perspective. May the promised rest in the future give me strength to work hard today.

THE LORD IS A WARRIOR

I saw heaven standing open and there before me
was a white horse, whose rider is called Faithful
and True. With justice he judges and wages war.
REVELATION 19:11 NIV

God is many things. He is love. He is the way, the truth, and the life. He is the Alpha and Omega, the beginning and the end. He is faithful, merciful, and kind. He is the Father, the Son, and the Holy Spirit. And God is a warrior.

Exodus 15:3 (NIV) says, "The LORD is a warrior; the LORD is his name."

Though people like to think about how loving and forgiving God is, He is still a just God who will pour out His wrath on His enemies. Uncomfortable as it may be to think of God in this way, Christians should find it a comforting thought. Would it be right to worship a God who didn't care about justice for victims? Would God still be loving if He didn't protect His people?

No matter what battle you face today, God is the ultimate warrior and He wants to protect His people. Don't worry about the outcome of your fight. God has it under control. So stand back and allow Him to fight for you.

Lord, my fight isn't mine. I belong to You and You
will take care of it. You are the Ultimate Warrior.

CLOSING THE DOOR ON THE PAST

He who was seated on the throne said, "Behold, I am making all things new." Also he said, "Write this down, for these words are trustworthy and true." And he said to me, "It is done! I am the Alpha and the Omega, the beginning and the end. To the thirsty I will give from the spring of the water of life without payment. The one who conquers will have this heritage, and I will be his God and he will be my son."

REVELATION 21:5–7 ESV

New Year's Eve is a great time to reflect on your walk with Christ over the last year. Have you been consistent in studying the Bible? Has your prayer life been more of a conversation with God than a stream of requests? Do you trust God more today than you did a year ago? Have you made fellowship with God's people a priority? Have you shared His love with others?

If your self-examination has turned up some areas in your life that still need work, remember that God is faithful. It's time to close the door on your past failures and allow Him to renew you. Let every day be New Year's Eve and resolve to let God work through you. Daily renewal is the key to spiritual endurance.

Go be new!

*Lord, I give myself to You. Make me new every day.
Bring me closer to You and to the person You want me to be.*

CONTRIBUTORS

Ed Cyzewski is the author of *A Christian Survival Guide: A Lifeline to Faith and Growth* and *Flee, Be Silent, Pray: An Anxious Evangelical Finds Peace with God through Contemplative Prayer* and is the coauthor of *Unfollowers: Unlikely Lessons on Faith from Those Who Doubted Jesus*. He writes about prayer and imperfectly following Jesus at www.edcyzewski.com. Ed's devotions are found in May and November.

Glenn A. Hascall is an accomplished writer with credits in more than a hundred books. He is a broadcast veteran and voice actor and is actively involved in writing and producing audio drama. Glenn's devotions are found in January and June.

Josh Mosey is the author of *3-Minute Prayers for Boys* and a contributor to other works. He's a husband, father, and reader. On any given day, Josh can be found in a bookstore, savoring coffee (one sugar, no cream) and the feeling of being surrounded by beautifully arranged words. He also enjoys delving into the truths of scripture and Vikings. On the web: joshmosey.com. Josh's devotions are found in December.

David Sanford's speaking engagements have ranged everywhere from the Billy Graham Center at the Cove to UC Berkeley. His book and Bible projects have been published by Zondervan, Tyndale House, Thomas Nelson, Doubleday, and Amazon. His professional biography is summarized at www.linkedin.com/in/drsanford. His personal biography features his wife of thirty-seven years, Renée, their five children, and their twelve grandchildren (and one in heaven). David's devotions are found in March and April.

Tracy M. Sumner is a freelance author, writer, and editor in Beaverton, Oregon. An avid outdoorsman, he enjoys fly-fishing on world-class Oregon waters. Tracy's devotions are found in July and September.

Dr. Marty Trammell and his wife, Linda, enjoy leading relationship retreats and serving at Corban University, redeemingrelationships.com, and Valley Baptist Church. He is the co-author of *Love Lock: Creating Lasting Connections with the One You Love* (CrossLink), *Redeeming Relationships* (CSS), *Spiritual Fitness* (Credo), *Speaking Matters* (Horizon) and *Communication Matters* (Corban/Amazon). Marty's devotions are found in October.

Lee Warren is published in such varied venues as *Discipleship Journal*, *Sports Spectrum*, Yahoo! Sports, Crosswalk.com, and ChristianityToday .com. He is also the author of the book *Finishing Well: Living with the End in Mind* (a devotional), as well as several Christmas novellas in the Mercy Inn series. Lee makes his home in Omaha, Nebraska. Lee's devotions are found in February and August.

READ THRU THE BIBLE IN A YEAR PLAN

1/1 . . . . Gen. 1-3	2/15 . . . . Num. 3-4
1/2 . . . . Gen. 4:1-7:9	2/16 . . . . Num. 5-6
1/3 . . . . Gen. 7:10-10:32	2/17 . . . . Num. 7
1/4 . . . . Gen. 11-14	2/18 . . . . Num. 8-10
1/5 . . . . Gen. 15-18	2/19 . . . . Num. 11-12
1/6 . . . . Gen. 19-21	2/20 . . . . Num. 13-14
1/7 . . . . Gen. 22-24	2/21 . . . . Num. 15-16
1/8 . . . . Gen. 25-27	2/22 . . . . Num. 17-19
1/9 . . . . Gen. 28-29	2/23 . . . . Num. 20-21
1/10 . . . . Gen. 30-31	2/24 . . . . Num. 22-24
1/11 . . . . Gen. 32-34	2/25 . . . . Num. 25-27
1/12 . . . . Gen. 35-36	2/26 . . . . Num. 28-30
1/13 . . . . Gen. 37-39	2/27 . . . . Num. 31-32
1/14 . . . . Gen. 40-41	2/28 . . . . Num. 33-34
1/15 . . . . Gen. 42-43	3/1 . . . . Num. 35-36
1/16 . . . . Gen. 44-45	3/2 . . . . Deut. 1-2
1/17 . . . . Gen. 46-48	3/3 . . . . Deut. 3-4
1/18 . . . . Gen. 49-50	3/4 . . . . Deut. 5-7
1/19 . . . . Exod. 1-3	3/5 . . . . Deut. 8-11
1/20 . . . . Exod. 4-6	3/6 . . . . Deut. 12-14
1/21 . . . . Exod. 7-9	3/7 . . . . Deut. 15-17
1/22 . . . . Exod. 10-12	3/8 . . . . Deut. 18-20
1/23 . . . . Exod. 13-15	3/9 . . . . Deut. 21-23
1/24 . . . . Exod. 16-18	3/10 . . . . Deut. 24-26
1/25 . . . . Exod. 19-20	3/11 . . . . Deut. 27-28
1/26 . . . . Exod. 21-23	3/12 . . . . Deut. 29-31
1/27 . . . . Exod. 24-27	3/13 . . . . Deut. 32-34
1/28 . . . . Exod. 28-29	3/14 . . . . Josh. 1-2
1/29 . . . . Exod. 30-31	3/15 . . . . Josh. 3-5
1/30 . . . . Exod. 32-33	3/16 . . . . Josh. 6-8
1/31 . . . . Exod. 34-35	3/17 . . . . Josh. 9-10
2/1 . . . . Exod. 36-38	3/18 . . . . Josh. 11-13
2/2 . . . . Exod. 39-40	3/19 . . . . Josh. 14-16
2/3 . . . . Lev. 1-4	3/20 . . . . Josh. 17-19
2/4 . . . . Lev. 5-7	3/21 . . . . Josh. 20-22
2/5 . . . . Lev. 8-10	3/22 . . . . Josh. 23-24
2/6 . . . . Lev. 11-12	3/23 . . . . Judg. 1-3
2/7 . . . . Lev. 13:1-14:32	3/24 . . . . Judg. 4-5
2/8 . . . . Lev. 14:33-15:33	3/25 . . . . Judg. 6-8
2/9 . . . . Lev. 16-17	3/26 . . . . Judg. 9
2/10 . . . . Lev. 18-20	3/27 . . . . Judg. 10-12
2/11 . . . . Lev. 21-23	3/28 . . . . Judg. 13-16
2/12 . . . . Lev. 24-25	3/29 . . . . Judg. 17-19
2/13 . . . . Lev. 26-27	3/30 . . . . Judg. 20-21
2/14 . . . . Num. 1-2	3/31 . . . . Ruth 1-4

SCRIPTURE INDEX